About Island Press

Island Press, a nonprofit publisher, provides the best ideas and information to those seeking to understand and protect the environment and create solutions to its complex problems.

Working with leading thinkers from around the world, Island Press elevates voices of change, shines a spotlight on crucial issues, and focuses attention on sustainable solutions.

Island Press gratefully acknowledges major support from The Bobolink Foundation, Caldera Foundation, The Curtis and Edith Munson Foundation, The Forrest C. and Frances H. Lattner Foundation, The JPB Foundation, The Kresge Foundation, The Summit Charitable Foundation, Inc., and many other generous organizations and individuals.

Generous support for this publication was provided in part by:

National Endowment for the Arts

The Richard H. Driehaus Foundation

AARP Livable Communities

Furthermore: a program of the J. M. Kaplan Fund

MISSING MIDDLE HOUSING

MISSING
MIDDLE
HOUSING

Thinking Big and Building Small to
Respond to Today's Housing Crisis

DANIEL PAROLEK

WITH

ARTHUR C. NELSON

◐ **ISLAND**PRESS | WASHINGTON | COVELO

Library of Congress Control Number: 2019957215

All Island Press books are printed on environmentally responsible
materials.

Manufactured in the United States of America
10 9 8 7 6 5 4 3 2

Keywords: Affordable housing, attainable housing, cohousing,
comprehensive plan, cottage court, courtyard building, duplex,
fourplex, impact fees, land use planning, live-work housing,
multifamily housing, Not In My Backyard (NIMBY), parking
requirements, urban design, zoning

CONTENTS

PREFACE

I HAVE SPENT MY ENTIRE LIFE BUILDING my understanding of what makes walkable urban towns and cities vibrant and investigating the many diverse types of places that people are happy to call home within them.

As a child, my hometown was the bustling "metropolis" of Columbus, Nebraska, with a population of around eighteen thousand. It had a gridded street network with tree-lined streets, a grassy town square in the heart of downtown, and an imposing Beaux Arts county courthouse engaging the square. In the pre-Walmart era while I was growing up, Columbus had a thriving and vibrant downtown with two hardware stores; Woolworth, JCPenney, and Sears department stores; a two-screen movie theatre; restaurants; two donut shops; and a bike shop that was always my favorite destination when I ventured out on my own or with friends and headed downtown. In Columbus, I walked and biked everywhere independently from the age of six. I remember meeting my best friend every morning at the end of the block to ride to school together, without parents, starting in kindergarten. My great-grandmother lived in a charming Victorian duplex in a one-bedroom, approximately 600 sq. ft. unit she called home, one block from the thriving main street. It was everything she needed in the elder stages of her life. This experience growing up in this Midwestern small town was my first informal introduction to walkable, bikeable communities and Missing Middle Housing.

As I grew older, I had the itch to leave small-town America and explore other places and bigger cities. Without really knowing what I was getting myself into, but knowing that I wanted to experience city life, I moved to the South Side of Chicago to start my college career. I lived in a dormitory on a campus designed by the famous architect Mies van der Rohe that did not feel like a home. This was the first time I lived in or experienced a place that was supposed to be home but didn't feel like that to me. During this time in Chicago I did not have a car, so I would hop on the el train, eager to explore different parts of the Windy City. I spent most of this time in the wonderful row-house neighborhoods north of the downtown Loop, such as Lincoln Park and Wrigleyville. This was my first introduction to an expanded palette of Missing Middle types at a more urban scale. The more I immersed myself in urbanism and these walkable neighborhoods rich in variety of housing, the more I liked them.

I then lucked out: after my freshman year, I transferred to the University of Notre Dame into one of the few architecture programs in the country that taught traditional and classical architecture with an emphasis on urbanism and city making. At the time, I had no idea how heavily this would influence my life's course.

The seed for the concept of Missing Middle was planted my fourth year at Notre Dame. I had a design studio led by Michael Lykoudis and Norman Crowe. As part of the studio, we took a multiple-day field trip to the small town of Madison, Indiana, and were asked to document the building types, street types, public spaces, and urban structure of the town. Madison was very similar in scale to my hometown, so I immediately felt comfortable with the place, but through this exercise of documentation, my eyes were awakened to the scale of the block, the neighborhood, and the town for the first time, and more importantly to the role of building types and housing types as building blocks for neighborhoods, towns, and cities. Madison has a rich and distinct Federal-style architecture and a range of housing types, including a vast variety of row houses. Some were attached; some were slightly detached; some had formal entries and eaves; others were very basic but still well proportioned and attractive; some had stoops that directly engaged the sidewalk; others had a small front yard; and many of the homes had wonderful side-yard porches that responded to the hot, humid summer climate. I was learning through careful observation and documentation. This was when urban design started to make sense to me as a profession and when the study of building types became a foundation of my architecture and urban-design training. That focus would follow me into my profession.

Upon graduation, I decided I needed more of an urban, big-city fix, and my classmate and new wife, Karen, was game, so we targeted New York City, and I was offered a job with Robert A. M. Stern Architects. I got to work on a wide variety of projects while at Bob Stern's office, including a baseball stadium, a federal courthouse, a storytelling center, and several custom homes. "Homes" for our clients and the clients of the other firm I worked for while in New York City meant huge custom mansions for the likes of Jon Bon Jovi, Michael Eisner, and other billionaires who were building 10,000+ sq. ft. compounds in the Hamptons. These did not feel much like home to me either. I enjoyed this work for a while but ultimately found it unfulfilling.

More influential to my thinking about housing types while I was working in New York City was my life in the Park Slope neighborhood in Brooklyn. I lived there with Karen in a small one-bedroom apartment within an eight-unit, three-story, Tudor-style co-op building. The scale of Park Slope felt very comfortable. It felt like a neighborhood. There was block after block of three- and four-story brownstones—some that functioned as single homes and others that had been divided into multiple apartments—and sprinkled in among these types were larger apartment buildings that you would not even notice unless you stopped to look closely. While living here I learned about the flexibility and evolution of the town house form and the important role of a neighborhood main street in a walkable neighborhood.

After three years practicing architecture in New York, I knew I wanted to work at the scale of the neighborhood and city doing urban design and was accepted into UC Berkeley's master's of urban design program. At UC Berkeley, I had an amazing faculty to mentor me: Donlyn Lyndon, who was a former partner with Charles Moore, codesigner of Sea Ranch and author of several books, including *The Place of Houses*; the brilliant Allan Jacobs, who wrote San Francisco's first urban design plan in 1971 and wrote several books, including *Great Streets* and *The Boulevard Book*; Michael Southworth, a Kevin Lynch protégé from MIT who coauthored *Streets and the Shaping of Towns and Cities* and who trained me in the importance of studying a city's morphology as the first step of urban design; Daniel Solomon, cofounder of the Congress for New Urbanism and author of *Building*, *Global City Blues*, and *Cosmopolis*, who furthered my understanding of housing types; and last but not least, Peter Bosselmann, who established urban-simulation laboratories in Berkeley, Milan, New York City, and Tokyo and authored several books, including *Urban Transformation*.

In one of Peter Bosselmann's courses I completed a personally influential report titled *The Perception of Density* with Bryan Suchy and Marshall Foster, who went on to be planning director in Seattle. This was the point at which I began questioning the validity of the use of density for framing planning, zoning, and more generally housing conversations and began trying to understand what form characteristics primarily established a person's perception of whether a place was or was not densely populated.

While I was exploring housing types at UC Berkeley, I was also experiencing Missing Middle in my personal life. When arriving in Berkeley, Karen and I found a wonderful 500 sq. ft. one-bedroom apartment in a three-story eightplex building. It was in a vibrant neighborhood called Northbrae on Hopkins Street across from the Monterey Market, which had an amazing selection of fresh produce, a cheese shop, a fish market, a bakery, a coffee shop, yoga studio, dry cleaner, and a restaurant. The unit was small, but it was exactly what we needed and had the walkability we wanted at this point in our lives.

For my graduate thesis, I entered a professional design competition, sponsored by the Great Valley Center based in Modesto,

California, called "Housing the Next 10 Million." It was an ideas competition that asked for ways in which California's Central Valley could accommodate the projected ten million more people without compromising its rural character and thriving agricultural economy. For my submittal, I decided to create a comprehensive growth strategy for Modesto. In addition to focusing on revitalization and infill in its downtown, I wanted to demonstrate how this medium-sized valley town could grow in a walkable pattern of neighborhoods with a variety of housing types. While preparing the proposal, I remember spending hours and hours studying the building-type diagrams from Peter Katz's *The New Urbanism*, and *Towns and Town Making Principles* by Andrés Duany and Elizabeth Plater-Zyberk. The two became mainstays on my desk in Wurster Hall.

This was also when I first started to think in greater detail about how to write more effective zoning for walkable places. As one part of the competition submittal, I wrote my first form-based code, at the time called a typological code, that introduced many of the Missing Middle Housing types and how to effectively regulate them. My submittal won the grand prize for the competition. The winning schemes traveled throughout the Central Valley, sharing ways for valley communities to grow more thoughtfully and compactly with a pattern of small towns and cities. This exposure opened the door to my branching out on my own and starting my architecture and urban-design practice, Opticos Design.

Opticos's first major project, and an opportunity to further explore housing types, was creating a master plan for the community of Isla Vista, which was adjacent to UC Santa Barbara. We were hired by Santa Barbara County to lead this job after winning the design competition appropriately called "RE: Vision Isla Vista." Isla Vista was one of those university-adjacent communities that had visually suffered from a few decades of poorly designed, high-density apartment buildings that were slowly creeping from the university into the community.

When we first stepped into this project, it was very clear that Isla Vista's citizen advisory group had the perception that everything above the density threshold of eighteen dwelling units per acre (du/acre) would not be compatible with the community and that anything lower would be. They demanded that our plan and new zoning set a cap of 18 du/acre. We were taken aback by this immediate pushback and could not figure out how they came up with this desired density number. Why was 18 du/acre perceived as good in their minds, but 18.5 was bad, or why did they not pick 15 or 16 du/acre? We needed to figure out a way to shift the housing conversation away from a somewhat random and misleading density number and toward the form, scale, and building types that would be appropriate. To initiate this conversation, we led community members on a walking tour of neighborhoods adjacent to nearby downtown Santa Barbara. Santa Barbara is a laboratory of great Missing Middle Housing types. On this walking tour, we saw duplexes, fourplexes, mansion apartments, and bungalow courts in a variety of styles that the advisory committee really liked.

One of the last buildings we visited was a quintessential two-story, C-shaped Spanish Revival courtyard building on a 100 x 110 ft. deep lot. Everyone in the group loved this building, and the more we talked about it, the more it became clear that this was the type of building they wanted in their community. After speaking for a while, I told them to give me five minutes to further explore the building: I counted mailboxes, doorbells, and meters to determine the number of units in the building. Then I calculated the density of the building and went back to them with a little surprise.

"If we can create a plan and form-based code that ensures this type of building," I said, "Would you be willing to support the plan?"

They all said yes.

Then I told them that this building that they loved so much generated a density of almost 45 du/acre—almost two and a half times higher than the maximum density they thought should be allowed in Isla Vista. This immediately made the point and shifted the process and conversation away from density and focused it on

Committee members said they did not want more than eighteen dwelling units per acre in their community. On a walking tour, however, they all loved this building and were shocked to find out it was forty-five dwelling units per acre, thus planting the seed for the concept of Missing Middle Housing.

form and building type. The resulting form-based code we drafted was building type–based, and it encouraged buildings such as the courtyard apartment and other Missing Middle Housing types (though we didn't yet call it that) that wowed the Isla Vista community leaders. At this point we knew we were onto something.

At this same time I was asked to coteach a graduate architecture studio at UC Berkeley with Donlyn Lyndon and Charles Correa, one of India's most famous architects, further exploring housing in California's Central Valley but with a focus on farmworker housing. Correa's amazing work on such projects in India, his simple, vernacular, kit-of-parts approach to design, with a focus on creating community, were an inspiration.

Over the next fifteen years I grew my company, Opticos Design, into an urban-design and architecture firm that influenced best practices and challenged standard practices in urban design and zoning and the policy, design, and delivery of a variety of housing choices. One of our early projects was an award-winning master plan for the beachfront community of Seaside, Florida. Over the course of seven years, I visited Seaside often and got to experience the range of different housing types built in Seaside under one of the country's first modern form-based codes.

Much of our work would focus on needed zoning reform to deliver walkable communities and a broader range of housing choices. To achieve these goals we delivered highly graphic and easy-to-understand form-based codes. I coauthored a book on this topic, called *Form-Based Codes*, that was published in 2008 by John Wiley and Sons. Most of these codes had a strong component of enabling Missing Middle Housing types.

Between 2008 and 2010, I began a concerted focus on effective zoning and form-based coding for the Missing Middle Housing types in our practice and through teaching. I really wanted to figure out why we were not building these important housing types and what zoning barriers needed to be removed to enable more of them to be built. Much of this teaching was through courses led by the Form-Based Codes Institute (FBCI), a nonprofit think tank that I had helped cofound, but also included presentations and teaching through the Congress for the New Urbanism (CNU), American Planning Association (APA), and the New Partners for Smart Growth. Most form-based codes at the time were focused on downtowns and delivering mixed-use places. As this zoning-reform work spread across the country, the breadth of the barriers in conventional zoning to deliver these types became evident. This work also reinforced how little understanding there was about these types among community members, developers, and even planners.

From late 2010 to 2012, I was creating the proper messaging and framing of my developing concept of Missing Middle Housing. A breakthrough came in February 2010 at the New Partners for Smart Growth conference. I organized a panel with Chris Leinberger and Linda Pruitt called "Getting to Small Footprint Density." Within my presentation I presented a slide labeled "Missing Middle Housing Types" with a photo collage of a range of types. A few months later I taught a course called "Building Types as the Building Blocks for Great Places," where I further developed the concept. In November 2011, I gave a presentation called "Missing Middle Densities" at California APA, and the following spring I gave a presentation called "Regulating Missing Middle Densities." All of these presentations had a similar message: there is a growing gap between what types of housing people want and need due to shifting household demographics and market demand for walkable urban living; An introduction to the full array of these types that existed in neighborhoods historically; and barriers in zoning and how to remove them and effectively regulate these types with form-based coding.

Two thousand twelve was a milestone year for Missing Middle and really the year that I fully branded, framed, and launched the concept. EPA's Smart Growth Network (SGN) had a call for ideas for a publication to be called *A National Conversation: New Ideas in Community Planning, Design, and Development*. Their request stated the intent of the collected articles was to "start a national conversation around the future of our communities and to engage new voices." SGN was "seeking ideas and innovative approaches to community planning, design and development that will emerge in the next 15 years." I knew that Missing Middle Housing was such an idea, and SGN agreed and selected the article on Missing Middle Housing that I had written to include in the publication. While I was drafting the article, and being a visual person, I had realized that in addition to providing photos of each of the types, I needed a diagram to communicate the Missing Middle Housing concept quickly and effectively. The concept, the first version of what now is a more refined Missing Middle diagram, came to me fairly quickly because my company had been utilizing and communicating so frequently about this range of housing types and we had a 3-D library of them already in the Opticos library.

In retrospect, making the Missing Middle Housing diagram was a critical milestone in the evolution of Missing Middle Housing and is what ultimately would allow the idea to go viral. Anyone can look at the diagram and understand the concept without an explanation. When my article was published in *A National Conversation* it gave people the first view of the Missing Middle diagram with the full description of the concept. This diagram has since shown up in publications and planning documents across the country as well as in Australia and Canada. This diagram and article started a Missing Middle Housing movement.

In response to our presentations at national conferences over three to four years, my article in Smart Growth Network's publication, and a growing housing crisis across the country, buzz began to build around the idea of Missing Middle Housing, and we started fielding frequent inquiries. In response, I considered writing a book, but knowing it would take too long to respond to the immediate demand, Karen Parolek, Stefan Pellegrini (my partners at Opticos Design), and I decided to gather and organize our vast research related to Missing Middle Housing to create an online resource. In spring of 2015 we launched MissingMiddleHousing .com. This site filled a niche for those needing more information related to these housing types. It gets over fifty thousand visitors a year and has had over one hundred thousand total visitors since its launch through mid-2019. In addition, the Opticos team went on a multiyear Missing Middle road tour of sorts: from 2015 to 2019, we did almost one hundred presentations across the country, including helping inform, support, and spread the efforts that early adopters such as Portland and Minneapolis had started or were about to embark upon. These efforts helped the concept and the diagram to spread globally: it now frequently appears in international planning documents and publications. The movement had spread in application around the world.

From December 2017 to early 2019, the National Building Museum hosted an exhibit called *Making Room: Housing for a Changing America*, and we were thrilled to be asked to help design an interactive exhibit related to housing choices, different household demographics, and Missing Middle Housing types as part of this larger exhibit. Then, reinforcing the reality of this topic becoming more mainstream, AARP (formerly the American Association of Retired Persons), an organization with thirty-eight million members, hired my firm, Opticos Design, in 2018 to help facilitate a conversation and educate its members about the need for more housing choices across the country. This work became a core part of their Livable Communities Initiative.

One primary issue related to this greater visibility of Missing Middle Housing is that the use of the term often leads to a conversation that is solely about middle-income housing and neglects the very important components of scale, form, and housing type that we like to emphasize as primary concepts. We try to stay ahead of this and direct and inform the conversion. This is a big part of the reason I decided that I needed to write this book.

As I write this, phase-one units in the country's first Missing Middle Neighborhood have completed leasing in our Prairie Queen project in Papillion, Nebraska, to great interest from renters, developers, planners, and decision makers, and the next ninety units are under construction. The ultimate build-out will be 640 units of all Missing Middle Housing types over forty acres. In addition, we are working on what will be the country's largest car-free community, which has a variety of exciting Missing Middle courtyard-based housing types within a plan that delivers desert-responsive urbanism in Tempe, Arizona. This should be under construction when this book hits the shelves in 2020. We have also clearly defined the scope for Missing Middle Scans™, a service we have started providing to cities and counties across the country. The *New York Times, San Francisco Chronicle, Chicago Tribune, Washington Post, Next City*, and other professional publications have covered this topic and included interviews with me about our work.

After a century of development and planning focused on delivering single-family homes to the detriment of our cities and the earth, and at prices that are less and less attainable to all but the wealthy, we all need to act to respond to the housing issues in our communities and to deliver housing choices in walkable urban environments at a variety of price points and that deliver more sustainable development patterns. Delivering homes is the goal. With this, I hope that this book plays a role in people working together to define a new, equitable, attainable, and sustainable American Dream.

Let's help everyone find home.

ACKNOWLEDGMENTS

THANKS TO my wife, Karen, and my kids, Abby and Noah, for supporting me and covering for me while I slowly chipped away at this manuscript.

Thank you to the Richard H. Driehaus Foundation for providing their generous support for the book. And thanks to AARP for supporting the Missing Middle Housing movement as well as providing financial support for this book.

A special thanks to Max Heninger, who made major contributions to this book, including interviewing developers; drafting the case studies; analyzing data from the American Housing Survey, American Community Survey, and the Terner Center's California land-use survey to provide supporting evidence for key concepts in the book; and editing several draft chapters. It was great to have his passion for this topic and his knowledge to support the book effort early on.

Thanks for all of the support I got at Opticos, especially from Beth Cichon, Roger Foreman, and Singeh Saliki, who produced many of the graphics for this book under the guidance of John Miki. Also Drew Finke and Xenia Alygizou for helping out when they found some time. And thanks to my business partners, Stefan Pellegrini and Karen Parolek, for letting our firm commit the resources to take on such an endeavor.

Thanks to Michael Lykoudis for inspiring me, as a fourth-year undergraduate at Notre Dame, to think about building types.

Thanks to Jim Heid, Jerry Reimer, David Spence, Eli Spevak, and Garlynn Woodsong for taking time out of their busy schedules to provide information for the case studies. And to my colleagues Jonathan Fearn, Michael Lander, and others for our "coffee talks" related to Missing Middle Housing as the manuscript was unfolding.

Thanks to Heather Boyer at Island Press for her thoughtfulness, assistance, and effort in getting the manuscript completed.

Thanks to my mom and dad, Mary and Robert Parolek, for making the sacrifices they did to ensure that I could take this career path that I love.

And a final thanks to my great-grandmother for showing me that a small, 600 sq. ft. duplex apartment could serve as a world-class bakery as well as a home.

*Highly desirable walkable
neighborhoods across the country
have a mix of single-family homes and
Missing Middle Housing.*

INTRODUCTION

IF YOU WALK DOWN ANY TREE-LINED STREET in a pre-1940s neighborhood in any city across the country and look very closely, you will notice some of the buildings are not quite like the others. Some buildings will look like and are the scale of single-family houses but have two doors or four gas meters, which means there are multiple units. These buildings are often a seamless part of a street and block with mostly single-family homes. Or you may see a wonderful collection of very small cottages oriented around a shared green space. These housing types, such as duplexes, four-plexes, cottage courts, and courtyard buildings, are examples of Missing Middle Housing. Many of us have lived in one of these types, currently live in one of these types, or have friends or family who live in one of them. They provide more housing choices and can help people to stay in the neighborhood as their lifestyle needs change. They can provide a broad range of affordability as well. They often consist of smaller but well-designed units and are within walking distance to amenities such as restaurants, coffee shops, small grocery stores, transit, and more.

Due to shifting household demographics and market interests, there is a tremendous mismatch between the available housing stock in the United States and the type of housing that people want and need. The post–World War II auto-centric, single-family-development model no longer meets the needs of a large percentage of the US population. The household and cultural demographics of the United States have shifted dramatically—nearly 30 percent of all households are now single-person.[1] By 2035, one in five

Americans will be over the age of sixty-five,[2] and households without children will make up 84 percent of change in households between 2015 and 2025.[3] Baby boomers and millennials are increasingly saying no to the suburbs and choosing a walkable urban lifestyle. (See chapter 2 for an in-depth analysis of shifting household demographics and the need for new housing choices.) Buyers are longing for a sense of community that is not being delivered.

In addition, cities across the country are struggling with the lack of affordable housing, while development pressures are delivering McMansions or other inappropriately scaled housing, and NIMBYs (not in my backyard) are pushing back strongly against any housing that is not single-family detached. It is difficult for developers and builders to deliver homes at attainable prices due to rising costs and increasingly complex entitlement processes.

The reality in most cities is that their planning and regulatory systems are barriers to delivering the housing choices that communities need. Density- and use-based planning and zoning were established to separate uses and create suburban environments, which makes it difficult, or impossible, to mix forms, uses, and types that result in walkable, mixed-use neighborhoods similar to the ones that formed organically before zoning was commonplace in the United States before the 1940s. These neighborhoods are typically highly cherished and in high demand, such as Park Slope in Brooklyn, Dundee in Omaha, Old Louisville in Louisville, Westbrae or Elmwood in Berkeley, East Walnut Hills in Cincinnati, Lincoln Park or Oak Park in Chicago, or Bishop Arts in Dallas.

(Photos, pages 2–5) Searching for and counting doors, doorbells, meters, and mailboxes are ways to discover Missing Middle Housing.

Cities have attempted to address these issues over time but have often failed and sometimes made the problem worse. For example, in the 1970s many cities began to make changes in the zoning in single-family neighborhoods adjacent to downtown to allow higher densities. Due to ineffective regulations, most of the new housing built was out of scale, poorly designed, and poorly constructed and resulted in community members up in arms. In most cities, the backlash led to dramatic downzoning as well as the creation of historic districts in some areas to protect those neighborhoods. Most cities still have not recovered from that misstep in planning and zoning.

Unfortunately, the solution is not as simple as building more multifamily or single-family housing using conventional housing models, making minor adjustments to our planning and zoning (such as simply increasing density), or making simple refinements to other systems related to building, financing, and selling homes. Rather, we need a complete paradigm shift in all of these systems and the way we think about and communicate about housing—no small task. Missing Middle Housing and, more specifically, Missing Middle Housing types are what many households

across the country are seeking to call home and struggling to find. Some local and state governments have recently started taking action. The State of Oregon just passed legislation removing single-family zoning statewide and allowing triplexes or duplexes, depending on a city's size, on all lots now zoned for single family. And the City of Minneapolis, Minnesota, adopted a policy to allow triplexes on all single-family-zoned lots citywide. The State of California has been attempting to pass similar legislation in SB 827 and SB 50 to address the dire housing needs across the state. All of these efforts have a strong component of enabling Missing Middle Housing to provide more housing and more non-single-family housing choices.

Understanding the role and characteristics of Missing Middle Housing types, the barriers to building them that need to be overcome, and how to effectively communicate about these housing choices will enable you to be part of the solution to the growing housing crisis whether you are a planner, architect, politician, developer/builder, city leader, or community member.

As you read through this book you will find yourself thinking differently about housing. This book will help get you beyond thinking about housing in the two overly broad categories of multifamily and single family. It will help you understand the benefits of living more compactly in a walkable environment. If you are a planner or city leader, it will help you realize why density-based policy and zoning is too blunt of an instrument to effectively regulate for twenty-first-century housing needs, and that a new, more refined approach is needed. If you are a builder or realtor, it will elucidate why complete industries and systems need to be rethought to help deliver the broad range of Missing Middle Housing needed to meet the growing demand for walkability, non-single-family living, and housing at attainable price points. If you are a renter or home buyer, you will see a whole new world of options available to you. You will just need to look closely to find them.

After reading this book, it is likely that you will walk down a

street and find yourself observing a neighborhood differently: noticing a second or third door, or multiple doorbells and mailboxes, on the building you thought was a single-family house; looking closely at the windows on the side of the building to try to understand the floor plan; walking through rear alleys to see how parking works or if there is any provided; then maybe even stopping to calculate what density that particular housing type generates.

Each of us plays a role in addressing the dire housing issues and need for a broad diversity of housing choices in communities across the country. Once you have a basic understanding of Missing Middle Housing, you will be empowered to make a difference in your own community, or maybe even across the country, as housing issues continue to grow for cities and towns large and small. You too can and need to be part of the solution.

WHAT IS MISSING MIDDLE HOUSING AND WHY IS IT IMPORTANT?

MISSING MIDDLE HOUSING IS A RANGE OF MULTIUNIT OR CLUSTERED HOUSING TYPES, COMPATIBLE IN SCALE WITH SINGLE-FAMILY HOMES, THAT HELP MEET THE GROWING DEMAND FOR WALKABLE URBAN LIVING, RESPOND TO

shifting household demographics, and meet the need for more housing choices at different price points. The majority of these types accommodate four to eight units in a building or on the lot, in the case of a cottage court. At the upper end of the spectrum they can have up to nineteen units per building.

We label these housing types "missing" because, even though they have played an instrumental role in providing housing choices and affordable options historically in towns and cities across the country, we are building very few of these housing types today and have built very few in the past thirty to forty years—even in cities such as Boston and other eastern cities whose early patterns of development were founded on these types. The term *middle* has two meanings. First, and most importantly, it represents the middle scale of buildings between single-family homes and large apartment or condo buildings, as explained in more detail below. The second definition of middle relates to the affordability or attainability level. These types have historically delivered attainable housing choices to middle-income families without subsidies and continue to play a role in providing homes to the "middle income" market segment that typically straddles 60 percent to 110 percent average median household income, in new construction, for-sale housing. This percentage will vary based on what market you are in. That being said, it is important to note that Missing Middle Housing is not exclusively targeting a middle-income market. There is a large, pent-up demand for these housing types at the upper end of the market as well as from downsizing baby boomers, single-person households, and millennials who want walkable living. Missing Middle can deliver a range of affordability but can also respond to the demand for different types of housing at the upper end. It is often not hard for a well-designed Missing Middle type to adapt to hit both an

Single-family homes on the left (small) and large, multiunit apartment buildings on the right (large) represent the two types of housing that primarily get built, thus providing a big gap in housing choices.

entry-level and a higher market. Within the same housing type or building, introducing a higher level of materials and finishes on the exterior and the interior of a unit, and sometimes adjusting unit sizes, is enough for the same unit to hit both market segments. Savvy developers are delivering Missing Middle Housing with higher-quality finishes and build-out to those at the very upper end of the market looking for walkability and quality over quantity. These type of projects tend to have very little competition in their markets.

On the left-hand side of the figure below are single-family homes. Cities and developers have had the zoning, construction, finance, and other systems set up to effectively deliver these housing types since the 1940s. There is no shortage of the single-family housing type. On the right-hand side of the figure are the large, five-to-seven-plus floor apartment, condo, or mixed-use buildings that, particularly in the past fifteen to twenty years, cities have enabled within their planning and zoning and developers have figured out how to deliver. This scale of building is being delivered in a majority of cities large and small across the country. It is often necessary, along with Missing Middle, for cities to meet their housing needs. But, due to the many barriers for Missing Middle, the larger buildings are the only rental buildings being built in many cities. The large size and boxy form and scale of this type of building, its nondescript character, the fact that it is often built in a short time period, and a fear of "density" have all resulted in pushback by residents in communities across the country.

This diagram represents the full range of housing types in-between the scale of single-family homes and large, multiunit buildings, known as Missing Middle Housing, that need to be built to address housing issues of today.

The previous figure shows the Missing Middle Housing types (in the middle of the diagram): duplex, fourplex, cottage court, multiplex: medium (mansion apartment), triple-decker, town house, live-work (flex house), and courtyard building. These buildings are all house scale, which typically means not more than two to two and a half stories, no more than 55 to 75 ft. wide along the street front, and a depth similar to that of a single-family home, typically 45–60 ft. maximum. Examples that are at the upper end of width along the street, around 75 ft. wide, usually are at the lower end of depth, or about 45 ft. maximum.

Although the core of Missing Middle Housing is at the scale of single-family homes, at the upper end of the spectrum they can reach three to four stories and deeper on a lot. It is important to differentiate these types and this scale from the core of the Missing Middle to build support for the idea of Missing Middle Housing. These should be clearly classified as Upper Missing Middle Housing, which is appropriate only in some locations. One zone

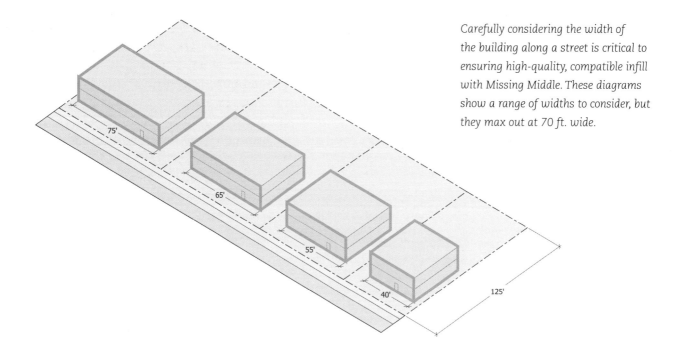

Carefully considering the width of the building along a street is critical to ensuring high-quality, compatible infill with Missing Middle. These diagrams show a range of widths to consider, but they max out at 70 ft. wide.

Existing Missing Middle units by decade built. This illustrates the steady decline in the number of Missing Middle units built in the recent past, thus why they are labeled "missing." (Source: American Housing Survey, 2013, US Census Bureau)

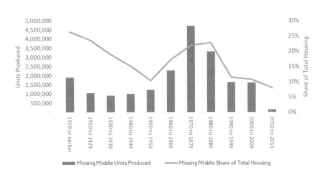

district will be needed to effectively regulate the core of Missing Middle, and another will be needed to regulate the slightly larger Upper Missing Middle. (Chapter 7 gives an overview of different planning and zoning techniques. See chapter 5, "Missing Middle Housing Types," for photo examples of types.)

Keep in mind it is the form and scale of the building that matters most, not the number of units. Think about the defined and regulated building form as a house-scale container. The same-sized container, or building, that accommodates four one-bedroom apartments could also easily accommodate eight studio apartments within that same container if zoning and parking standards allow it to. This contradicts a common belief that buildings need to get bigger as the number of units increases.

If you are going to take one concept away after reading this book it should be that Missing Middle Housing is about *house-scale* buildings that happen to have more than one unit within them. House scale has a maximum width, depth, and height. There will be some variation based on local examples, but the maximum scale is fairly consistent across examples. This concept counters the belief that as you add more units to a building it needs to get bigger and that multiunit buildings are always bigger than a single-family home.

When communicating about Missing Middle Housing, and the need for more housing choices generally, it is important to first emphasize the scale and form parameters of these housing types because it can help build support from community members to

Alliance for Housing Solutions, a housing-advocacy group in Arlington, Virginia, created its own interpretation of the Missing Middle diagram to help communicate the organization's mission and message effectively. (Source: Alliance for Housing Solutions)

allow more housing, but doing so without introducing large buildings into sensitive contexts. It is also this middle scale that allows the buildings to be built more cost efficiently to deliver attainability by design.

It is important to understand that housing types represent a specific form, scale, and layout of a building, which is very different than thinking of them as an allowed use without specific form implications or intent. As a use, all Missing Middle types could fit under an attached single-family or multifamily category, but their form is quite different across the Missing Middle spectrum.

Many Missing Middle Housing types have unique histories in different cities or parts of the country in terms of who built them, when, and why, which could be a research project or book in and

---

Box 1-1

Missing Middle and Cohousing

One of the questions that often comes up is how Missing Middle Housing relates to cohousing (an intentional community of private homes organized around shared space). Generally speaking, there is overlap between the two concepts in terms of the physical design and layout, including the range of housing types that are often used, and site plan layout characteristics, such as shared community spaces. People who live in Missing Middle Housing and in cohousing often want similar characteristics and community-focused elements and are willing to make trade-offs, such as unit size and privacy. But there are also differences in physical design elements, and cohousing generally involves the residents in the design process and requires a level of formalized or structured social contracts. The Cully Grove case study in chapter 6 is a great example of a cohousing project that also fits within the Missing Middle classification.

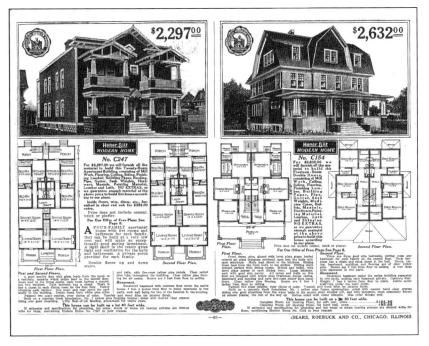

Missing Middle types such as duplexes and fourplexes could be ordered out of the Sears, Roebuck and Co. catalog in the early 1900s at affordable prices. Similarly time- and cost-efficient delivery methods of Missing Middle Housing need to be found today.

of itself. In the early to mid-1900s, Sears, Roebuck and Co. sold house plans and, later, kit houses to the American market, and some of these houses were Missing Middle Housing types such as the fourplex. One example is the Modern Home No. 264P247, also called the Atlanta. This was a craftsman-style fourplex, with two-bedroom, one-bath units. Sears reported that more than 70,000 of these homes were sold in North America between 1908 and 1940. More than 370 different home designs in a wide range of architectural styles and sizes were offered over the program's thirty-three-year history.[1] In Chicago, two- and three-flat buildings make up a quarter of the overall buildings. In the 1910s and '20s, Bohemian immigrants may have worked hard and saved enough money to build or buy one of these buildings. For these households, buying a two flat didn't just mean more breathing room and more pleasant living conditions; they were always intended as wealth-building investments. Rental income could cover the mortgage and provide a degree of economic security.[2] There is a lesson in this example that applies to today's conditions and how a household can creatively build equity with the purchase of a Missing Middle type.

Proximity to vibrant commercial main street environments like this one that can deliver social centers, amenities, transit, and entertainment is ideal for Missing Middle Housing. Walkability is about walking to destinations like this, not simply walking for recreation on paths, trails, and the like.

THE CHARACTERISTICS OF MISSING MIDDLE HOUSING

The exact architectural elements (materials, roof forms, window patterns, eave details, and so on), the patterns of where they were applied, and the forms of Missing Middle types vary from city to city and region to region, but there is a shared set of characteristics that are inherent in most of these types.

Located in a Walkable Context

Missing Middle Housing types are best located in an existing or newly built walkable context to meet the growing demand. Walkable does not mean recreational walking such as on paths and trails, but rather walkable to a destination like work, a coffee shop, restaurants, bars, entertainment, and other amenities. Linda Pruitt of the Cottage Company, who is building innovative pocket-neighborhood communities in the Seattle region, says the first thing her potential customers ask is, "What can I walk to?"

In the context of Missing Middle, walkable urban is delivered at the neighborhood scale, two to three stories, rather than the city scale. Buyers and renters of these housing types are looking for walkability and are willing to make tradeoffs on other house characteristics, such as unit size. Missing Middle types can be built in an isolated auto-oriented context, but they will not attract the same kind of buyer or renter, will not deliver more compact, sustainable patterns of development, and will not achieve the same returns or rents for developers. The higher the walkability of a project context, the smaller the units can be, and the less off-street parking that is needed.

Lower Perceived Density, but Enough to Support Services and Amenities

One of the most important characteristics of Missing Middle Housing types is that, because they have the scale and form of a single-family house, the density is perceived to be lower than it is. They can generate average densities at or above 16 du/per acre—the general threshold needed to create a supportive environment for public transportation and also much desired neighborhood-serving main streets that provide services and amenities that more and more buyers and renters are looking for within walking distance of their homes.

One objective of the Missing Middle concept is to shift the housing conversation away from metrics like density that, contrary to what many believe, do not ensure predictable built results, and toward aspects that *can* deliver predictable results, such as form, scale, and building types—or the perceived density. Therefore, it is highly encouraged that density not be used as the primary way to frame a discussion about housing options or Missing Middle Housing, but as a general reference point these building types typically range in density from 16 du/acre to up to 35 du/acre with one- and two-bedroom units. Some Missing Middle buildings with smaller units integrated, even though they are only two stories, can generate densities as high as 85 du/acre. This type of framing can be challenging. Effective communication strategies for introducing Missing Middle Housing to communities are discussed in chapter 7.

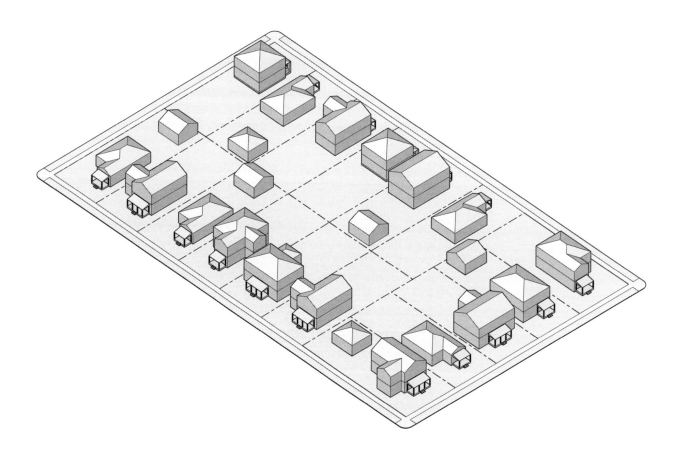

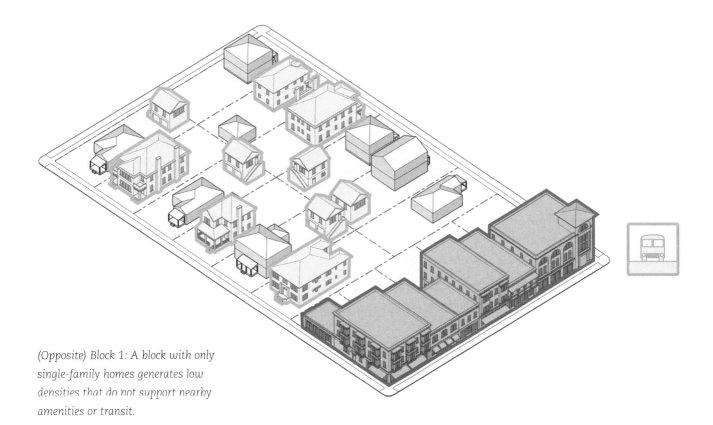

(Opposite) Block 1: A block with only single-family homes generates low densities that do not support nearby amenities or transit.

(Above) Block 2: Missing Middle Housing can be thoughtfully integrated into single-family neighborhoods to increase the population density to reach a threshold that will begin to support neighborhood commercial amenities and transit.

Table 1-1: Density of Blocks, Compared
Block 1 with all single family compared with block 2 with a mix of Missing Middle and single family and a main street.

	SINGLE-FAMILY BLOCK	MIXED BLOCK
DENSITY OF RESIDENTIAL	7.0 du/acre	18.6 du/acre
DENSITY OF HOUSING ABOVE RETAIL		46.0 du/acre
DENSITY AVERAGE	7.0 du/acre	26.6 du/acre

Small Building Footprints (Width and Depth of Building)
This characteristic directly ties into its lower perceived density but has its own section because it is very important to emphasize. Most community discussions about housing focus primarily on maximum height, but maximum width and depth are just as important, and maybe even more important, in terms of compatibility with existing buildings. Missing Middle Housing types typically have small-to-medium-sized footprints, with a body width, depth, and height no larger than those of a single-family home. This concept of house-scale buildings should be used when framing a discussion with a community about what Missing Middle is and how it can be compatibly integrated into more neighborhoods, even those with primarily single-family homes. This discussion should shy away from agreeing upon a certain number of units per lot and focus more on building scale (maximum width, maximum depth, and maximum height) as defined in the Missing Middle Housing types chapter (chapter 5).

House-scale buildings have maximum width, depth, and height.

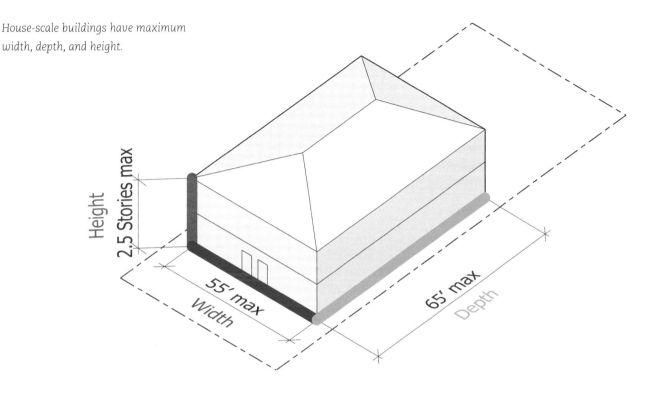

Smaller but Very Livable Homes

Small in the context of Missing Middle Housing starts as low as 600 sq. ft. (not quite tiny house scale, but we love that type as well), but the ultimate unit size will depend on the context. Smaller-sized units can help developers keep their costs down and attract a different market of buyers and renters who are not being provided for in all markets. This is an important strategy today as developers struggle to deliver attainability with rising land, materials, and labor costs across the country. Opticos's Mews Homes in the Daybreak Community in South Jordan, Utah, which delivered units starting at 900 sq. ft. (not the smallest size recommended in more urban contexts, but much smaller than the average new home in its broader suburban context), achieved a price point around $25,000 less than a conventional tuck-under town house, and at the same time achieved the highest per-square-foot sales price points of any attached housing in this community by delivering smaller, quality units. Keep in mind that these smaller units are very attractive to 30 percent of US households that are single-person households, downsizing baby boomers, and other households choosing to live small for environmental reasons. The Mews Homes (see case study in chapter 6), like many other similar projects across the country, attracted primarily single-woman households and downsizing baby boomers who wanted quality but in a small, well-designed unit.

Thoughtfully designed small units can provide highly livable spaces with tall volumes, built-in furniture, and elements like nooks within a floor plan.

The challenge is to create small spaces that are well designed, comfortable, and very livable. One common starting point is using taller ceiling heights and larger volumes to make smaller spaces feel larger. Thoughtful integration of small, intimate spaces such as breakfast nooks, built-in furniture such as pantries to maximize storage in a small space, and creative approaches to layout such as providing sleeping nooks or lofts for occasional guests, are all design strategies that are recommended for maximizing livability of these smaller spaces.

Live Like a Single Family Home

The final and maybe most important characteristic in terms of market viability is that these types provide a similar living experience to single-family homes, such as entering from a private door on a front porch or stoop versus entering from a long, dark corridor to get into your home. Therefore, the mental shift for potential buyers and renters to Missing Middle from single family is much less dramatic than moving to a large mid-rise or high-rise apartment or condo building or a conventional suburban garden apartment.

Rental or For-Sale Homes

The question is always asked: is Missing Middle Housing rental or for-sale housing? The answer is that Missing Middle Housing types can be either or, even better, a mix of both within larger projects or a neighborhood. Many of the historic examples, including some of those documented in this book, are income properties owned by one person who rents them out. Sometimes the building has been divided into individually owned units through the creation of condominiums. The best and most sought-after neighborhoods in cities across the country are a mix of ownership and rental-housing choices, and this is a concept that holds true in Missing Middle Housing application.

More and more people are choosing to rent longer or choosing to rent permanently rather than buying a home and dealing with the hassles of homeownership, but they desire a place that is not a large condo building or a suburban garden apartment. A report by the Pew Research Center found that rental rates have increased among some groups that have traditionally been *less* likely to rent, including whites and middle-aged adults.[3] The Prairie Queen case study in chapter 6 tapped into this segment of the market by delivering a Missing Middle neighborhood.

TIP

In the context of Missing Middle it is important in many communities to have a conversation to counter concerns about rental housing and its perceived impact on home values, because more and more Americans are choosing to rent by choice.

Thoughtful Approach to Parking

Thoughtful parking approaches are necessary to enable Missing Middle both in terms of the quantity of on-site parking and how the parking is integrated onto the site and or into the type(s). A nonstarter for Missing Middle Housing is having to provide too much parking on a lot. Reducing parking is usually viable because these units are, ideally, being built in a walkable urban context, many of the households have only one person, and adjacent streets have on-street parking. If too much parking is required, not as many units can be built on a lot, often making Missing Middle projects not viable economically and shifting neighborhoods below the 16 du/acre density threshold. Architects can often get creative and force the parking onto a site, but the quality of design and living experience is compromised: often spaces that would be otherwise shared community spaces or courtyards become

driveways (not the same), and the ground floors of units are primarily parking so they do not effectively activate the streetscape or ground-level outdoor spaces.

Within multifamily and medium-density zones, parking standards often result in only single-family homes being physically viable on small-to-medium-sized lots. Therefore, as a starting point in most markets, these units should typically be required to provide no more than one off-street parking space per unit. A good example of this is newly constructed mansion apartments in the new East Beach neighborhood in Norfolk, Virginia, shown in the following figure. See chapter 7 for techniques to effectively adjust parking requirements.

This recently built fourplex in the East Beach project in Norfolk, Virginia, designed by Brown Design Studio, provides one off-street parking space per unit.

A majority of older Missing Middle examples were built with little or no off-street parking. Therefore, an effective strategy for framing the parking conversation in your community related to Missing Middle Housing is to document several of these historic examples in your community and to create posters, presentations, and online summaries of these documented, local case studies to illustrate how these types function with little or no parking on-site without impacting the neighborhood. This documentation can be done with participation from local architects utilizing your American Institute of Architects (AIA) chapter, planners through the American Planning Association (APA) local chapters, and community members. Documentation templates can be downloaded at MissingMiddleHousing.com.

Simple Construction

In the terminology of developers, Missing Middle Housing types are type V construction, meaning it is simple wood construction and comparatively less expensive to build, less risky, and often easier to finance than other urban-housing types that fall into the type I or III categories. If the height is kept to two stories, which is a sweet spot for Missing Middle, they provide even greater cost efficiencies for builders (see the Mews Homes case study in chapter 6). This makes them a very attractive alternative for developers to achieve good yields (this is where trying to avoid the *density* term is tough) without the added financing challenges and risk that come with more complex construction types. As construction costs have risen and it has become harder for builders to build and sell single-family homes, and in some markets town houses, at attainable price points, Missing Middle types are an excellent alternative for them to be able to achieve lower price points without having to completely rethink their business model.

Because of their simple forms, smaller size, higher yields, and type V construction, Missing Middle building types can help developers maximize affordability and returns without compromising quality.

Simple wood/stick construction, especially when contained to two stories, provides cost efficiencies for Missing Middle types.

Focus on a Strong Sense of Community

Americans are longing for a sense of community that is missing from their lives. Missing Middle Housing helps to create community through the integration of shared spaces within the building type or simply from being located within a vibrant neighborhood with a strong social fabric, diversity, and places to eat, drink, and socialize. This is an important aspect considering the growing number of single-person households that want to be part of a community.

This characteristic becomes extremely important in site layout and selection of a Missing Middle type early in the design phase. It reinforces the fact that there are diminishing returns on forcing too many units onto a lot so that it feels forced, fails on place making, and does not deliver a sense of community.

Shared community spaces within Missing Middle types provide great opportunities to foster a strong sense of community. This is highly desirable to a large percentage of renters and buyers, especially single-woman households. (Source: The Cottage Company)

Box 1-2

AARP Livable Communities and Missing Middle Housing

AARP (formerly the American Association of Retired Persons) has been a champion of Missing Middle Housing through its Livable Communities initiative. AARP Livable Communities supports the efforts of neighborhoods, towns, cities, counties, and entire states to become more livable and age friendly for people of *all* ages. According to AARP, a livable community is "safe and secure, contains housing that's affordable and appropriate, features transportation options, access to needed services, and opportunities for residents to engage and participate in community life."

To help create communities that are livable for people of all ages and life stages. AARP works with communities throughout the nation to increase transportation options, so work, cultural activities, volunteering, visiting with family and friends, shopping, and other daily activities are doable without always needing to drive or have access to a car. The availability of housing choices at different price points and sizes enables both older and younger adults to relocate within their community if or when their housing needs change.

AARP Livable Communities provides free publications and online resources through its website—AARP.org/livable—and works with AARP's fifty-three state offices to support, inform, and inspire local leaders.

The initiative's AARP Network of Age-Friendly States and Communities program provides a framework for towns, cities, counties, and states that have committed to becoming more age friendly and livable for all.

The AARP Livability Index—a free, data-driven interactive tool—tracks dozens of policies and indicators to calculate the livability of a state, county, town, city, or street or specific address.

Missing Middle Housing has fit into and informed this important discussion about housing choices that accommodate the changing needs of the nation's rapidly aging population. In addition, since Missing Middle Housing is a core component of walkable communities, it delivers these housing choices in locations that give older residents easy, nearby access to services and amenities, as well as the strong sense of community and community support that is inherent in locations with car-free or car-light living.

As older homeowners sell their large single-family homes in car-centric suburbs, Missing Middle Housing provides a great alternative by featuring smaller homes that require less maintenance but have just the right amount of space and convenient access to needed services and amenities.

With its national livability efforts and local community work throughout the United States, AARP is able to bring the voices of millions into the Missing Middle Housing discussion.

WHERE DO YOU FIND MISSING MIDDLE?

Since Missing Middle Housing typically has a footprint not larger than a large single-family home, it is easy to integrate it into existing neighborhoods. There are a number of places where Missing Middle Housing typically exists.

Distributed Throughout a Block with Single-Family Detached Houses

Due to their house scale, Missing Middle types can be thoughtfully integrated onto blocks with single-family homes and other Missing Middle types. Note that it is not appropriate to cluster one single type on a block, but rather a mix of types should be used to provide variety in form and scale. Architecture alone cannot mitigate the impact of repetition of one type.

On the End-Grain of an Otherwise Single-Family Detached Block

One way to thoughtfully integrate Missing Middle types onto a block without blending them with single family homes is to place them on the end-grain of a block that otherwise has single-family homes.

Missing Middle types are similar in scale to single-family homes, making it possible to integrate them onto blocks with single-family detached homes. Many neighborhoods built prior to the 1940s that people think include primarily single-family detached homes actually have a mix of Missing Middle types within them that are "hidden density," a term often used by Brent Toderian to explain Missing Middle.

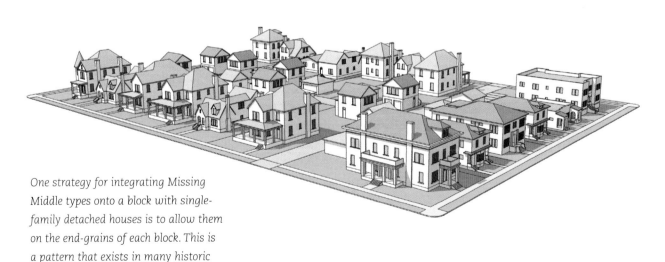

One strategy for integrating Missing Middle types onto a block with single-family detached houses is to allow them on the end-grains of each block. This is a pattern that exists in many historic neighborhoods and is replicable in new neighborhoods as well.

On Lots Adjacent to a Commercial Corridor to Transition into a Single-Family Detached Neighborhood

As you turn the corner from a neighborhood commercial corridor or main street, the first few lots on the perpendicular street are a great location for Missing Middle Housing as a transition from the commercial forms and uses into a single-family neighborhood.

In a Transition Area from Single-Family Homes to Higher-Density Housing

Missing Middle types are great to serve as transitions from higher-intensity housing into single-family neighborhoods. This can be done on a few lots or an entire block depending on block orientation.

Learning from these existing patterns and taking steps to adapt and evolve them to meet current needs and demands or goals is an important strategy for local jurisdictions. Chapter 7 discusses policy, planning, and zoning approaches that have been and can be used to determine where cities have targeted and should strategically target for the application and delivery of Missing Middle types.

Missing Middle types are more resilient to the physical and other impacts inherent in commercial uses, so they make a great means for neighborhood commercial areas to transition into neighborhoods.

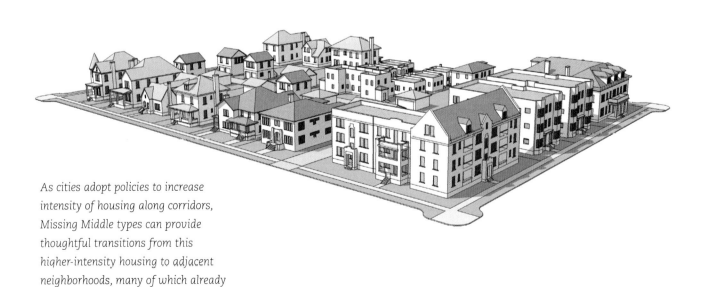

As cities adopt policies to increase intensity of housing along corridors, Missing Middle types can provide thoughtful transitions from this higher-intensity housing to adjacent neighborhoods, many of which already have a mix of types.

DEMOGRAPHIC CHANGES AND GROWING PREFERENCE FOR MISSING MIDDLE HOUSING

By Arthur C. Nelson

THE NUMBER AND MARKET SHARE OF NEW SINGLE-FAMILY DETACHED HOMES HAS BEEN FALLING STEADILY SINCE THE GREAT RECESSION (2007-2009). CHANGING DEMOGRAPHICS and housing preferences are slowly reshaping housing markets. One thing is certain: the preference for living in walkable communities and especially in Missing Middle Housing will drive housing markets over the next several decades and likely beyond. Therefore, both cities and developers need to respond.

Why these changes from building mostly single-family detached housing on large lots in the suburbs? Simple demographic changes mean that more than 80 percent of the growth[1] in households between 2018 and 2040 will be those without children. And the largest change will occur among multi-adult households with no children. These trends will affect the demand for existing stocks of housing.

Sweeping demographic changes will occur between 2017 and 2040 that will continue to increase the demand for Missing Middle Housing.[2] Tens of millions of baby boomers (born between 1946 and 1964) as well as Generation Xs (born between 1965 and 1980) will become empty nesters and singles. Many, perhaps most of them, will want to exchange their large homes on large lots for smaller homes on smaller lots or attached homes. Tens of millions of millennials—born between 1981 and 1997—will be forming households with children but may not want to buy boomers' large-lot homes, opting instead for smaller homes on smaller lots or attached homes. The newest generation—Generation Z, born between 1998 and 2015—will become starter-home households seeking mostly attached homes and then mature into multi-adult households.[3] Unlike prior generations, most of these baby boomers, Generation Xs, millennials, and Generation Zs will prefer to live in walkable communities. Millions of householders prefer to live in walkable communities with many millions of them preferring Missing Middle Housing. The problem is that even if every home built between 2020 and 2040 were built in walkable communities (including Missing Middle Housing units and all other attached units), it simply will not be enough to meet the growing preference for housing in walkable communities.

THE BIG PICTURE—SHIFTING HOUSEHOLD DEMOGRAPHICS

A large part of America's household demographic changes have their root in the "baby boom." With more than seventy-three million babies born between 1946 and 1964, "boomer" babies were equivalent to more than half (52 percent) of the 1946 population. No generation before or since has been as large proportionate to the base year of the generation. America's households, and along with them housing demand, swelled by eighteen million (from thirty-eight million to fifty-six million), nearly doubling the number of households and making it the largest numerical and percentage increase during any comparable period in the nation's history.

Cities were unable to meet such unprecedented demand for housing in such a short period of time. And newly formed households wanted something different: safer places than cities were perceived to be, open spaces, clean air, healthier environments, yards for children to play in, and new homes. For their part, suburban communities were poised to accommodate the needs of millions of baby boom households.[4] By 1970, suburbs had more people than central cities.

When boomers grew up and formed households of their own, they typically chose to settle in the landscapes with which they were most familiar: suburbs. Because they also enjoyed unprecedented incomes and housing-finance options, boomers led the national wave to homeownership, which peaked at 69 percent in 2005. The height of the boomer-driven surge in housing demand, especially for owner-occupied single-family detached homes, occurred during the period 1990 through 2010.[5] Between those years, the housing demand for mostly boomer households with children accounted for 82 percent of the market for new housing. Indeed, to meet this demand, 85 percent of all new homes built were single-family detached homes.[6]

Table 2-1: Change in Total Households by Type and Householder Age, 2018–2040

Household (HH) Type and Age	2018	2040	Change	Share
Households by Type				
Households with Children	34,958	39,387	4,429	19%
Households without Children	58,110	68,046	9,936	42%
Single-Person Households	34,739	44,025	9,286	39%
Total	127,807	151,459	23,651	
HHs with Children Share				19%
HHs without Children Share				42%
Single-Person HHs Share				39%
Households by Householder Age				
HHs <35	26,499	26,718	219	1%
HHs 35–64	68,439	73,358	4,918	21%
HHs >64	32,869	51,383	18,514	78%
Total	127,807	151,459	23,651	
HHs <35 Change				219
HHs <35 Share				1%
HHs 35–64 Share				21%
HHs >64 Share				78%

Figures in thousands.

Source: Adapted from Spader (2019) by extrapolating figures 2018–2038 to 2018–2040

Household Change by Type and Householder Age

Jonathan Spader at the Harvard Joint Center for Housing Studies has projected households by type and age, and by tenure (owner and renter) for the period 2018 to 2038.[7] I adapt this analysis extensively to help show the nature of change in housing demand associated with change in households by type and age. I also extrapolate projections to 2040. Table 2-1 shows changes in households by type and householder age between 2018 and 2040. This is key to understanding how the demand for Missing Middle Housing will unfold. There are two key findings. First, there will be 4.4 million more households with children in 2040 than in

2018, but 19.2 million (or 81 percent of the growth) will be households without children. Households with more than one adult will account for 9.9 million (or 42 percent of the net change) while single-person households will comprise 9.3 million (or 39 percent). This shift is important because households without children and especially single-person households prefer walkable communities and Missing Middle Housing options.

Second, of the 23.7 million growth in households, only about 200,000 of the growth will be among householders less than thirty-five years of age (in 2018 and in 2040) accounting for less than 1 percent of the change. This age group comprises mostly the children of millennials, who are deciding to have children later or perhaps not at all. For their part, householders aged thirty-five to sixty-four in 2018 and in 2040 will increase by 4.9 million or 21 percent of the change. The largest change, being the 18.5 million new householders between 2018 and 2040 who are more than sixty-four years of age, will account for 78 percent of the change. These trends are illustrated in the following figure.

Share of change of households by type and householder age. (Source: Adapted from Spader [2019])

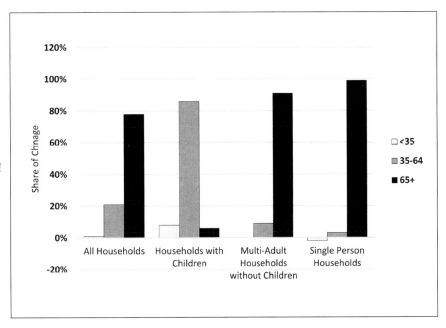

Housing Tenure Change by Householder Age
The projected number of households and change by tenure between 2018 and 2040, based on our extrapolation of Spader's base- and low-ownership scenario, show similar trends.

Overall, the home-ownership rate is projected to fall from 64.3 percent in 2018 to between 62.6 percent and 64.0 percent in 2040. While on the surface this may not seem to be a large difference, there are indeed substantial changes afoot when considering householders under sixty-five years of age.

For instance, in both scenarios, the number of householders under thirty-five years of age who own homes will fall between 2018 and 2040 even as the number of total householders in this age group grows by more than 200,000. What this means is that the net change in householders who rent will range from about 600,000 to more than 1.3 million. This signals a very large shift toward rental options by 2040 for this householder group.

Nearly equally surprising is the small change in owners among householders between the ages of thirty-five and sixty-four. With about 4.9 million householders entering this age group, those who become owners will range from about 80,000 (2 percent) to 1.6 million (33 percent). Remember that this was the age group that drove homeownership to record levels in the 2000s.

In contrast to younger age groups, householders who are sixty-five years of age and over will increase by about 18.5 million, with 12 million (70 percent) to 13.3 million (72 percent) owning homes, though the overall ownership rate may fall from 78.8 percent in 2018 to 75.8 percent in 2040.

The influence of the baby boom generation (and to a lesser extent Generation X) on future housing markets is clearly evident. What seems more evident is that younger generations are clearly moving away from homeownership. One reason is that while seniors will tend to own their typically suburban detached homes for a long time, younger generations will not be buying those homes anyway but instead seek alternatives such as Missing Middle Housing, which is mostly rental housing in locations they prefer. But both younger and older generations will want more walkable communities in which to live.

MISSING MIDDLE HOUSING TRENDS 2011–2017

Overall, attached units accounted for about 30 percent of all occupied housing units in 2011 and 31 percent in 2017 but comprised 59 percent of the change in housing units over that period of time. In contrast, single-family detached units comprised just 44 percent of the change. (The number of manufactured homes and other housing units fell by three percent.) Clearly, what was being built shifted during the 2010s away from single-family detached units, which dominated the 2000s, toward attached units.

I divide attached units into large attached structures and Missing Middle Housing. "Large attached" are those with twenty or more units, including townhome developments comprising twenty or more units. These units accounted for 43 percent of the entire change in occupied attached units.

Missing Middle Housing units comprise townhomes in structures of fewer than twenty units, plexes including duplexes, threeplexes, and fourplexes, and all other units in structures of fewer than twenty units, called "small attached." They accounted for 57 percent of the change in occupied attached units. We will now focus on Missing Middle Housing before adjusting for those that are in truly walkable communities.

While Missing Middle Housing was 77 percent of all existing attached units in 2011, its share fell to 75 percent in 2017, accounting for 57 percent of all newly occupied attached units. The loss of share is attributable to plexes that lost 610,000 units. Although units in small attached structures increased, they did not gain share as much as units in large attached structures. As plexes and units in small attached structures combined lost about 40,000 units, townhomes accounted effectively for all the change in Missing Middle Housing.

Why has there been a decline in two-, three-, and fourplex units? For one thing, communities have been modifying zoning codes to eliminate this housing type, especially duplexes, in single-family residential areas. For another, because they have fewer units, these types are difficult to scale for production. So, even if they are allowed, economics works against building them. Finally, older two-, three-, and fourplex structures are often in the path of redevelopment so they may be replaced by more intensive development—perhaps high-rises comprising more than twenty units.[8]

What share of all attached units would be reasonably allocated between large attached and Missing Middle Housing units? While data from 2011 and 2017 suggest Missing Middle Housing could make up about three-quarters of the total attached housing share, new Missing Middle Housing units accounted for only 57 percent of all new attached units. Indeed, there were 7 percent fewer two-, three-, and fourplex units in 2017 than in 2011, a loss rate of 1 percent per year. We suspect there is reason to believe that large attached units will gain considerable share over time for several reasons:

- Though urban infill and redevelopment is becoming increasingly common, it is also more costly and requires large scales of development to be financially feasible; this favors large attached units over Missing Middle Housing.
- Because of their small, neighborhood-level scale and by design if not intention, Missing Middle Housing will be a series of niche products in the form of small lot infill and redevelopment into townhome and small attached structures, and conversions of larges homes into two-, three-, and fourplexes.

For these reasons, and to be conservative, I assume that roughly half the total attached-unit production between the late 2010s and 2040 will be Missing Middle Housing.

PREFERENCE FOR LIVING IN WALKABLE COMMUNITIES

There is a pent-up preference in America for more walkable communities. This is reflected in what the market is willing to pay for locating in them. I use the word *preference* instead of *demand* because demand implies what people want in the absence of choices, while preferences are based on what people prefer when given reasonably plausible choices.

For this, I turn to the National Association of Realtors' (NAR) Community Preference Survey. It has been conducted every odd-numbered year since 2011.[9] Among the first questions asked by the NAR is the kind of home in which a respondent would choose to live, with choices being a single-family detached home, town-home, apartment, condominium, or other. More than 70 percent of respondents choose the single-family detached home. The survey then confronts respondents with reasonably plausible choices in two sets of questions. Respondents choose between (a) small detached lots[10] in walkable communities or conventional lots that are auto-dependent and (b) attached homes (such as town houses, condominiums, and apartments) in walkable communities or conventional auto-dependent lots.

However, we do not know how respondents are distributed by household type and householder age with respect to preferences for large-lot drivable-only homes, small-lot homes in walkable communities, or attached homes also in walkable communities. (To see the table with the results of my reanalysis of the NAR's raw survey data, please see the "resources" tab on the IslandPress .org page for this book).

Not surprisingly, the largest preference shares are for any kind of detached home, whether drive-only or walkable to places, ranging from 62 percent for single-person households to 71 percent for households with children. But, with one exception, people prefer to live in walkable communities by larger shares. Among all households, the walkable preference is 70 percent, reaching a high of 76 percent for single-person households though falling to 63 percent for multi-adult households without children. The exception is households with children, where most (58 percent) still prefer to live in walkable communities.

The bottom line is that based on insights from the NAR's Community Preference Survey, nearly 51 million households would prefer to live in attached-housing units that are walkable to places, a key element of Missing Middle Housing.

- 11.7 million households with children
- 23.1 million multi-adult households without children
- 16.6 million single-person households, most of whom are sixty-five years of age or older

This is the demand for Missing Middle Housing in 2050. (To see my table with the detailed distributions of preferences by household type and householder age, see the "resources" tab on the book page for this book at IslandPress.org.

Deriving True Missing Middle Housing: The Walkability Factor
In 2013, the American Housing Survey asked a special set of questions about whether selected destinations could be accessed by walking or biking.

For the most part, members in households of large attached residential units walk or bike to those destinations more than twice as much as those in detached homes. Members of all types of Missing Middle Housing households walk or bike to those destinations a little less than twice the rate of detached households and only moderately less so than for large attached units. However, somewhat more attached Missing Middle Housing units than townhome units are in walkable communities.

Table 2-2 shows that the weighted average of the accessibility to destinations by walking or biking ranges from 18 percent (about a fifth) for detached units to 32 percent for all Missing Middle Housing units (about a third) to 40 percent for large attached units (about two-fifths).

Table 2-3 derives the supply of true Missing Middle Housing units in walkable communities. It shows a little more than nine million Missing Middle Housing units in 2017.

Put differently, we know from the NAR that about a third of American households prefer to live in attached units in walkable communities. As there were 121.6 million households in 2017, the

Table 2-2: Non-Work Walk/Bike Accessibility among Housing Types, 2013

ACTIVITY	ALL UNITS	DETACHED	MMH TH	MMH ATTACHED	MMH ALL	LARGE ATTACHED
DESTINATIONS						
Grocery store	26%	22%	33%	39%	37%	45%
Personal services	24%	19%	30%	36%	35%	42%
Retail shopping	21%	17%	27%	33%	31%	40%
Entertainment	23%	19%	29%	36%	34%	42%
Health care services	16%	13%	20%	26%	24%	31%
Personal banking	21%	17%	26%	31%	30%	38%
Weighted Average	22%	18%	28%	33%	32%	40%

Source: American Housing Survey, 2013

Table 2-3: Deriving True Missing Middle Housing Supply in Walkable Communities, 2017

METRIC	FIGURE
Missing Middle Housing before Adjustment, 2017	28,383
Walkable Share 2013	0.32
True MMH Walkable Missing Middle Housing, 2017	9,083

Figures in thousands of units.

Source: American Housing Survey

implication is that about 40 million households preferred to live in attached units in walkable communities. We can derive from table 2-5 that only about 34 percent of the occupied attached units were considered walkable in 2017, or about 12.8 million attached units.[11] Missing Middle Housing units account for about 70 percent of the existing supply of attached units in walkable communities. This also means that about 27 million households who wanted to live in attached units in walkable communities do not.

Average Annual Missing Middle Housing Absorption Needed to Accommodate Preferences to 2040

Relative to production in 2017, new Missing Middle Housing units would need to account for about 62 percent of all new housing completions between then and 2040 to meet the demand for these housing types (see table 2-4). In addition, considering that we are allocating only 50 percent of the total preferences to Missing Middle Housing, all new housing built to 2040 would need to be in walkable communities, split roughly between Missing Middle Housing and large attached structures to meet the demand for walkable living.

There are some other ways in which preferences can be accommodated even if new housing starts are insufficient. For instance, conversions of existing single-family detached homes into two-, three- and fourplexes in walkable communities can help expand supply. This would occur on a scattered, ad hoc basis, but if local land-use and building codes were modified perhaps just slightly, many more households could be extended Missing Middle Housing options perhaps more cost effectively.

Moreover, local governments by themselves or through public-private partnerships could convert existing developed areas, including the existing housing stock, into walkable communities.

There may also be the possibility of converting surplus strip-center land into small-scale Missing Middle Housing projects albeit perhaps with considerable brownfield remediation investment from federal, state, and local governments. The tradeoff is converting nonproductive urban land into Missing Middle Housing that can stabilize neighborhoods if not make them more vibrant.

In other words, with the right policy direction, there may be reasonably straightforward ways to convert existing non-walkable communities into walkable ones, in addition to focusing on infill in existing walkable urban areas and creating new walkable communities, in order to increase the supply of Missing Middle Housing units to the level needed to meet the demand.

The Fall of Detached and the Rise of Attached Housing

Over the past century, new detached-home construction has outpaced attached-home construction, but trends may be reversing. The following figure shows that the share of new detached homes to all new homes has been declining in recent decades. From the

Table 2–4: Average Annual Share of New Housing Absorption to Accommodate MMH Preferences to 2040

METRIC	CALCULATION STEP
50,851	Total preferences for attached housing in walkable communities, 2040, from table 2-3
50%	Share allocated to Missing Middle Housing in walkable communities
25,426	Amount share allocated to occupied Missing Middle Housing in walkable communities
9,083	Occupied supply of Missing Middle Housing in 2017, assuming no losses to 2040
16,343	Unmet future preferences for occupied Missing Middle Housing units
23	Years between 2017 and 2040
711	Average annual absorption needed to meet future MMH preferences
1,153	Total new occupied housing added 2017
62%	Average annual Missing Middle Housing absorption compared to new occupied units built 2017

Source: Arthur C. Nelson

period before the 1940s into the 1950s, detached homes increased from 59 percent to 77 percent of the share of all new occupied dwellings, falling steadily back to 57 percent in the 1980s. Home-finance innovations in the 1990s and 2000s led in part to an excess supply of new detached homes into the 2000s, but in the 2010s, the new-detached-home share fell to 56 percent, which is the lowest level. As the supply of detached homes wanes, the supply of attached homes increases; we anticipate that these trends will continue for the foreseeable future.

Even as the share of new detached homes to all new homes falls, their average size increases. Notably, census data show that the average size of new detached homes increased from 1,500 sq. ft. in the 1970s to 2,500 sq. ft. in the 2010s—a 60 percent jump. The increase has garnered media attention, with some claiming that the increasing size of new detached homes is a key signal of overall economic health and validation of the market demand for ever-increasing new-home sizes.[12]

Closer examination of this shift reveals troubling trends. First of all, the sheer number of detached homes built on an average annual basis fell from nearly 1.5 million homes during the 1970s to less than 400,000 homes in the 2010s. Moreover, while only 6 percent of the homes built in the 1970s were over 3,000 sq. ft., in the 2010s this share was four and a half times higher at 27 percent. Put differently, during the 1970s, 74 percent of all new homes built were less than 2,000 sq. ft., but only 39 percent were in the 2010s. Indeed, there were nearly as many homes over 3,000 sq. ft. built annually in the 1970s (about 99,000) as in the 2010s (about 101,000), yet those homes accounted for a far larger share. It is little wonder the mismatch between new-detached-home prices and incomes keeps growing.[13] In contrast, American Housing Survey data show that the average size of new attached units, including townhome and small and large attached structures, has not changed much over the past several decades.

I surmise that newly built attached structures are meeting shifting housing demand better than detached products.

New detached dwelling share of all new dwellings by decade. (Source: American Housing Survey)

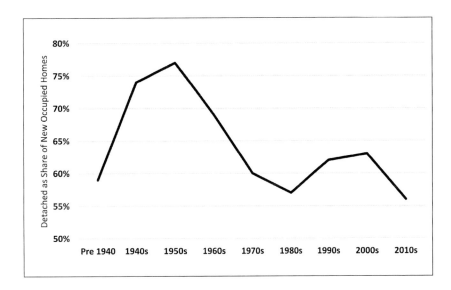

Structural and Occupancy Differences with a Nod to the Missing Middle Housing Niche

Detached homes have more persons per unit than townhomes, which have more persons per unit than Missing Middle Housing attached, which have more persons per unit than large attached ones. While sensible, these differences help one understand the niche Missing Middle Housing can fill.

For the most part, larger households will prefer larger homes albeit not necessarily on larger lots, though perhaps categorically not necessarily in walkable communities. But larger households are on the wane. Smaller, especially single-person households of sixty-five years of age or older, may be attracted to large attached units especially for the on-site amenities and security they provide. In the middle, of course, is Missing Middle Housing, which may be attractive to smaller households, empty-nesting or downsizing households, and households who seek a walkable lifestyle.

Detached have 1.21 bedrooms per person, the largest rate among all housing types. By and large, these are larger homes with more bedrooms per unit than the other types, but the bedroom ratio may also suggest that for many households, these homes have more space than is needed. In contrast, the bedroom-per-person ratio for Missing Middle Housing is close to 1.0, suggesting a closer match between household size and needs. Large attached units have the smallest bedroom-to-person ratio, which is consistent with the smaller households occupying those units. From the perspective of unit size based on the bedroom ratio, Missing Middle Housing options would seem to cater to smaller, multi-person households while large attached units would seem to cater perhaps to older couples or single-person households.

Table 2-5 generally supports my expectations. Households without children and especially single-person households dominate

Table 2-5: Key Demographic Comparisons between Housing Types

METRIC	ALL UNITS	DETACHED	MMH TH	MMH ATTACHED	MMH ALL	LARGE ATTACHED
Minority	34%	28%	56%	45%	51%	48%
Householder (HH) Type						
HHs with Children	32%	34%	33%	30%	31%	18%
HHs without Children	68%	66%	67%	70%	69%	82%
Single-Person HHs	27%	20%	31%	42%	38%	53%
Householder Age						
HH <35	18%	12%	22%	35%	18%	31%
HH 35–64	55%	58%	54%	49%	53%	43%
HH65+	27%	29%	25%	15%	29%	26%
HH Income	$84,393	$94,823	$76,902	$48,818	$57,978	$64,593

Figures may not sum due to rounding.

Source: American Housing Survey

occupancy of large attached units. On the other hand, there are large differences when it comes to householder age. Middle- and upper-aged householders are concentrated among detached homes more so than other types. There is also a large difference with respect to incomes, with households occupying detached, town house, and large attached units earning more on the whole than households living in small attached Missing Middle Housing units.

Reducing Automobile Dependency and Improving Housing Affordability

There is another factor to consider: the role of true Missing Middle Housing located in walkable communities in reducing commuting costs. This is not a trivial issue because lower transportation costs means more money in the pockets of households thereby making housing itself more affordable. For instance, table 2-6 shows the transportation mode to work for workers living in different types of housing. Literature shows consistently that the greater the dependency a household has on the automobile in the commute to work, the higher that share of income that household spends on the automobile. Notice in table 2-6 that 89 percent of the workers living in single-family, detached homes commute to work in single-occupant vehicles (SOV). In contrast, only about three-quarters of all workers living in Missing Middle Housing commute in single-occupant vehicles, while an even smaller number, 59 percent of those living in large attached units, do. In contrast, the share of people commuting to work in non-drive modes (transit, walk, or bike) living in Missing Middle Housing is more than double that of detached units, while for those living in large attached units, that share is nearly double that of Missing Middle Housing.

These are large differences. Not shown, because it is part of ongoing, unfinished research, is the commuting distance and cost and the number of vehicles by unit type. Prior research suggests that, based on our continuum of residential units, total Missing Middle Housing transportation costs will be about 60 percent lower than costs for the average detached home, while costs for large attached units will be about a third of those costs.[14] And it is

Table 2-6; Commuting Modes among Housing Types, 2017

METRIC	ALL UNITS	DETACHED	MMH TH	MMH ATTACHED	MMH ALL	LARGE ATTACHED
Single-Occupant Vehicle	83%	89%	80%	73%	75%	59%
Carpool	4%	3%	4%	6%	5%	3%
Transit	8%	5%	10%	13%	12%	25%
Walk/Bike	5%	3%	6%	9%	8%	13%
Transit/Walk/Bike	13%	8%	16%	22%	20%	38%

Figures may not sum due to rounding.

Source: American Housing Survey, 2017

not just transportation cost savings: reduced automobile dependency reduces greenhouse gas emissions, reduces the land needed for parking vehicles, and can increase the value of real estate.

SPECIAL ROLE OF MISSING MIDDLE HOUSING TO MEET AMERICA'S FUTURE HOUSING NEEDS

Americans want something different than what was provided from the mid-1940s into the early 2000s: places where people can walk or bike (or increasingly, scooter) to shops, restaurants, services, transit stations, and even work. Though on the one hand, people might prefer detached homes (even on large lots), if the tradeoff means not living in walkable communities, attached homes in those communities prevail. Though large attached structures can also facilitate walkability, they can often isolate residents from their community. Missing Middle Housing requires householders to accept living in their communities, but that may not be for everyone, which is why choices are important.

But choices are constrained by the ability of markets to respond. We noted above that to meet the market preference for

Missing Middle Housing, more than 60 percent of all new housing would need to be built as Missing Middle Housing units in walkable communities over the next several decades. Will the market deliver? Though this seems unlikely, we know the order of magnitude of emerging housing preferences that need to be met.

3.

THE MISSING MIDDLE HOUSING AFFORDABILITY SOLUTION (WITH CASE STUDIES)

With Karen Parolek

THE LACK OF AFFORDABILITY OF HOUSING IS AN INCREAS-

ING PROBLEM IN MANY PLACES ACROSS THE COUNTRY—

PARTICULARLY IN THOSE THAT ARE WALKABLE AND HAVE

TRANSIT SERVICE. (HOUSING IS GENERALLY DEFINED AS

affordable when householders do not have to spend more than 30 percent of their income on housing.) While there is outsized media attention on the affordability woes of San Francisco, New York, and other high-cost cities, the reality is that a one-bedroom apartment in 99 percent of counties in the United States is not affordable for a full-time minimum wage worker. While the federal minimum wage has remained stuck at $7.25 since the aftermath of the financial crisis, rents have risen at a steady clip between 2.5 and 4 percent since 2012, according to Harvard's Joint Center for Housing Studies.[1] Solutions to the affordability crisis lie on a spectrum that includes subsidized housing on one end, an increase in supply on the other, and Missing Middle Housing in the middle.

At one end, it's imperative we increase the supply of subsidized housing for households with lower incomes, particularly those that make at or below 60 percent of area median income (AMI). These households do not make enough to pay the true cost of building housing, so the market will not be able to meet the need for this sector without subsidy. For many families the availability of subsidized housing can be the only bulwark against being extremely housing-cost burdened or even homeless.

Barbell of affordable housing solutions showing subsidized housing on left, increasing supply on the right, and providing Missing Middle Housing in the middle.

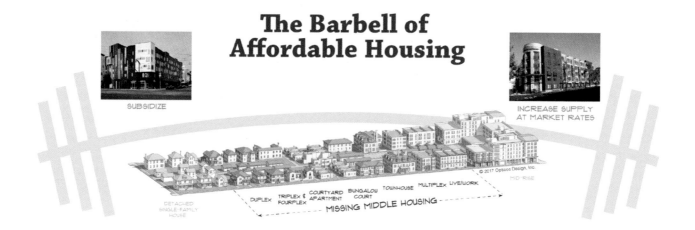

The Barbell of Affordable Housing

SUBSIDIZE

INCREASE SUPPLY AT MARKET RATES

© 2017 Opticos Design, Inc.

MID-RISE

DUPLEX TRIPLEX & FOURPLEX COURTYARD APARTMENT BUNGALOW COURT TOWNHOUSE MULTIPLEX LIVE/WORK

DETACHED SINGLE-FAMILY HOUSE

MISSING MIDDLE HOUSING

However, absent a massive influx of government (likely federal) spending on housing subsidies, the market must be part of any realistic supply-side solution to the housing crisis, and the supply simply has not kept up with the growing demand. The reasons for this, as addressed elsewhere in this book, include a zoning paradigm that drastically limits where and what type of new housing can be built, and resistance from existing residents (known as NIMBYs, or, "not in my backyard"). Fortunately, a growing number of planners and policy makers at the local and state levels are recognizing the dire need for more housing supply, especially in jobs- and transit-rich areas, and are proposing policies to remove barriers to delivery.

Instead of focusing solely on already dense, mid-rise, urban contexts, cities should also look to add housing to their existing walkable but smaller-scale neighborhoods, some of which may be primarily single family. The key is to focus on areas that already deliver walkability or could deliver it with the introduction of more housing, improvements to the public realm, and access to amenities. This is where Missing Middle can be most impactful in delivering housing that is more affordable. Heather Hood from Enterprise Community Partners states, "We used to build smaller and medium-sized housing structures that were the building blocks of integrated neighborhoods. These are those 'missing middle' sizes somewhere between the single-family home and the nineteen-plus-unit, multifamily apartment buildings. Now," Hood goes on, "we can see the genius in this old settlement pattern and find ways to bring it into our futures to achieve both affordability, flexibility, and variety in neighborhoods. Tucking such sizes into neighborhoods can create all levels of affordability, depending on financing, and take some of the pressure off the housing markets where communities are experience displacement's fatal sting."

Since Missing Middle Housing types are typically affordable for households with incomes at 60 percent the average median incomes or higher, we often call it attainable housing rather than affordable housing. Here are ways that Missing Middle Housing delivers more attainable housing.

AFFORDABLE BY DESIGN FOR MIDDLE-INCOME HOUSEHOLDS

Missing Middle Housing is affordable by design, which means that it can achieve affordable price points for rental or for-sale units without subsidies. It achieves this by increasing supply and filling the gap for neighborhood living; using simple, lower-cost construction methods; reducing reliance on automobile ownership; using land more efficiently with shared and smaller units; and providing more income opportunities for residents. All of these factors result in an end product that is much more attainable for households, typically those making 60 percent or more of the area median income, or middle-income households.

A number of the case studies in this book highlight Missing Middle projects that are affordable for these income levels, and

Box 3-1

Understanding the Small and Medium Multifamily Housing Stock

In 2017, Enterprise Community Partners, Inc. released a report titled *Understanding the Small and Medium Multifamily (SMMF) Housing Stock*. This report focuses on buildings of fifty units or less, which is bigger than what is classified as Missing Middle, but this research and findings are informative about the role of this segment of the market in the United States in delivering naturally occurring affordable housing choices, and also very telling about the long-term impact on affordable housing of the market building fewer and fewer small and medium apartment buildings. This report classifies SMMF housing as any multiunit building with fewer than forty-nine units. According to this report, SMMF accounted for more than a quarter of all units built in the 1970s and 1980s, but since 1990 it has represented only about 15 percent of new construction. In addition, this report finds that buildings with more than fifty units account for less than 10 percent of all rental units, emphasizing the important role of smaller buildings, such as Missing Middle Housing, in the rental market historically, and confirming that smaller SMMF forms define the most affordable segment of the housing stock, with the most affordable rents found in buildings with two to nine units. Within this same data set we can see that Missing Middle buildings, which we define as two to nineteen units, make up 45 percent of all rental units, thus reinforcing Missing Middle Housing's role in delivering rental housing historically.

the case studies in this chapter are projects that are subsidized and thus affordable to households with lower median incomes. And in almost all cases Missing Middle Housing is more affordable than a single-family home or town house built on the same lot. The Prairie Queen case study delivers attainability by providing units that lease for $995 per month in triplex and fourplex building types, which is affordable for a household making just over 60 percent of AMI for the city it is located within, while at the same time having larger units in town houses sited on the same block that rent for as high as $3,000 per month. The Mews Homes were able to sell for around $25,000 less than a typical town house in the same market due to smaller unit sizes; simple, easy-to-construct design; and the typical two-story height compared to the three-story town house.

REDUCING THE COST OF TRANSPORTATION

Building parking is expensive, especially with the high cost of land in high-demand markets. The cost of building parking is passed on to the buyer or renter, thus increasing the cost of housing. By one estimate, parking costs the average renter $225 per month.[2] Missing Middle Housing is inextricably tied to walkable places, so the need for parking is less, which can lower the cost per unit in multiple ways: 1. Decreasing the lot size and overall amount of land needed for each unit; 2. Increasing the number of potential units on a site; 3. Eliminating or reducing the cost of building garages. (For example, a small two-car garage is 625 sq. ft. At $75 per sq. ft., the cost for building this garage is almost $47,000. This additional cost can easily be the difference between a household being able to afford to buy or rent a unit or not); and, 4. Providing an option for households to live without a car, and thus eliminating the cost of car ownership. In the United States, the average annual cost of owning a car is nearly $10,000.[3] Approaches to reducing parking requirements are summarized in chapter 7.

SHARING LAND COSTS AND BUILDING SMALLER UNITS

Missing Middle Housing delivers multiple units on the same-size lot as a single-family home, therefore allowing distribution of land cost across multiple units, making them inherently more affordable. Even though they have multiple units, the scale of the buildings can be thoughtfully regulated with maximum widths, depths, and heights, or with floor-area-ratio standards. The units are often smaller than conventional single-family housing, thus making them less expensive to build.

The economic benefits of Missing Middle Housing are only possible in areas where land is not already zoned for large, multiunit buildings, which will drive land prices up to the point that Missing Middle Housing will not be economically viable regardless of how many units can be integrated into a Missing Middle type.

In every market, based on real estate values, the number of units in a building or project needed to deliver units that are affordable by design will be different and should be carefully considered. In some markets a fourplex may deliver the desired target of affordability, and in other markets it may take eight units on the same-size lot to effectively hit affordability targets.

OPPORTUNITIES FOR ADDITIONAL INCOME, OWNERSHIP, AND BUILDING EQUITY

Missing Middle Housing has added bonuses. While it helps contribute affordable-housing solutions, it can also put ownership within reach of more households and provide local business opportunities. Federal home loans can be used for buildings up to four units, which means a homeowner can qualify to purchase a Missing Middle Housing building that could contain their own, more affordable unit, plus up to three additional units, which can provide additional rental income to help subsidize their housing cost.

Historically, Missing Middle types provided lower-income households an opportunity to attain higher-quality living, to build equity, and to move up the social ladder. One such example was in Chicago in the early 1900s, where many two-flat and

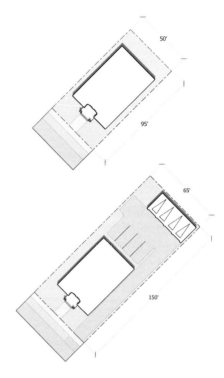

The impact of parking on affordability is large. This illustration shows how much more space is required to fit a fourplex on a site when two parking spaces are required per unit versus one without parking. This additional cost of land is directly passed along to renters or buyers.

three-flat building types were built that provided Bohemian immigrants, with some diligent saving and hard work, to earn enough money to buy one of these two-flat buildings and move out of the crowded tenements. This was a great step up from the tenements. The primary reason this was possible for them was that the rent generated from the second and sometimes third units helped them pay their mortgage. Often times, after having spent time in the two flat and saved even more money, many of these households then moved onto Chicago's highly desirable bungalow neighborhoods.

The biggest challenge with this opportunity is the potential buyer or builder having or finding the capital to fund the construction loan for a new building or for a down payment to purchase an

Box 3-2
Hope VI Program and Missing Middle Housing

The Hope VI program was started in 1992 by the United States Department of Housing and Urban Development. The intent of the program was to redevelop the most unsafe and poorly maintained public-housing projects into mixed-income neighborhoods. These projects were not without controversy, but the projects that were implemented under the Hope VI program integrated a broad variety of Missing Middle housing types, including duplexes and fourplexes that were delivered as both subsidized affordable housing as well as market-rate housing. A few examples of Hope VI projects that are seen as successful are the Park DuValle neighborhood in Louisville, Kentucky, and Townhomes on Capitol Hill, in Washington, DC.

Park DuValle integrates 1,050 housing units, including single-family homes, duplexes, town houses, and bungalow courts. Forty percent of the rental and homeownership units are for households earning no more than 50 percent of the area median income (AMI); 30 percent of the units are for households earning up to 60 percent of AMI; and the remaining 30 percent are for households earning more than 60 percent of AMI.

In the Townhomes at Capitol Hill there are 134 units, more than half of which are reserved for households making less than $54,300 (which is half of DC's area median income of $108,600). A quarter are reserved for households falling below 25 percent of AMI ($27,150), a quarter between 25 and 50 percent of AMI ($27,150–$54,300), and half between 50 and 115 percent of AMI ($54,300–125,976).

existing building. But much can be learned from these examples about how Missing Middle types can be used today to creatively deliver attainable housing options.

Small, incremental Missing Middle infill is also an excellent business opportunity for a small local business, and I often recommend that community-development corporations or local banks consider supporting or even incubating these small businesses. This could lead to a groundswell of incremental Missing Middle

The two flat provided opportunities for hardworking immigrants in Chicago in the early 1900s to purchase a home and move up the social ladder. The rent from the second unit was critical in helping them pay their mortgage. Similar strategies to utilize Missing Middle Housing to make homeownership accessible to more households should be created.

Housing development, contributing large numbers of affordable, locally owned housing units. It's the development version of a successful fundraising strategy: making big change through lots of small contributions. It also puts the power to make that change in the hands of the many rather than only a few. Finally, it empowers locals to build equity and benefit from improvements to a neighborhood and broader community.

COMMUNITY LAND TRUSTS

Creative approaches can be used to limit the impact of the cost of land on the short- and long-term affordability of a unit. A community land trust (CLT) is one approach. A community land trust is a nonprofit organization formed to hold title to land to preserve its long-term availability for affordable housing and other community uses. A land trust typically receives public or private donations of land or uses government subsidies to purchase land and develop housing. They are often used for single-family homes but can be a great tool to deliver a broad range of Missing Middle types at even more affordable price points than single-family homes while providing a similar quality of living experience. The homes/units are sold to moderate-to-lower-income families, but the CLT retains ownership of the underlying land and provides long-term ground leases to homebuyers. The CLT typically limits the price homeowners can sell the homes for and also retains a long-term option to repurchase the homes at a formula-driven price when homeowners later decide to move.[4]

CLTs are particularly efficient with the use of public funds. For example, if a home-buyer assistance program subsidizes the purchase of a home for a low-income person, and that person then owns the home outright, he or she could theoretically sell it a few years later and retain the full value of the subsidy while terminating any long-term affordability of the home itself. Thus, home-buyer subsidy programs are efficient at building wealth in individual homeowners but are very inefficient at creating and preserving affordable-housing supply in a geographic area. In this sense, traditional individual homeowner subsidies are more people-based, and they create an ongoing need for subsidies to deliver the same number of affordable units in a community. On the other hand, the CLT is a place-based alternative that creates permanent affordable-housing stock for generations to come through a one-time subsidy at the outset.[5]

AFFORDABLE MISSING MIDDLE HOUSING CASE STUDIES

The following are a few case studies that demonstrate how Missing Middle is being used in various scales and types of projects across the country with housing subsidies in order to deliver affordable-housing choices to a broader range of households.

MISSING MIDDLE PILOT PROJECT, DECATUR, GEORGIA: A City-Driven Missing Middle Affordable-Housing Pilot Project

It is not unusual for the development community in a city to initially respond to discussions about the need for more housing diversity or Missing Middle by saying, "It is not viable here." One approach to counter this response is for a city to take the lead on developing a Missing Middle Housing pilot project. As a pilot project, it introduces a housing product that is not already in the market that is intended to prove economic viability and market demand, thus making it easier to finance and reducing the risk for any other developers to begin building Missing Middle Housing.

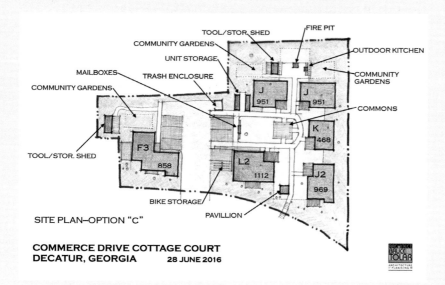

The six units on a half-acre site are oriented around a shared courtyard. (Source: Bruce B. Tolar, architect)

The cottages range from 468 to 1,100 sq. ft. (Source: Bruce B. Tolar, architect)

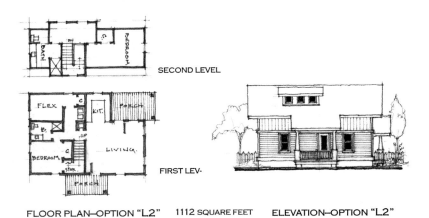

SECOND LEVEL

FIRST LEV-

FLOOR PLAN—OPTION "L2"   1112 SQUARE FEET   ELEVATION—OPTION "L2"

COMMERCE DRIVE COTTAGE COURT
DECATUR, GEORGIA   **25 AUG 2016**

One example got underway in Decatur, Georgia, in 2016. The City of Decatur purchased a half-acre vacant infill property within walking distance to jobs, amenities, and services with the intent to build a cottage court with six homes that will be sold to buyers who make 80–100 percent of the median household income in Decatur, selling at price points ranging from $100,000 to $250,000. Buyers will be determined through a lottery, with the City targeting city employees, city school employees, and employees of the Decatur Housing Authority as potential homeowners. The smallest unit is 468 sq. ft., the largest at 1,100 sq. ft., and the remaining homes are 900–1,000 sq. ft.

The City paid for and led the design for a six-unit cottage court with an architect, Bruce B. Tolar, and then went out to an RFP to find a developer and builder partner to build the designed project. This approach, of a city-led design process, is highly recommended. This also enables a city to get a more detailed and solid estimate in proposals from builders and to get a builder on board that is committed to delivering a shared vision. Decatur assistant city manager Lyn Menne stated in an article, "We don't intend for this project to be a one-off.

Phase one in the implementation of the vision to provide much-needed housing in Sonoma County, California, particularly after the wildfires there, completed. (Source: Sonoma County Habitat for Humanity)

We really want this to be a catalyst for these types of projects throughout our community."[6]

More than a year into the process, gaining full support from the city and the community, the project ran into a potential roadblock that demonstrates why these types of projects are still missing in communities across the country. The street that the pilot project is located on is a state road, and the one proposed residential-scale curb cut is considered changes within right of way by the Georgia Department of Transportation (GDOT), who manages this right of way. They reviewed the plans and have expressed concerns about the curb cut and wanted a deceleration lane added to address the problem. This not only would have been a bad solution for this context, compromising the compact walkable nature of the place, but also would have reduced the area of the project site. A compromise was made, and the project is now on track for construction.

SONOMA WILDFIRE COTTAGES, SANTA ROSA, CALIFORNIA:
Using Missing Middle Housing for Effective Disaster Relief

In October 2017, devastating wildfires torched at least 245,000 acres of Northern California, claiming forty lives, causing nearly $10 billion in property damage, and destroying over five thousand homes in Sonoma County alone, exacerbating an already dire housing crisis in the Bay Area. Habitat for Humanity of Sonoma County embarked on an effort to rapidly rehouse displaced residents. They envisioned a pilot project that would showcase different prefabricated building technologies and models of development in order to quickly and inexpensively deliver homes to residents throughout the county. They were interested in exploring whether Missing Middle Housing could play a role in their approach.

Habitat partnered with Cypress Community Development Corp, led by Marianne Cusato, the celebrated designer of the Katrina Cottages, to design and manage the construction of nine cottages clustered around a shared community space. Opticos Design joined the team to lead the site planning. (The ten-acre pilot-project site was graciously donated by Medtronic at their Santa Rosa, California, corporate campus.)

The primary design approach was to create a cottage court with a series of small detached units oriented around a shared community green space. The cottages are one- and two-bedroom units, ranging from 380 to 744 sq. ft. of livable space. Due to the need for quick construction while controlling construction costs, it was important for the team to compare the performance of a variety of different construction-delivery systems. These systems ranged from complete off-site fabrication to partially off-site fabricated systems that would enable quicker construction.

Construction began in February 2019 and was completed in August 2019. The built homes showcase four different building technologies, including: 1. A components system with light-gauge-steel-and-rigid-foam walls coated in stucco; 2. Structural insulated panels (SIPs) that are prefinished with windows, siding, and drywall before arriving on-site; and, 3. Two different modular manufacturers who built the units completely off-site. The process started

Residents are given keys to their homes on opening day. (Source: Sonoma County Habitat for Humanity)

with six vendors, but due to pricing and backlog, two dropped out early in the process.

The homes are designed to meet the State of California's strict sustainable-design requirements, CalGreen Title 24, including being solar ready. They also meet the Wildland-Urban Interface Code for hazard areas at risk for wildfires.

Initiated as a demonstration on a donated site in Santa Rosa, the cottages will be rented temporarily to families that lost their homes in the wildfires. The cottages will be relocated in two to five years and sold to Habitat-qualified families. The goal of this pilot

(Photos, pages 64–65) Before-and-after photos show the thoughtful historic rehabilitation that happened as part of the Iberville Off-Site Housing project to deliver affordable housing and reinforce the existing neighborhoods of Treme and Seventh Ward in New Orleans, Louisiana. (Source: Kronberg Wall Architects)

project is to employ the lessons learned to deliver more of these cottages on scattered opportunity sites around the county. This will help Sonoma County Habitat to respond to the high demand for housing by providing much-needed housing supply at attainable price points.

A key component of the project is affordability. The total project cost was approximately $2 million, including substantial site improvements, units, and fees, with the cost per unit on average just over $220,000. The one-bedroom units will rent between $950 and $1,250 per month, and the two-bedroom units will rent for $1,650 per month. By comparison, the average rent for a one-bedroom apartment in Santa Rosa is $1,730. Residents will only pay one-third of their before-tax income; the rest of the rent will be offset by Section 8 vouchers. Some families are paying less than $400 a month once vouchers are added. Families' income levels range from 13 percent to 79 percent average median income (AMI).

Ultimately, Habitat and Cusato envision the project will serve as a model for rapid response to disaster-recovery needs throughout the state of California and the United States.

IBERVILLE OFF-SITE HOUSING, NEW ORLEANS, LOUISIANA: Utilizing Existing Historic Resources to Deliver Affordable Housing and to Rebuild Neighborhoods

When this project began in 2013, more than two hundred thousand residents had returned to New Orleans after Hurricane Katrina. Many of them struggled to find affordable-housing options and to reestablish their communities. Rents had doubled in the previous four years, while median household income was static.

This project took an unconventional approach to developing low-income housing. Instead of tearing down blighted homes (there are 47,738 vacant housing units in New Orleans), the development company Redmellon rehabilitated the homes on the project sites to offer affordable housing while maintaining the distinct architecture of the community. The company sensitively rehabilitated forty-six buildings on twenty-six separate lots—vacant creole cottages, shotgun houses, and bungalows—in the Treme and Seventh Ward neighborhoods, preserving their character while providing modern amenities and sustainable features.

Completed in 2014, the project was a public-private partnership between the Housing Authority of New Orleans (HANO), New Orleans Women's and Children's Shelter, and Redmellon Restoration and Development. Financing for the $12.1 million scattered-site development was provided in part by affordable-housing and historic-preservation subsidies and low-income-housing tax credits.

(Opposite Left) One of the historic shotgun duplexes in a tremendous state of disrepair and almost near collapse prior to this project. (Opposite Right) The renovated duplex celebrates the historic structure with attention to detail. (Source: Kronberg Wall Architects)

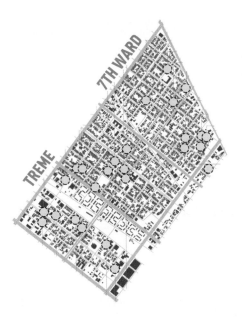

Map showing the scattered-site approach to renovating buildings in an effort to also stabilize and revitalize the historic Treme and Seventh Ward neighborhoods. (Source: Kronberg Wall Architects)

Redmellon executed the Iberville Offsite Home project in three separate phases that included a total of more than one hundred units. The homes are part of a larger Choice Neighborhoods Redevelopment Plan, a program by the US Department of Housing and Urban Development that supports locally driven strategies to address struggling neighborhoods with distressed public housing through a comprehensive approach to neighborhood transformation. In 2011, HANO and the City of New Orleans were granted $30.5 million as part of the US Department of Housing and Urban Development Choice Neighborhoods Initiative. The grant award included plans to revitalize the Iberville-Treme neighborhood.

Redmellon partnered with HANO to find former Iberville residents and low-income tenants in need of housing. Based on the location of the particular site, HANO qualified low income as a household making between 20 and 60 percent of the area median income of New Orleans, which the US Department of Housing and Urban Development values at $60,767. HANO rental subsidies allow residents to pay as little as $0 to $360 per month, depending on their household incomes. Long-term affordability is guaranteed via a thirty-five-year legal restriction on the properties that limits occupancy to low-income occupants.

A few of the happy new residents of the Iberville Off-Site Housing project. (Source: Kronberg Wall Architects)

The homes were designed by Kronberg Wall Architects of Atlanta and incorporate original design details such as decorative wood brackets and moldings as well as sustainability features such as new solar panels, tankless water heaters, and energy-efficient heating and cooling systems. The renovations met the challenging guidelines of the National Park Service Secretary of the Interior's Standards for Rehabilitation for historic tax credits as well as the Enterprise Green Community Criteria.

This affordable-housing project focuses on the core goals of the HUD Choice Neighborhoods program, which are housing, people, and neighborhoods. More specifically, the project replaces distressed housing with high-quality mixed-income housing that is well managed and responsive to the needs of the surrounding community. This project demonstrates that it is possible to use an innovative but replicable model to sensitively rehabilitate large numbers of single- and two-unit homes and provide affordable housing in the process.

This project won a Rudy Bruner Award for Urban Excellence and a National Trust Secretary's Award for Excellence in Historic Preservation.

A POWERFUL AFFORDABILITY HOUSING SOLUTION TO HAVE IN YOUR TOOLBOX

Missing Middle Housing is a proven, affordable-by-design housing solution that meets the growing demand for walkable neighborhood living and the need for housing choices at a broad range of price points. It provides a "missing middle" option between subsidized housing at one end and market-rate mid-to-high-rise housing at the other, but does so at a small, neighborhood scale or within house form. The Missing Middle types can also be utilized creatively in subsidized projects to deliver neighborhood-focused affordable-housing options. Therefore, Missing Middle should be a tool in every city's affordable-housing toolbox.

4.

UNDERSTANDING BARRIERS TO MISSING MIDDLE HOUSING

THE LIST OF BARRIERS PREVENTING THE DELIVERY OF

MISSING MIDDLE HOUSING IS, UNFORTUNATELY, LONG,

WHICH IS WHY THESE HOUSING TYPES ARE STILL MOSTLY

MISSING FROM RECENT AND NEW CONSTRUCTION. OFTEN

the challenge is not one single barrier but the accumulated costs, complexity, and risk added by several of these barriers that make Missing Middle infeasible, especially for smaller developers.

PLANNING AND ZONING BARRIERS

Keep in mind that many of the neighborhoods that have Missing Middle types were built prior to the advent of zoning in the early 1900s. The common approach to zoning (often called Euclidean zoning) was created to separate uses and to separate different housing types, such as single family and multifamily. Zoning varies from city to city, but few zoning codes effectively enable Missing Middle Housing. Some of the major issues include the lack of zoning districts that enable Missing Middle, metrics in development standards that are wrong, such as minimum lot sizes that are too large, densities that are too low, parking requirements that are too high, and the fact that very little of the geographic area of most cities is zoned to allow anything but single-family homes.

Below is a more detailed explanation of those zoning barriers. Efforts from city and state legislators are targeting much-needed changes to remove these barriers. In 2019, the City of Minneapolis approved a comprehensive-plan policy that will allow up to three units on any lot in the city, including those zoned single family, and in 2019 the State of Oregon passed legislation that will allow three to four units on any lot in the state, depending on the size of the jurisdiction. These efforts and other strategies to identify planning and zoning barriers and employ techniques to remove them are discussed in detail in the following chapter.

Lack of Zoning Districts that Enable Missing Middle Housing

This barrier is much larger than most people, even planners, realize. Few cities have zoning districts and the correct set of development standards that truly enable Missing Middle Housing types. In many instances, a city's entire group of zoning districts jumps from single-family zoning, which may allow duplexes, to districts that allow buildings that are much taller and larger than the Missing Middle types. Some cities, like Novato, California, are making

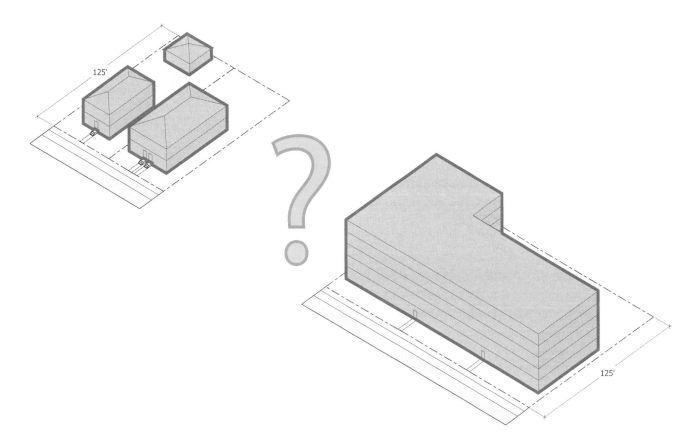

Zones that enable Missing Middle–scale buildings between single-family homes and larger apartment and condo buildings are often missing completely from a city's zoning code.

targeted additions of one or several new, effective Missing Middle zoning districts. Other cities, such as Flagstaff, Arizona, and Denver, Colorado, have tackled the issue as part of a larger citywide zoning code or land-development code update.

The Metrics in Multifamily or Medium Density Zoning Districts Hinder Missing Middle

Very few multifamily or medium-density zones have the intent of delivering small-scale buildings with multiple units on small-to-medium-sized lots. Most of them assume multiunit buildings are going to be big buildings on bigger lots. Often, even if a city has zones intended to deliver small-scale, multiunit buildings, the actual development-standard metrics include setbacks, maximum densities, minimum lot sizes, and so on that hinder Missing Middle

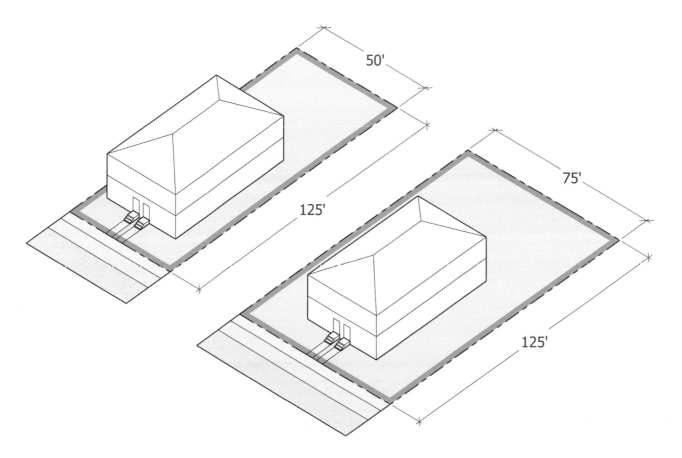

Housing. This gap is often present even in recently updated zoning codes. These metrics can make Missing Middle types economically unviable or physically impossible, especially on smaller lots. Local organizations, cities, and counties across the country, such as in Greenville, South Carolina, are leading efforts to analyze their zoning codes to identify gaps in the metrics of their existing zoning, often using graphic testing of potential development scenarios on existing lot sizes. Specific recommendations for the right metrics to include in your zoning are included in chapter 6 as well as in the Missing Middle types overview (chapter 5).

Ineffective Mapping of Zones
Another issue with zoning is related to how and where zones are mapped to allow Missing Middle. Just about every US city has

Minimum lot sizes required by zoning are often too large to truly enable Missing Middle Housing. As a start, a fourplex should be allowed on any lot 50 ft. or wider. If the minimum lot size is larger than one typical lot, which means a builder needs to buy two lots for a building, it makes building the type more challenging and often economically infeasible.

mapped single-family zones on a majority of the land in a city or county, thus prohibiting any other housing type in most of the city or county. A 2019 article in the *New York Times* titled, "Cities Start to Question an American Ideal: A House with a Yard on Every Lot" states, "Today the effect of single-family zoning is far-reaching: It is illegal on 75 percent of the residential land in many American cities to build anything other than a detached single-family home."[1] And often the small percentage of land zoned for multifamily housing is in non-walkable locations that are far from ideal for the application of Missing Middle and other non-single-family housing types.

Efforts in cities such as Medford, Oregon, are highlighting these issues with where multiunit buildings are allowed and on how much land. One of the findings of a study in Medford is that downtown-adjacent neighborhoods, which historically had a mix of Missing Middle and single-family homes, are currently zoned for single family but are the perfect location for this type of diverse housing.

Density–Based Planning and Zoning Discourages Smaller Units

This is a topic that is rarely discussed but may be one of the primary causes of a lack of housing choices and affordability across the country. Historically, smaller units or homes, generally 600–1,000 sq. ft., enabled a household to buy a smaller unit, build equity, then buy a larger home when needed. A system based on allowed density (either dwelling units per acre, or square footage of the lot required for each unit) inherently discourages the creation of smaller units and encourages developers to build as large of units as the market will accept, often high-end, expensive units. This biased zoning system has been in place since the 1920s.

As an example, if a developer has a 50 x 125 ft. lot, and the density-based zoning has a maximum density of 14 du/acre and allows only two units, the developer is incentivized to build two of the largest units that fit within the broadly defined allowed building envelope and that the largest and highest end of the market will accept. If zoning were changed to define a house-scale form as defined above without a density cap, the developer could choose to build four smaller units within that same building form.

Even outside of the affordability and attainability conversation, the simple realities that 30 percent of all households across the country are single persons, that family sizes are decreasing, and that a large percentage of the population is aging and wanting to downsize are reasons enough to want to incentivize and remove the existing density-based barriers and disincentives for the delivery of small units.

Progress on this front has been slow, but cities and counties across the country are increasingly taking a more form-based approach to their land use and zoning to remove this barrier. These approaches have been applied broadly to cities and counties ranging from Cincinnati, Ohio, and Miami, Florida, to rural contexts such as Beaufort County, South Carolina, and Kauai County, Hawaii, as well as small- and medium-sized towns such as Flagstaff, Arizona, and Paso Robles, California.

The Challenge of Parking Requirements

Off-street parking requirements have a tremendous impact on the financial and physical feasibility of Missing Middle Housing. In most instances requiring more than one parking space per unit, with no guest parking, is a barrier. Ideally, parking requirements will be removed completely, allowing the market to determine the amount of parking needed or not.

Requiring off-street parking has the biggest impact on small-lot residential infill. When you analyze neighborhoods platted before the 1940s, the lots are typically 25–50 ft. wide and the depths vary greatly but are typically between 100 and 150 ft. deep. For lots of this size, even if the development standards are intended to deliver Missing Middle–scale infill, the space needed to fit off-street parking on the site typically makes it physically impossible to provide the required parking and get multiple units on the site. If an architect can make the parking fit, often times there is not enough development potential for the project to make financial

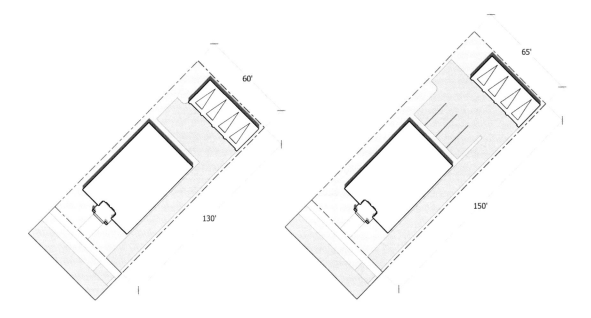

This set of drawings illustrates the impact of required off-street parking spaces on the minimum lot that a fourplex can fit onto.

The image on the left shows a fourplex and one space per unit.

The image on the right shows the larger lot required for a fourplex and two spaces per unit.

sense to pursue. This barrier is a primary reason most residential infill that cities are experiencing is on larger lots.

Parking requirements can have secondary and unintended impacts as well, often making it impossible for a project in a zone that is intended to allow multiunit buildings to achieve the maximum allowed densities or number of allowed units, and making it such that a single-family home is the only physically viable option on this lot. This house can also often have an unlimited number of bedrooms, thus encouraging the type of housing that is not desired rather than smaller multiunit buildings.

In the United States, San Francisco is leading the way with citywide elimination of parking requirements. But even small cities such as Hudson, New York, took the step of eliminating parking requirements citywide. Other cities, such as Flagstaff, Arizona, are reducing parking requirements in defined walkable urban contexts or in targeted areas such as along transit, as in Kansas City, or in downtown-adjacent neighborhoods, such as Davis, California. Other cities are approving developer-driven projects and standards to reduce parking, such as the Prairie Queen case study in chapter 6 in Papillion, Nebraska. General parking strategies and how to communicate to a community about them are also discussed in chapter 5.

Impact Fees Make Multiple Smaller Units Economically Infeasible

Impact fees are charges paid by the developers of new developments to a municipality to provide new or expanded public facilities (such as roads, sewers, schools, fire and emergency response) required to serve that development. The big issue with impact fees, in terms of them providing a barrier for Missing Middle Housing, is that the fee charged for a unit is typically the same regardless of whether it is 5,000 sq. ft. or 500 sq. ft. Therefore, there is a large economic impact for small, multiunit buildings (Missing Middle), particularly those with smaller units, often making them economically infeasible simply due to the extent of impact fees. This is because a high fee that can be absorbed by the sale or rent generated from a larger unit often cannot be absorbed by a smaller unit. And the more small units you include in the project, the higher the economic impact.

These abnormally high fees can dramatically change how developers design and deliver housing.

TIP

Adjust impact fees based on unit size, so smaller units pay less, and by context (infill versus greenfield).

COMMUNITY OR NEIGHBORHOOD OPPOSITION

You have to be living in a cave to be unaware of the polarized discussion related to new development, specifically around multifamily housing in or adjacent to existing neighborhoods. This type of pushback from communities prevents many developers, especially those who focus on delivering smaller, Missing Middle–scale projects, from even considering building in these communities because of the increased time and risk of getting a project

Yard signs showing support for and opposition to Missing Middle Housing efforts.

approved. This is particularly a problem in cities with zoning that requires a public, negotiated process such as a use permit or a rezoning. But it can also be a problem where the Missing Middle project is allowed by right and still challenged. A developer could spend years and hundreds of thousands of dollars on a project and not get their entitlement. This risk is too high for small projects. The irony is that the unintended consequence of this type of pushback is that larger projects are incentivized because they are the only ones that have the funding and the tolerance to risk making it through entitlements.

Local groups are organizing to get ahead of the housing conversation and using Missing Middle Housing to find a middle ground within communities to allow for much-needed housing. For example, Bend, Oregon's nonprofit organization Building a Better Bend and Arlington, Virginia's Alliance for Housing Solutions organized events to effectively frame the conversation and educate community members and decision makers about Missing Middle Housing. Groups of realtors and other development-industry stakeholders in communities such as Greenville, South Carolina, and Coeur d'Alene, Idaho, have raised money to host events and to complete the early phases of presenting and introducing the concept of Missing Middle Housing to their communities as well as funding studies that define the local planning and zoning barriers for Missing Middle Housing and address community concerns. In addition, large, visible organizations such as AARP have stepped up with education and advocacy related to Missing Middle Housing as part of their Livable Communities initiative (see box 3-2).

Techniques cities and organizations can use to effectively frame the conversation about the need for more diverse housing choices, utilizing the concept of Missing Middle Housing, are discussed in chapter 7.

MISSING MIDDLE HOUSING IS NOT EASILY CLASSIFIABLE BY INDUSTRY STANDARDS

Currently there is not a single large-scale builder that is focused on delivering Missing Middle Housing types like there are for single-family homes and larger multifamily housing. Missing Middle types are mostly built by small, local builders. The primary reason is likely that these types have been illegal under most city's zoning codes for three to four decades, so there was no reason for an industry to exist.

In order to address this barrier and meet the demand for these housing types, industries and professional organizations need to adapt and focus on this important niche, much as they did in the early 2000s to deliver vertical mixed-use projects. Various groups within the housing industry are trying to position this conversation with builders, but the response has been slow. *Professional Builder Magazine*, as part of their Housing Giants Conference, introduced the concept of Missing Middle Housing with a focused session on this topic and a few targeted articles that highlighted several successful recently built case studies. Some Urban Land Institute (ULI) Product Councils are beginning to discuss this topic, but it does not easily fit within the specific categories that define the Product Councils. One response to this has been the creation of the Small Scale Development forum within ULI, started by Jim Heid, that gets smaller, creative developers together at venues across the country to discuss project experiences and lessons learned. There are various efforts to train non-developers how to develop Missing Middle Housing, such as the nonprofit Incremental Development Alliance's efforts with courses being held across the country. Industry leaders such as RCLCO are completing market research and analysis that is proving the demand for Missing Middle Housing and highlighting the successes of builders who are building these types.

PERCEIVED COST INEFFICIENCIES FOR BUILDING SMALL

It's a fact that building larger buildings, say a 125–150 unit apartment or condo building, provides easier-to-identify and often larger cost efficiencies than building a four-, eight-, or even a sixteen-unit building or series of these buildings.

"Overall, a 50-unit project requires about the same amount of development work to execute as a 150-unit project, but the margins for the developer on the 50-unit project are lower, and the cap rates/valuations are also generally lower," says Curt Gunsbury, owner of the Solhem Companies, a Minneapolis-based developer that specializes in building sustainable residential properties. "Small projects have a hard time paying their way in a cost and regulatory environment that requires such a high level of developer sophistication, capital, and risk."[2]

This is one major reason larger builders and developers, who are looking for higher returns on their investments, are not building Missing Middle types, and why they are mostly being built by smaller builders and developers.

A solution takes some creative thinking, outside of a conventional pro forma approach and project approach, but it is possible. Efficiencies can be found elsewhere, such as repeating unit plans and counting on-street parking toward parking requirements as shown in the Prairie Queen/Urban Waters case study included in chapter 6.

ADDITIONAL RISKS OF SMALL CONDOMINIUM PROJECTS

There is greater complexity and added risks in building for-sale Missing Middle projects as condominiums, which is a primary reason few of them have been built recently across the United States.

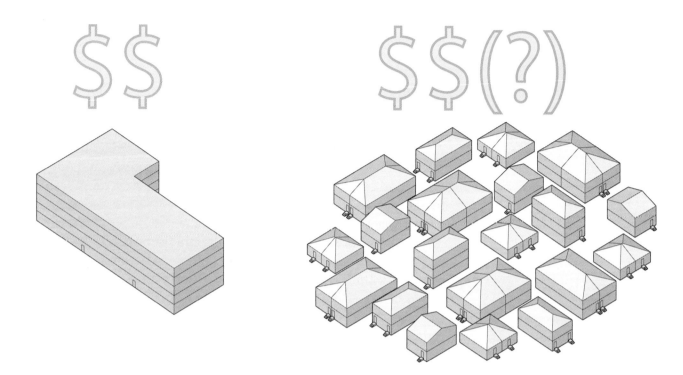

Condominium Liability and Construction Defect

Construction defect laws—such as California's Senate Bill 800: Construction Defect Liability, passed in late 2002—were established for good reason, to protect buyers from poor construction and to curb litigation between builders, homeowners, and the insurance industry. California builders and all entities affiliated with the construction of condos now have to take on additional liability, often with a statute of limitations of up to ten years. Based on recent history, the conventional wisdom is that if you build condos, you will get sued. Dan Bertolet from Sightline Institute, referring to the State of Washington's Condominium Act, explains why this is the case: "The law sets a higher construction-warranty standard for condos than for houses or apartment buildings." Over time, this "has spawned

It is more expensive to build more smaller Missing Middle buildings than larger conventional apartment buildings, but creative developers are finding cost savings in other components of their projects to compensate.

a legion of attorneys who specialize in persuading condo association board members to sue their builder for something—anything!—because it's better to be safe than sorry when the statute of limitations is running out." Therefore, condo projects generally require builders to secure additional insurance coverage, which makes development more expensive and riskier. This additional cost and risk can be absorbed into a larger fifty-to-one-hundred-plus-unit project, but for a Missing Middle project with nineteen units or less, the added risk and cost are too large to take on.

Even in the most highly valued markets, the construction of for-sale units, especially smaller-scale ones, is missing. For example, from 2012 to 2017 in the Seattle market, less than 4 percent of all new dwellings were condos, while more than 80 percent were apartments.[3] And Seattle is by no means the exception. Nationally, new multifamily units are overwhelmingly built for rentals rather than for ownership, and this trend has only accelerated since the Great Recession. In 2017, for every new multifamily unit built for ownership there were over fifteen built for rentals, up from 5:1 in 1999.

A few states are beginning to acknowledge this barrier, and some are taking strides to thoughtfully remove it. In early 2019 the State of Washington proposed a bill that would tighten what qualifies as a warrantable defect and would more explicitly shield condo association board members from personal liability so they would be less inclined to file frivolous lawsuits just to protect themselves. In the San Francisco Bay Area, the multidisciplinary group CASA, formed by the Metropolitan Transportation Commission (MTC) and Association of Bay Area Governments (ABAG), released the "CASA Compact, a 15-year Emergency Policy Package to Confront the Housing Crisis in the San Francisco Bay Area" in January 2019. The compact defined construction-defect liability as a priority issue for the state to address within its "Compact Element #7—Expedited Approvals and Financial Incentives for Select Housing."

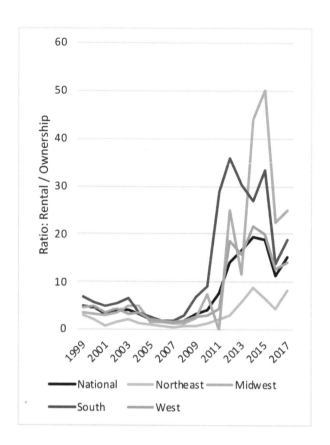

The amount of for-sale multifamily housing constructed in the past eighteen years has decreased. (Source: American Housing Survey 2017, US Census Bureau)

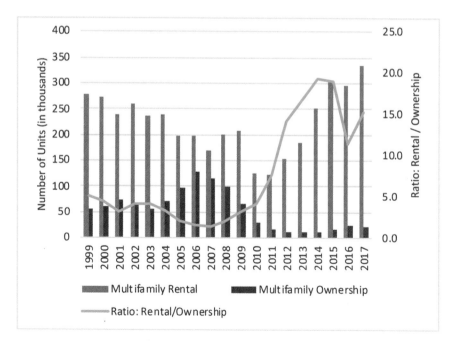

> **TIP**
>
> It is important for states to revise or refine condo-liability laws to reduce liability for projects that are under sixteen to twenty units to truly enable for-sale Missing Middle Housing types.

Difficulty for Builders to Get Financing for Condos

Financing condominium development involves a great deal of risk as a result of the nature of a condominium and the government's involvement in the process of creating, selling and, sometimes, operating residential condominiums. For condos, the due diligence required prior to making the loan, the drafting of the loan documents, and the supervision of the sales process require unique knowledge and experience because of the potential for lenders to unintentionally become involved in either a state investigation or unit-owner disputes even after the construction is completed and the loan repaid. In most instances the loans are repaid without incident, but the lenders are careful because numerous parties have interests in the property besides the borrower and lender, the loans are complex, and other unpredictable events may occur.

Construction lenders also require more than 50 percent of the units on average to be presold prior to any construction draws being advanced to lower the risk of the project.[4]

Once again, these added complexities increase the costs and risk at all project scales, and make smaller, Missing Middle–scale projects difficult to justify or simply too complex to take on.

Difficult for Buyers to Get a Mortgage for a Condo

Condos can be more difficult to buy (at least with a mortgage) than single-family homes. And that has been especially true if you want to use an FHA loan to buy a condo because they required special underwriting. When you apply for a mortgage, the bank begins the underwriting process, in which it evaluates whether the buyer has the means and credit to repay the loan, and it

> **Box 4-1**
>
> **FHA Financing for Buildings Up to Fourplexes**
>
> The Federal Housing Administration (FHA) can help meet the demand for Missing Middle Housing for duplex, triplex, and fourplex structures. It will finance the purchase of these buildings with as little as 3.5 percent down. The program assumes the owner occupies one unit while the rental income of the remaining units is calculated as income; this helps the buyer to qualify, though the owner needs to live on the property. Fortunately, there is no maximum sales price, but there are loan limits depending on the state and county where the property is located.

assesses the property that the buyer wishes to buy. This assessment is complex, but the result is, it is simply more difficult to get a loan to buy a condo than a single-family home.

First-time buyers often look to loans backed by the Federal Housing Administration (FHA) because they have relaxed credit requirements and require down payments as low as 3.5 percent of the purchase price (see box 4-1). In order to secure an FHA loan to buy a condo, however, the condo you are purchasing must have FHA approval. Unfortunately, this FHA approval process includes a variety of factors that you, as a buyer, cannot control. Some of the current requirements include: 1. At least 50 percent of the condo units must be owner occupied; 2. No more than 15 percent of the units in the complex can have association dues that are more than thirty days behind; and, 3. No more than 30 percent of the units in the complex secure existing FHA loans. And of the more than 150,000 condominium projects in the United States, only 6.5 percent were approved to participate in FHA's mortgage-insurance programs.[5]

This has become increasingly problematic as prices for single-family homes have escalated across the country, which makes condo purchases more important as an option for entry-level buyers who want to purchase and build equity but for whom the cost of a single-family home or even a town house is out of reach.

FHA has recently responded to this issue and has modified its rules. The new rule, which became effective on October 15, 2019, will allow a home buyer to obtain an FHA mortgage for an individual condo unit in an unapproved condominium project if that project is completed and meets the following criteria:

- In a development with fewer than ten units, *no more than two* can be insured by FHA.
- In a development that exceeds ten units, a *maximum of 10 percent* can be insured by the FHA.
- A minimum of 50 percent of project units must be *owner occupied*.

HUD estimates the new rules will make an additional twenty thousand to sixty thousand condo units eligible for FHA insured loans each year.[6]

Cost and Complexity of Setting Up a Condominium Association for Small Projects

When you have a for-sale residential project that requires shared maintenance as part of a building or buildings, shared outdoor space, or other amenities that are provided to owners, there is often a condominium association or a homeowners association (HOA) established to manage the maintenance and to collect monthly fees to help pay for this maintenance. For smaller projects, the cost of setting up this system can impact financial feasibility and be too intimidating for smaller, less-experienced builders. This is one reason why most small-scale infill is fee-simple town house projects that do not typically require the creation of a condominium association or an HOA.

According to attorney Doris Goldstein, "Formation of a condominium is always cumbersome. With few exceptions, the legal requirements are the same whether there are four units or four hundred. There are some ways to make it a little easier, but there is no truly simple way to form a condominium." Goldstein notes that "Fewer than half the states have adopted one of the forms of model legislation known as the Uniform Common Interest Ownership Act or the Uniform Condominium Act (which are not identical even among those states, as the legislatures are free to modify the provisions of the uniform act). The remaining states have their own idiosyncratic acts, including the populous states of Florida, California, and New York—and Indiana. This makes it really hard to produce a set of form documents that can be used in different jurisdictions and almost certainly requires the involvement of a local attorney."

One developer in Michigan is building a cottage court with fee-simple buildings, using a shared-easement agreement for any shared property outside of the building footprint, thus leaving the coordination of long-term maintenance up to the future owners. This approach does not require the added and ongoing cost and complexity of a condominium association. Owners simply have to either maintain shared space themselves or set up an informal system for doing so. This is not ideal, because the ongoing maintenance of shared spaces can be hard to coordinate, but it is one alternative solution.

ADDED COST AND COMPLEXITY OF INTEGRATING ACCESSIBILITY

Any residential building with four units or more triggers Fair Housing Act (FHA) requirements, which is a complex set of requirements that necessitate additional construction costs and often specialized consultants to help navigate the requirements effectively, thus also adding cost. So if you are developing a Missing Middle type other than a duplex or triplex, these additional standards apply. A good architect is used to working within these parameters and can accommodate them and deliver a great design while meeting these standards. These are defined as a barrier primarily because they add additional cost and complexity that can make it difficult for small builders to deliver Missing Middle types, compared to historic examples. That said, FHA requirements are important for providing housing choices for people with special needs and housing for our rapidly aging population, which is a larger and larger percentage of the market.

Same Building Code Requirements as Larger Multifamily Buildings

Any Missing Middle type that has more than two units triggers the use of the International Building Code (IBC) rather than a more lenient and more cost effective International Residential Code (IRC), and the IBC categorizes all multifamily buildings the same whether they are 3 units or 150 units (yes, the classification Missing Middle building types is even missing from building codes). Builders of Missing Middle should carefully assess the impact of these additional requirements on the cost of construction early in a project. The IBC is complex, but fire separation and exiting are two primary areas of difference between the two codes that can impact cost and complexity of building Missing Middle.

Another challenge related to this IBC building code trigger is that residential builders, who have the best experience building at the single-family home and Missing Middle Housing scale, do not want to build Missing Middle Housing projects because of these additional IBC building code requirements that they are unfamiliar with, and the commercial builders, who are used to building under the IBC code requirements, will often charge more to build Missing Middle projects because they are used to building much larger, more complex projects and are less familiar with the smaller-scale buildings.

A possible remedy would be the completion of a specific analysis of Missing Middle–scale buildings, three stories and nineteen units maximum, related to these building code requirements to determine if it would be possible for them to qualify for existing IRC requirements or similar, rather than more restrictive and costly IBC compliance. As far as the authors know, no such analysis is being considered.

MISSING MIDDLE HOUSING TYPES

IN ADVOCATING FOR MISSING MIDDLE HOUSING, IT IS IMPORTANT TO START THINKING ABOUT HOUSING AS A RANGE OF TYPES AND FORMS. THIS MEANS SHIFTING THE DISCUSSION AWAY FROM CONVENTIONAL DEVELOPMENT

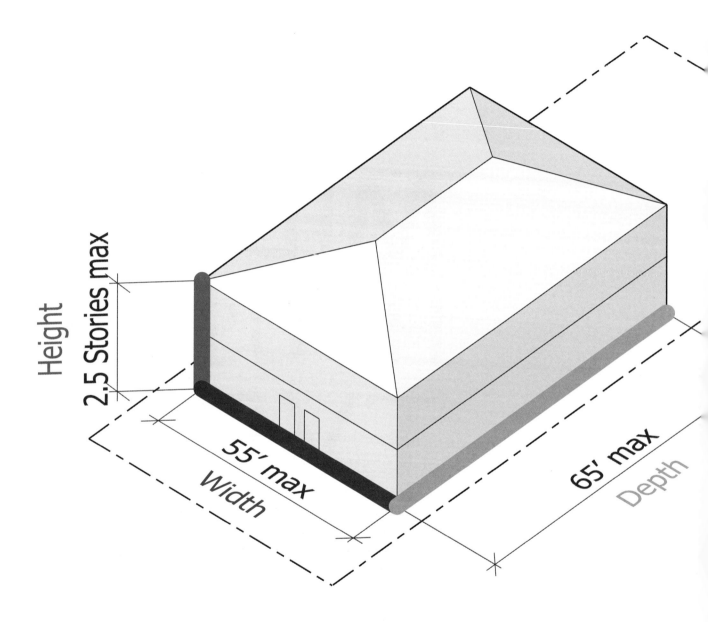

Height

2.5 Stories max

55' max
Width

65' max
Depth

Diagram illustrating the importance of considering maximum width, height, and depth in applying Missing Middle Housing.

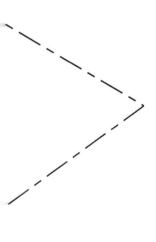

concepts such as density, FAR (floor area ratio), lot coverage, and multifamily and instead focusing on desired housing forms, scale, and types.

Developing an understanding of Missing Middle Housing types and their characteristics can help to inform general conversations about providing housing choices within communities. It will create an excellent foundation for planning, designing, and creating development strategies for Missing Middle Housing. The list of housing types in this chapter is extensive, but it does not cover every possible variation of good Missing Middle Housing types. Each type has a set of form characteristics that are most important in defining the type. These form characteristics do not prescribe one output or design but rather a series of forms that will vary based on lot size, location (whether a type is on a center block or corner lot, for example), and other context-specific characteristics that will enable the ultimate form to vary but still achieve the stated characteristic of the type.

Even though each type has different form characteristics that define them, all of the core Missing Middle Housing types share the following form characteristics :

- **Height:** Two to two and a half stories maximum (Third story as an exception; only allow with careful consideration of form and scale impact and differentiate as Upper Missing Middle Housing.)
- **Units per building:** Maximum of nineteen units per building, typically twelve units or less per building
- **Footprint:** House scale is 55–75 ft. maximum width along the street. Sometimes with wings that takes the total width up to 85 ft. along the street; 55–65 ft. maximum depth. Both the maximum width of the main body and the maximum width including the wings are important and thus crucial to regulate.
- **Off-street parking:** Maximum of one off-street parking space per unit. This is possible because of Missing Middle Housing's proximity to services, retail, and transit and

the availability of on-street parking. Parking is also not typically embedded in the building in the best examples.

- **On-site open space:** Private open space is not needed and should not be required. Shared open space exists in the form of a rear yard most often, sometimes as a side yard, or a courtyard.
- **Driveways:** Single-wide or narrow driveways if no alley is present. Note that narrow drives are often not allowed by city standards.

The following information is included for each of the Missing Middle Housing types in this chapter:

- **General definition:** This establishes the parameters for the building type. The general type is sometimes defined by the number of units, such as a fourplex. Other times it is form-driven, such as in the courtyard building.
- **Design characteristics:** This section defines the general form characteristics of the type that the reader should become familiar with.
- **Photo examples:** For each type there is a series of photographs that show variations of the defined type from cities large and small across the country. Most of these photos are historic examples because many of these types are still missing from recent construction, meaning few new examples have been built.
- **Idealized versions of the type:** For each type there are two 3-D examples. One version is front-loaded with driveway access from the street, and the second is an alley-loaded version where parking is accessed from the rear through an alley. For each of these versions a combination of the drawings and tables show the typical minimum lot widths and depths, building footprints, typical site-plan layout, and densities generated by the examples. The metrics and program information in the tables can be used to refine zoning standards to

effectively enable these types. These parameters are based on years of documentation and study of a variety of these housing types but represent only one of many ways the type can be designed and laid out on a lot.

- **How to regulate the type:** This section includes tips for adjusting or creating new zoning standards to enable the type. Note that there is some overlap in these recommendations, but many types have a specific set of form-based standards necessary to effectively regulate the type. These issues are addressed more generally in chapter 7.

Keep in mind that there are often local names for many of these types that are different than the names defined here. For example, in Chicago a "duplex: stacked" has historically been called a two flat. It is best to use these local names as long as there are no negative connotations associated with them. Locally generated names for the types can also be created if it is likely that the concept will resonate better with different names. In all instances, any relationship with the concepts of density or multi-family should be avoided in classifying these types.

DUPLEX

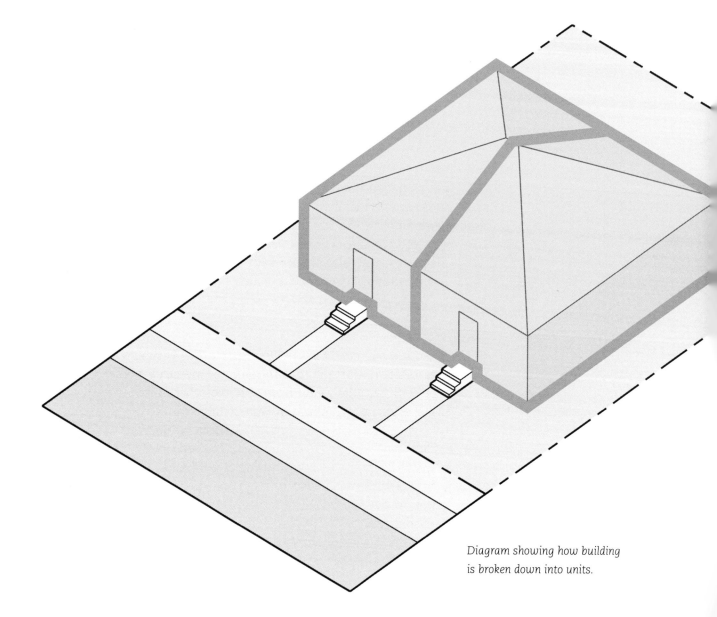

*Diagram showing how building
is broken down into units.*

SIDE-BY-SIDE

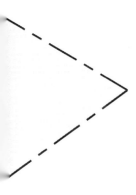

This type has two units next to each other with one shared wall. It is often important to differentiate one-story versions of this type with smaller units from the two-story versions with larger units, especially in planning and zoning strategies that are trying to deliver more housing choices and attainability.

The one-story version of this type was built historically to deliver attainable housing, but what is typically delivered today is a duplex with two two-story, large units because there is no incentive in a density-based system to build smaller units, thus not truly delivering attainability. This result of two large units often delivers more attainability than a single-family home but it is not an ideal solution in terms of delivering attainable housing.

(Photos, pages 98–99) Examples of side-by-side duplexes.

Design Characteristics

- The width, depth, and height are the same as a typical single-family house.
- The entry for both units may face the street. Another option, which is especially good for corner lots, is to have one entry face the street with the other facing the side yard.
- Sometimes there is a shared stoop or porch for both units at the center of the building. Other times each unit will have its own stoop or porch.
- Other configurations: Around a shared court or series of courts

How to Regulate This Type

- **Enable in areas where the additional unit allowed is an incentive:** New land-use and zoning districts often need to be created that enable both units to be built on

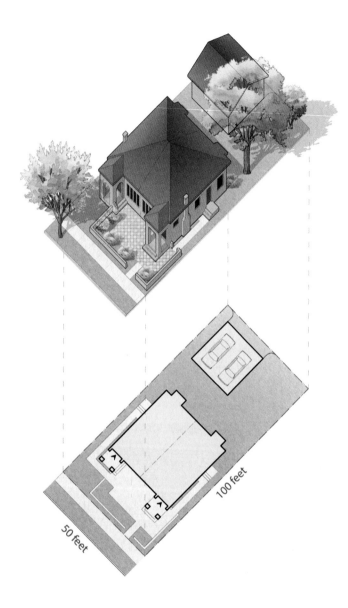

Table 5-1: DUPLEX: Side-by-Side, Alley-Loaded

LOT	
Width	50 ft.
Depth	100 ft.
Area	5,000 sq. ft.
	0.115 acres
UNITS	
Number of Units	2
Typical Unit Size	612 sq. ft.
DENSITY	
Net Density	17 du/acre
Gross Density	12 du/acre
PARKING	
Off-street Ratio	1.0 space per unit
On-street Spaces	2
Off-street Spaces	2
SETBACKS	
Front	15 ft.
Side	5 ft.
BUILDING	
Width	36 ft.
Depth	34 ft.
Height (to Eave)	14 ft.
Floors	1

Idealized alley-loaded axonometric drawing with data table.

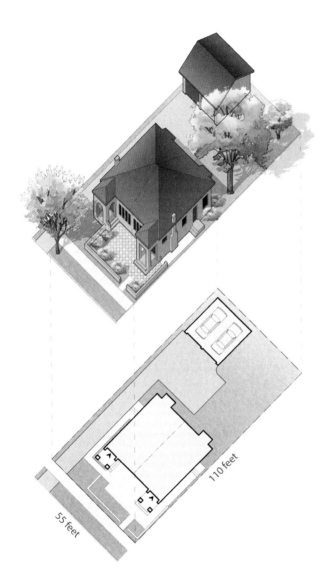

Table 5-2: DUPLEX: Side-by-Side, Front-Loaded

LOT	
Width	55 ft.
Depth	110 ft.
Area	6,050 sq. ft.
	0.139 acres
UNITS	
Number of Units	2
Typical Unit Size	612 sq. ft.
DENSITY	
Net Density	14 du/acre
Gross Density	11 du/acre
PARKING	
Off-street Ratio	1.0 space per unit
On-street Spaces	2
Off-street Spaces	2
SETBACKS	
Front	15 ft.
Side	5 ft.
BUILDING	
Width	36 ft.
Depth	34 ft.
Height (to Eave)	14 ft.
Floors	1

Idealized front-loaded axonometric drawing with data table.

Example of side-by-side duplex around courtyard.

a single lot. This will most likely make the most sense in the conversation of single-family zones to allow duplexes.

- **Be careful what you enable:** Do not allow two full-sized, detached houses on a lot. The bulk and scale of the built form will likely not be compatible with its context. This can be controlled with FAR maximums in addition to the form standards.
- **Consider not allowing more than one story of height for multiunit buildings in a zoning district in exchange for allowing a second unit:** This is a strategy for changing zoning from single family to allow for duplexes in a way that will not result in out-of-scale buildings. This should be done with careful form standards to define a maximum footprint as well.
- **Allow more FAR for non-single-family units:** In areas of high property values, you may need to set a maximum FAR for single-family homes that is lower than FAR allowed for a duplex so the economics of a duplex can compete with them.
- **Allow attached/integrated ADUs:** Allowing accessory dwelling units (ADUs) to be integrated into an existing house is an indirect way to enable a duplex. But there are often size limitations on the second unit in this approach.
- **Allow conversions:** Carefully consider allowing conversions of single-family homes into this type.
- **Consider allowing a fourplex instead:** If you are not regulating a maximum of one story in a zoning district, consider allowing four small units within the same building envelope/size to truly incentivize the delivery of smaller, more affordable units.

DUPLEX

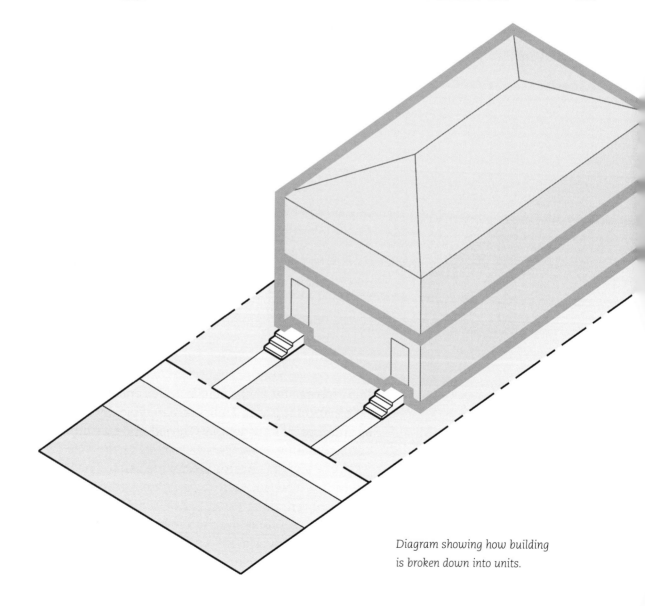

*Diagram showing how building
is broken down into units.*

STACKED

This type has two units stacked, with one on the ground floor and the other on top of it. This type can typically fit on a narrower lot (as small as 30 ft. wide) than the side-by-side duplex because it is stacked.

This is a great type for builders to sell to one buyer. The owner can rent the second unit to generate income from short-term or long-term rentals or use it to house aging parents or boomerang children or to simply have other family members close by. Buyers of this type can use a conventional single-family mortgage if they are going to live in the unit.

Design Characteristics

- The width, depth, and height is the same as a house.
- With an alley configuration, this type can fit on a lot that is 30 ft. wide.
- The location of the entryways is important for this type to encourage activation of the public realm. (Either both entries facing the street or one facing the street and one facing the side yard and visible from the street.) The ground floor unit is entered directly, while the upper unit is accessed by a flight of stairs.

(Photos, pages 106–107) Examples of stacked duplexes.

- Sometimes there is a shared stoop for both units along one side of the front facade of the building. The units may have entries on opposite sides of the front facade.

How to Regulate This Type

- **Regulate a house-scale building:** Establish a maximum depth and width that are house scale, but allow a second unit within that defined form.
- **Reduce minimum lot size:** This should be allowed on the same lot size as a single-family home. Minimum lot sizes should be reduced accordingly, otherwise you will not get this type.
- **Allow attached/integrated ADUs:** Allowing accessory dwelling units (ADUs) to be integrated into an existing house is an indirect way to enable a duplex. But there are often size limitations on the second unit in this approach.
- **Allow conversions:** Carefully consider allowing conversions of single-family homes into this type.

Table 5-3: DUPLEX: Stacked, Alley-Loaded

LOT	
Width	35 ft.
Depth	100 ft.
Area	3,500 sq. ft.
	.080 acres
UNITS	
Number of Units	2
Typical Unit Size	1,008 sq. ft.
DENSITY	
Net Density	25 du/acre
Gross Density	18 du/acre
PARKING	
Off-street Ratio	1.0 space per unit
On-street Spaces	1
Off-street Spaces	2
SETBACKS	
Front	15 ft.
Side	5 ft.
BUILDING	
Width	24 ft.
Depth	42 ft.
Height (to Eave)	21 ft.
Floors	2

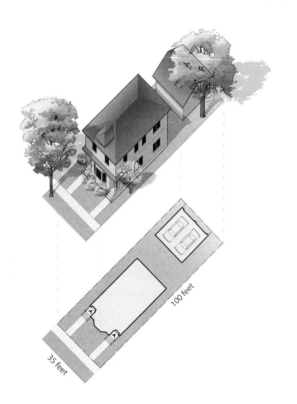

Idealized alley-loaded axonometric drawing with data table.

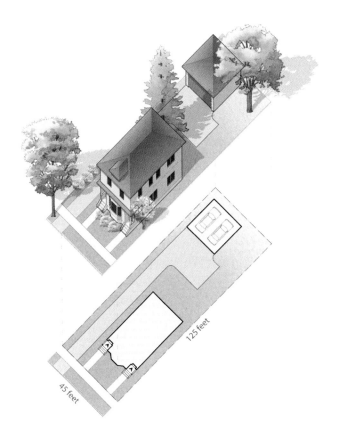

Table 5-4: Duplex: Stacked, Front-Loaded

LOT	
Width	45 ft.
Depth	125 ft.
Area	5,625 sq. ft.
	0.129 acres
UNITS	
Number of Units	2
Typical Unit Size	1,008 sq. ft.
DENSITY	
Net Density	16 du/acre
Gross Density	13 du/acre
PARKING	
Off-street Ratio	1.0 space per unit
On-street Spaces	1
Off-street Spaces	2
SETBACKS	
Front	15 ft.
Side	5 ft.
BUILDING	
Width	24 ft.
Depth	42 ft.
Height (to Eave)	21 ft.
Floors	2

*Idealized front-loaded axonometric
drawing with data table.*

COTTAGE

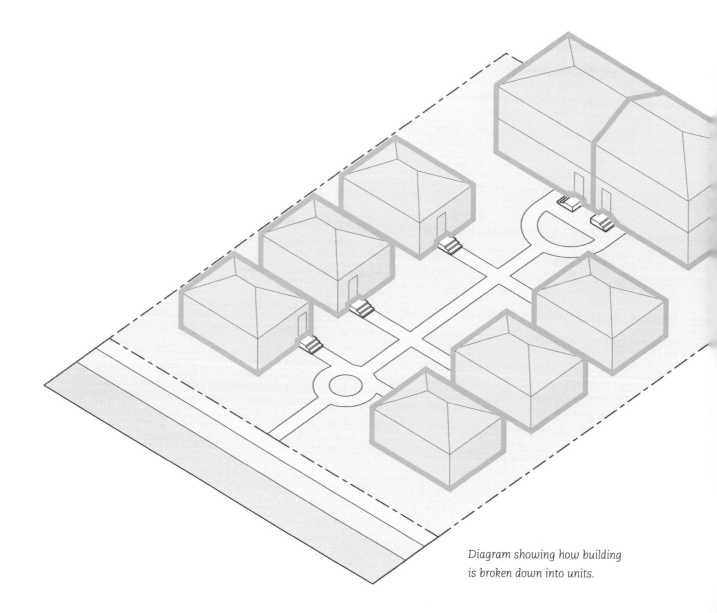

Diagram showing how building is broken down into units.

COURT

This type consists of a series of small (one to one and a half stories and small footprint) homes that are typically detached, oriented around a small shared court that is usually perpendicular to the street. The units to the rear of the lot, perpendicular to the street, are more often attached, sometimes even two stories, and in a slightly larger building that is parallel to the street.

In addition to accommodating units, the rear building sometimes houses a shared laundry room, storage space, or parking that is often accessed off of an alley. This type is ideally applied in walkable contexts. Since cottage courts are limited to one to one and a half stories and very small-footprint buildings, they are compatible with single-family homes, so it is the easiest type to justify allowing in single-family zones, even in neighborhoods with larger lots.

Design Characteristics

- Often found on an aggregation of one to three lots in pre-1940s neighborhoods, typically ranging from 100 to 200 ft. wide.

- One to one and a half stories maximum
  - Exception: If the rear building is parallel to the street, often along an alley, it is sometimes two stories tall. Since there is only 20–25 ft. of this building facing adjacent lots, this second-story element to the rear of the lot does not cause compatibility issues.
- Small-footprint units: Homes that are one room wide by two rooms deep are not uncommon (around 500–600 sq. ft.).

(Photos, pages 112–113) Examples of cottage courts.

- If the homes are full size, or on lots generally larger than 200 ft. in width, it becomes more of a pocket neighborhood or house cluster, neither of which are at the small scale of the cottage court (see comparison of cottage court and pocket neighborhood on page 119).
- Parking, if it is provided on-site, is often off of an alley or with a cluster-parking area. It should always be detached from the homes so that residents have to walk through the courtyard to get into their home. This type is really hard to make efficient if it is not loaded (parked) from an alley.
  - If residents can drive into a garage and walk into a unit directly, the casual interactions that occur when walking from car to unit are missed. It also takes much of the living space that engages the shared courtyard and pushes it up to the second floor. This may seem like a small deal, but it is not.
- Detached units are typical, but some examples have some attached units. Units are on the side or rear of the lot. (Be sure to clarify if attached units are allowed in your development standards.)
- Side setbacks are often very small at 5–6 ft. because

Table 5-6: Cottage Court, Alley-Loaded

LOT	
Width	110 ft.
Depth	150 ft.
Area	16,500 sq. ft.
	0.379 acres
UNITS	
Number of Units	8
Typical Unit Size	840 sq. ft.
DENSITY	
Net Density	21 du/acre
Gross Density	16 du/acre
PARKING	
Off-street Ratio	1.0 space per unit
On-street Spaces	5
Off-street Spaces	8
SETBACKS	
Front	15 ft.
Side	5 ft.
BUILDING	
Width	24 ft.
Depth	35 ft.
Height (to Eave)	15 ft.
Floors	1

*Idealized alley-loaded axonometric
drawing with data table.*

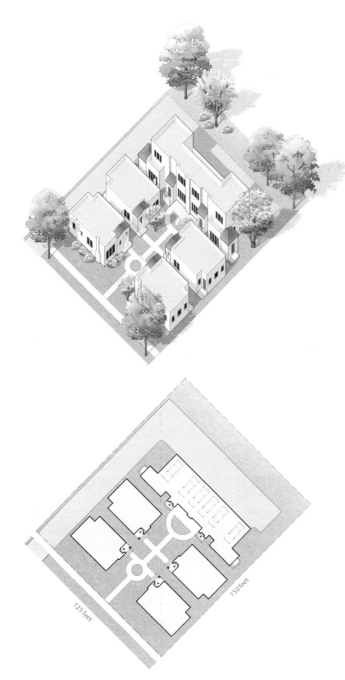

Table 5-6: Cottage Court, Front-Loaded

LOT	
Width	125 ft.
Depth	150 ft.
Area	18,750 sq. ft.
	0.430 acres
UNITS	
Number of Units	6
Typical Unit Size	840 sq. ft.
DENSITY	
Net Density	14 du/acre
Gross Density	12 du/acre
PARKING	
Off-street Ratio	1.0 spaces per unit
On-street Spaces	5
Off-street Spaces	6
SETBACKS	
Front	15 ft.
Side	5 ft.
BUILDING	
Width	24 ft.
Depth	35 ft.
Height (to Eave)	15 ft.
Floors	1

*Idealized front-loaded axonometric
drawing with data table.*

(Photos, pages 116–117) Various courtyard sizes and entry configurations.

no rear yards are desired. To maximize the size of the courtyard, the buildings push as close to the side property line as possible. There is typically an exception to minimum side setbacks for this type. This is okay because the houses are only one story.

- Private yard spaces ideally are not provided because they will compromise the use and activation of the shared court.
- This type often has a small 5–8 ft. deep dooryard between the porch/stoop/entry and the court. This space can be defined by a small 6–8 in. rope fence or by landscaping, or a taller hedge or fence. The hedge or fence should not be too tall or it will make spaces on both sides feel constrained and compromise the community feel.

Box 5-1
Comparing Pocket Neighborhoods and Cottage Courts

The Cully Grove case study in chapter 6 is an excellent example of a pocket neighborhood. They are a series of detached, attached, and sometimes stacked homes oriented around a shared green space that often integrate shared amenities, such as a community house or workshop.

Here are the primary ways a cottage court is different than a pocket neighborhood.

- Overall scale: Cottage courts are typically built on smaller lots, often an individual lot or a couple typical lots combined. Cottage courts create a strong sense of community but do not create a neighborhood. They are a component of a larger neighborhood.
- Cottage courts typically have smaller houses: This includes height and footprint.
- Cottage courts have smaller courtyard spaces.
- Cottage courts typically generate higher densities (if you are keeping track or regulating with density).

The reason that these differences matter is that you may need a separate set of standards, likely multiple zoning districts, to regulate the full variety of cottage courts on smaller infill lots, where you want smaller-scale buildings, and an ordinance to encourage pocket neighborhoods on larger lots. Pocket neighborhoods, which can typically happen on slightly larger lots, likely above one acre, often require larger community spaces and integrate two-story buildings.

How to Regulate This Type

- **Regulate a maximum height:** Establish a maximum height of one to one and a half stories.
- **Rear building heights:** When alleys are present, allow the rear building to go up to two stories, but regulate a maximum depth of the two story element.
- **Regulate a minimum width and depth of the courtyard:** It is not unusual to see examples that are 25 ft. from building face to building face. This minimum distance needs to be regulated in your development standards/ zoning.
- **Reduce side setbacks:** An exception often needs to be made to the required side setbacks in a zone. You could have a smaller side setback on one-story buildings than two-plus-story buildings.
- **Allow for narrower drives:** When alleys are not present, a city needs to allow narrow driveways for buildings and projects of less than ten to fifteen units to enable this type, including front-loaded versions. This is often controlled by a city's engineering or public works department.
- **Driveways are not courtyards:** Regulate such that access to garages or driveways do not count as courtyards. This is important within a good design of this type, because it provides outdoor space since there are no private yards. The courtyards function as the focal point for the residents, where formal activities and informal interactions happen that build a sense of community.
- **Allow attached units:** Allow these types with attached units in areas transitioning from single family to areas with larger buildings/higher densities. Otherwise require detached homes with a maximum of 8 ft. between them.
- **Enable further housing choices:** To cover a full spectrum of housing choices you may have multiple zones that enable different variations of cottage court types.

Minimum courtyard sizes and maximum size (height and footprint) of buildings may vary between the zones.

- **In a nuanced approach a city would have multiple zones that allow different variations of this type:**
    - **Zone one (small form and scale):** Caps the height at one story, requires detached units, and caps building footprints at 500 sq. ft.
    - **Zone two (medium form and scale):** Caps heights at two stories, requires detached units, but allows footprints as large as 1,200 sq. ft.
    - **Zone three (larger form and scale):** Caps heights at one and a half or two stories, allows attached units, only regulates building depth, and allows a smaller courtyard width.

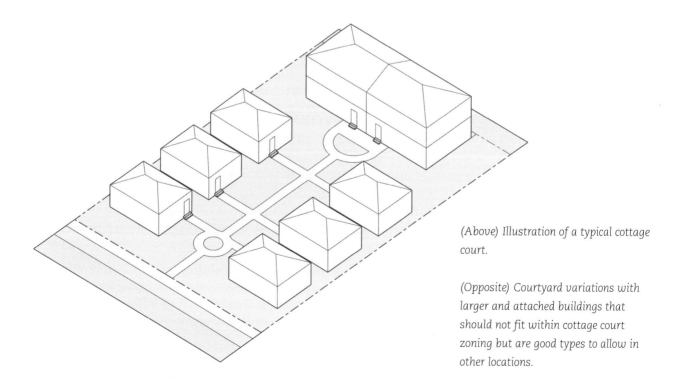

(Above) Illustration of a typical cottage court.

(Opposite) Courtyard variations with larger and attached buildings that should not fit within cottage court zoning but are good types to allow in other locations.

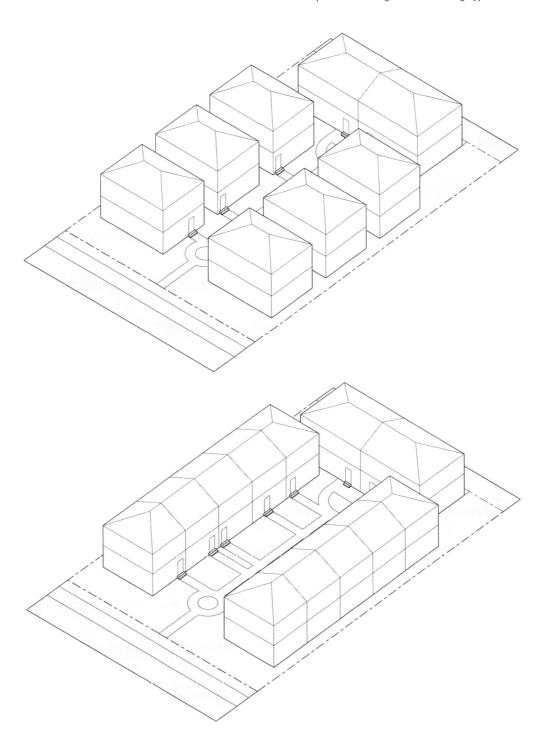

FOURPLEX

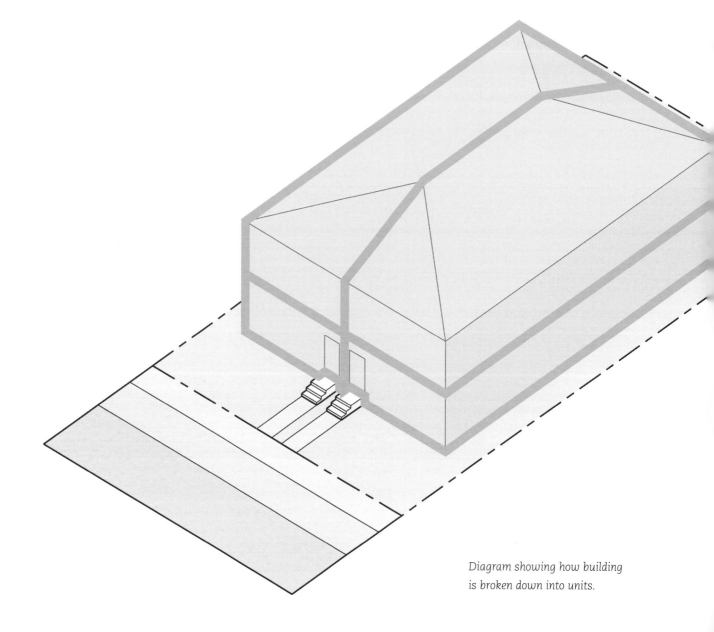

*Diagram showing how building
is broken down into units.*

STACKED

This type has a small-to-medium-sized structure that consists of two units on the ground floor and two units stacked directly above them. Generally speaking, this type could fit into a more generalized "multiplex: small" category. But it is important enough to define as a separate type because it generates enough units to make it attractive to builders on smaller lots, it is popular with renters and buyers because it feels and lives much like a single-family home, and it is a scale that is often compatible with existing single-family neighborhoods.

This type is considered the holy grail of Missing Middle Housing: very few for-sale fourplexes have been built recently due to many obstacles, and even newly constructed for-rent fourplexes with this stacked configuration are rare. Figuring out how to enable and deliver more of these types is critical for cities of all sizes.

Fourplexes are more efficient than four side-by-side town houses, because the top units are stacked on the lower units; therefore the building can fit onto a narrower lot. This type also delivers a broader range of housing choices because the one-story units are often smaller than the two-story town house units. The one-story units delivered by a fourplex are also often more desirable to older renters and buyers who want a one-story unit without stairs as they age and their mobility decreases.

The value of this type is that it reads like a house from the street, but it has four units, thus generating medium to high densities or, more importantly, enough people to support transit and

(Photos, pages 124–125) Examples of stacked fourplexes.

local-serving commercial amenities. Historically this type was often built on the same block as single-family homes and is indiscernible from those homes.

In many instances, these types have historically been built on corner lots with little setbacks on both sides and little or no parking. This is a good strategy for cities to start with.

This type is most likely to occur on alley-loaded lots because when a driveway is required to access parking, it makes this type inefficient, thus not enabling it to be economically feasible for development/new construction.

This type can generate a broad range of densities based on required setbacks, parking access from an alley, and level of parking required.

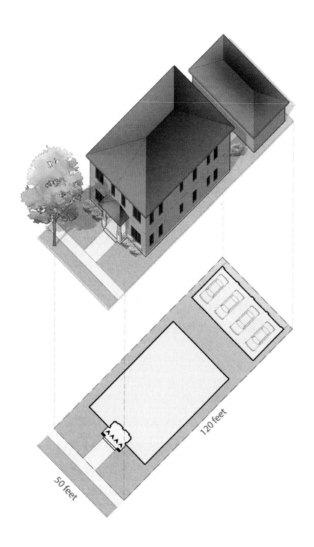

Table 5-7: Fourplex, Alley-Loaded

LOT	
Width	50 feet
Depth	120 feet
Area	6000 sq. ft.
	0.138 acres
UNITS	
Number of Units	4
Typical Unit Size	1200 sq. ft.
DENSITY	
Net Density	29 du/acre
Gross Density	22 du/acre
PARKING	
Off-street Ratio	1.0 space per unit
On-street Spaces	2
Off-street Spaces	4
SETBACKS	
Front	15 feet
Side	5 feet
BUILDING	
Width	40 feet
Depth	60 feet
Height (to eave)	21 feet
Floors	2

*Idealized alley-loaded axonometric
drawing with data table.*

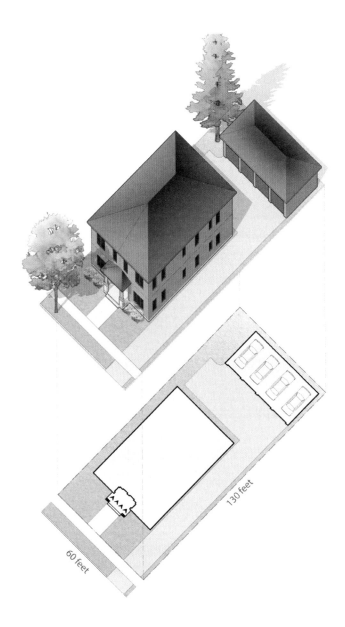

Table 5-8: Fourplex, Front-Loaded

LOT	
Width	60 feet
Depth	130 feet
Area	7800 sq. ft.
	0.179 acres
UNITS	
Number of Units	4
Typical Unit Size	1200 sq. ft.
DENSITY	
Net Density	22 du/acre
Gross Density	18 du/acre
PARKING	
Off-street Ratio	1.0 space per unit
On-street Spaces	2
Off-street Spaces	4
SETBACKS	
Front	15 feet
Side	5 feet
BUILDING	
Width	40 feet
Depth	60 feet
Height (to Eave)	21 feet
Floors	2

*Idealized front-loaded axonometric
drawing with data table.*

Design Characteristics

- Often found on lots 50 ft. wide
- Two to two and a half stories maximum
- The depth is similar to that of a house, which allows it to fit four units onto a lot but still be in scale with surrounding single-family homes. One-bedroom units in this type are typically around 40–45 ft. deep. A deeper building can accommodate two-bedroom units.
- These types typically have long, shallow units, which is good for providing natural lighting along the long side of the unit.
- Entries:
  - There is often one shared door that leads to a shared foyer or a recessed porch with four doors. The two doors facing the street each go up a flight of stairs to the upper units. To the left and right are the doors that enter into the ground floor units.
  - These buildings can be designed with four separate doors to provide private stoops or porches and entries for each unit.

How to Regulate This Type

- **Reduce allowed minimum lot width:** This type should be allowed on any lot at least 50 ft. wide in existing zones regardless of lot depth.
- **Regulate a maximum building width and depth:** A width of 45–55 ft. wide maximum and 50–60 ft. deep maximum is typical, but these numbers should be locally calibrated based on your typical lot sizes, sizes of existing fourplexes, and desired scale and form.
- **Where to allow this type:** This type is likely the most economically viable in existing single-family zones.
- **Consider allowing this type in multiple zones:** This type can be enabled in a range of zones. Starting on the lower-

intensity end with a zone that requires slightly larger front setbacks and side setbacks and maybe even rear yard, then on the most aggressive end, with little or no front or side setbacks and no off-street parking.

- **Increase allowed density:** With small units, this type can generate up to 35–40 du/acre, so a minimum density needs to be enabled in current medium-density/multifamily zones, or density barriers need to be removed and replaced with form or building type, or at the very least the densities need to be increased.
- **Enable fourplexes on corner lots, even in existing single-family zones:** As a starting point allow fourplexes on corner lots of single-family zones without parking, and with smaller front and side setbacks.
- **Do not require private open space.**
- **Consider exceptions for deeper lots:** On deeper lots, consider allowing additional fourplexes to the rear of the lot after a 10 ft. break. This is not typically recommended on lots less than 150 ft. deep, and this application needs careful consideration of the impacts on privacy for adjacent residences.

FOURPLEX VARIATIONS

NO PARKING
(0 Spaces/Unit)*

FOURPLEX ONE-BEDROOM UNITS

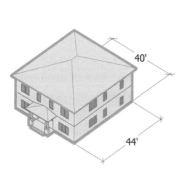

40'

44'

800 sf/unit

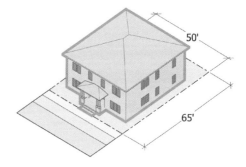

50'

65'

54 du/acre

FOURPLEX TWO-BEDROOM UNITS

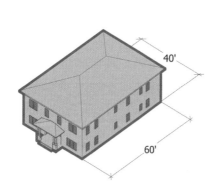

40'

60'

1,200 sf/unit

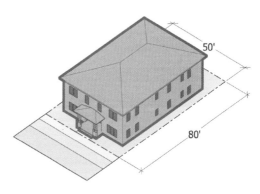

50'

80'

44 du/acre

Overview of a range of densities that can be generated by a fourplex with different parking accomodation and unit sizes.

ALLEY-ACCESS
(1 Space/Unit)*

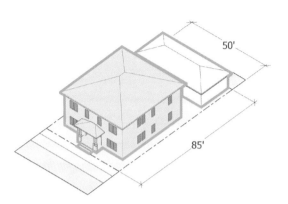

41 du/acre

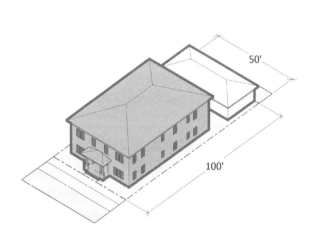

35 du/acre

FRONT-ACCESS
(1 Space/Unit)*

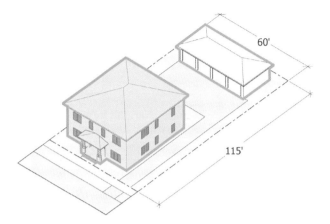

25 du/acre

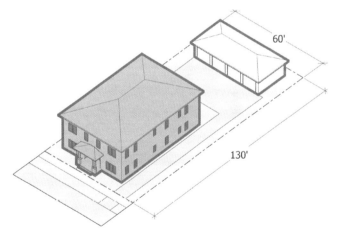

22 du/acre

*SETBACK ASSUMPTIONS:
—Front setback 8' with allowed encroachments
—Side setback: 5'
—Rear setback: varies with parking configuration

TOWN

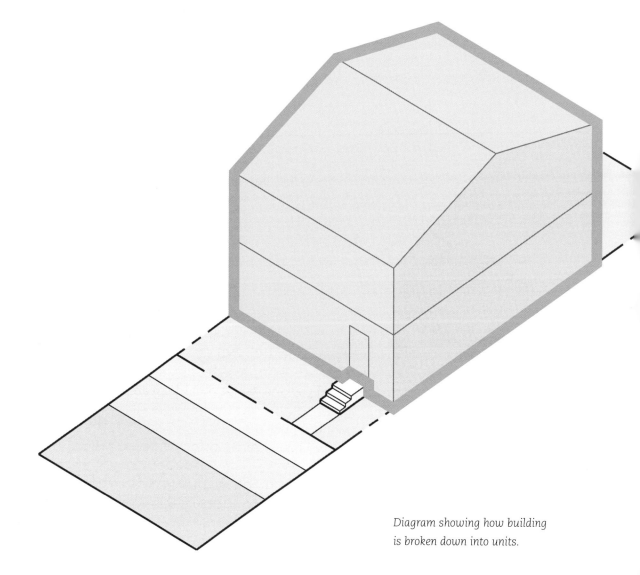

*Diagram showing how building
is broken down into units.*

HOUSE

This is a small-to-medium-sized structure with two or more multi-story units with shared side walls on both sides. They typically have entries facing a street and a rear yard or small court with detached parking garage or parking area loaded from an alley.

These types are not missing from all markets, especially in East Coast cities such as Boston and Philadelphia. In the Midwest in cities like Chicago and Cincinnati they were built as an important part of the original urban fabric of the neighborhoods, but they are missing in smaller-to-medium-sized cities, especially west of Chicago. These types represent the largest-growing percentage of new housing built between 2011 and 2017, far outpacing other Missing Middle types.[1]

(Photos, pages 134–135) An array of town houses.

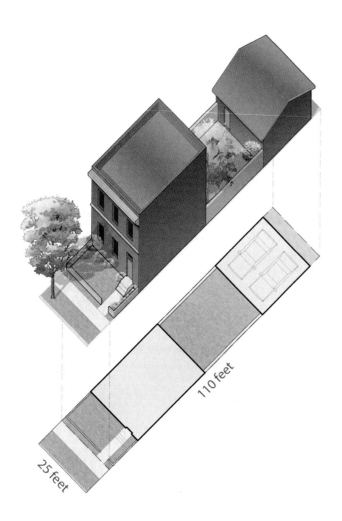

Table 5-9: Townhouse, Alley-Loaded

LOT	
Width	25 ft.
Depth	110 ft.
Area	2,750 sq. ft.
	0.063 acres
UNITS	
Number of Units	1
Typical Unit Size	1,750 sq. ft.
DENSITY	
Net Density	16 du/acre
Gross Density	12 du/acre
PARKING	
Off-street Ratio	2.0 spaces per unit
On-street Spaces	1
Off-street Spaces	2
SETBACKS	
Front	10 ft.
Side	0 ft.
BUILDING	
Width	25 ft.
Depth	35 ft.
Height (to Eave)	28 ft.
Floors	2

Idealized alley-loaded axonometric drawing with data table.

The major benefits of town houses today is that due to their more efficient use of land, small footprints, and shared walls, they can often be built and sold at a price point lower than detached single-family homes. They can be sold as fee-simple units, meaning the buyer owns the land the unit is on, and they are not stacked, which avoids perceived or actual concerns about privacy and noise and eliminates the need for establishing a condominium association and taking on the added risk of condominium construction. The Mews Homes case study in chapter 6 is a great example of a newly constructed adaptation of a town house type that delivered attainable price points to entry-level buyers.

Another benefit of these types historically was that they adapted over time in great neighborhoods like those in Brooklyn and Chicago to accommodate multiple units within the town house building envelope, often one per floor.

The tuck-under town house, which is three stories with the majority of the ground floor taken up by parking and two floors above, does not classify as a good Missing Middle type. It should be allowed only in targeted locations. These locations typically do not include small-lot infill in historically single-family neighborhoods but rather are focused in newly planned and built communities, or larger, multiple-acre infills. An exception is in an existing neighborhood where a process is undertaken to determine that transformation in scale, form, and intensity is desired and is reinforced by city policy.

Design Characteristics:

- Typically two stories
- Always fronting onto a street or a courtyard. The minimum courtyard width should be defined.
- Fronts of buildings always face fronts of other buildings, either across a street or across a courtyard or shared community space/mews.
- Narrow side of the unit typically faces the street with the larger side along the depth of the lot that is attached.

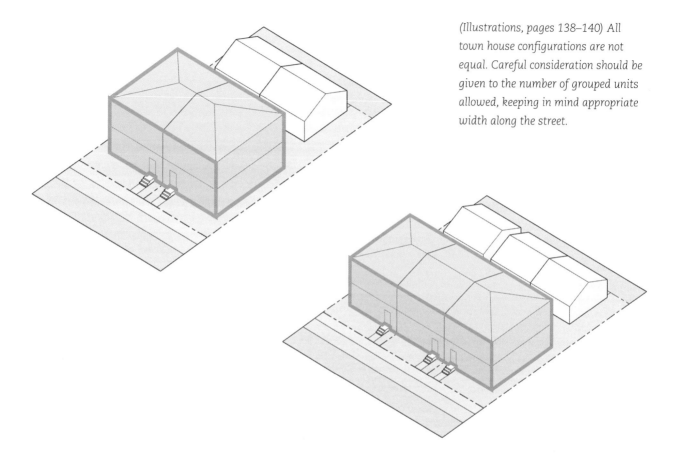

(Illustrations, pages 138–140) All town house configurations are not equal. Careful consideration should be given to the number of grouped units allowed, keeping in mind appropriate width along the street.

- Front setbacks can vary greatly within this type depending on the form intent of the area. In some areas, 0–5 ft. front setbacks are best, enabling the units' stoops to spill directly onto the sidewalk; in other areas, a deeper front setback makes sense with an 8–12 ft. front setback with a small hedge, wall, or fence along the sidewalk edge defining a dooryard that serves as a private space.

- Each unit has an individual entry.
- Widths of individual units typically range from 16 to 25 ft. Twenty-four feet of width or wider allows for two bedrooms across the front and/or rear of the building.

Variations of this type include an L-shaped configuration on corner lots, orientation around a courtyard, or integration into pocket neighborhoods with single-family homes or other Missing Middle types.

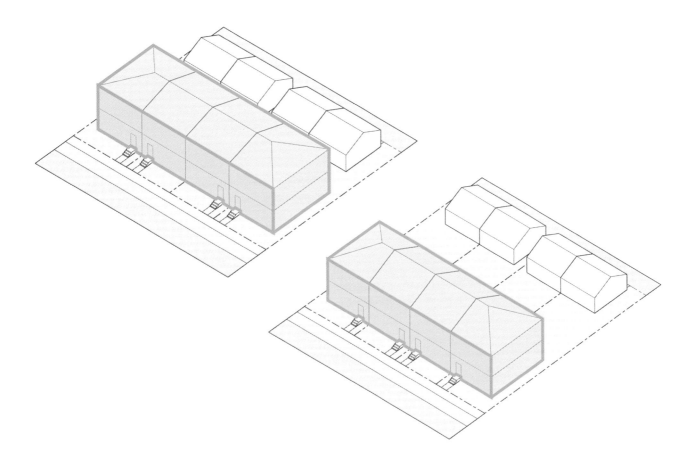

How to Regulate This Type

- **Do not allow garages on the front of buildings, even if with reduced garage widths.**
- **Thoughtfully regulate maximum length of grouping of town houses:** The number of types allowed in a row (maximum width along street) varies and should be considered carefully when regulating these types. Allowing two to three units attached is appropriate in some areas where reinforcing the scale of a house is important. In other areas, an entire face of a block (approximately 400 ft. or sixteen units) may be a continuous run of town houses.
- **Regulate deep-lot configurations:** Do not allow this type perpendicular to the street unless it is creating a courtyard that meets minimum size regulations.
- **Be careful where you allow the tuck-under town house:** Think carefully

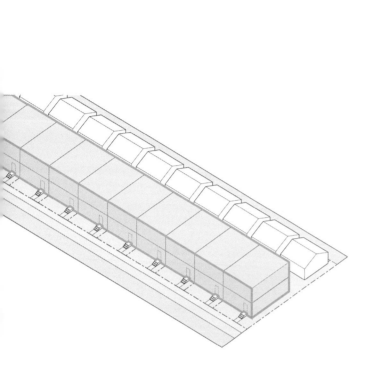

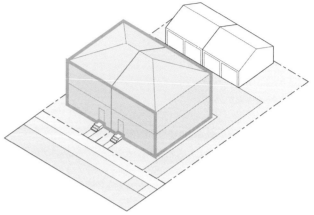

about whether or not you want to allow the tuck-under town house in a zone. Because of its three-story form and lack of activation on the ground floor because most of the ground floor is parking, it is not a great type. If your regulations do not explicitly prohibit it, it will be what most builders will build.

- **Site-plan standard:** Regulate so that fronts of town houses do not face backs of other town houses in site plans.

- **Reduce front setbacks:** Allow little or no front setback, especially on corner lots, and in larger lot applications should be encouraged.
- **Consider flexibility within desired form:** Consider allowing a town house form but allowing multiple units within it (no density cap). The town house form is very versatile and accommodates a lot of units without the perception of being higher density.

Examples of a bad town house configuration: slot home (tuck-under town houses perpendicular to the street). One example is loaded in the middle of the lot, and the other is loaded at lot edges.

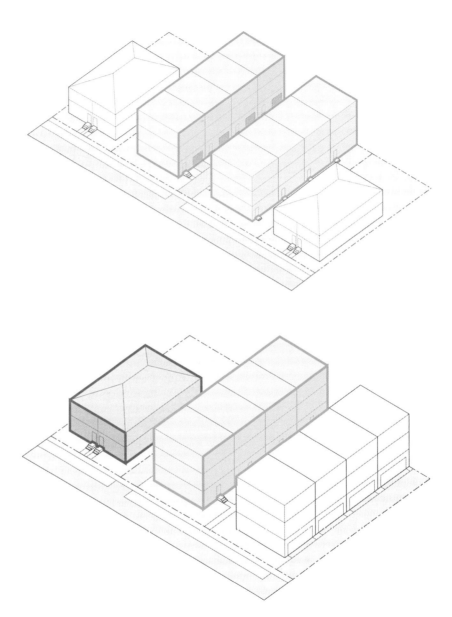

TRIPLEX

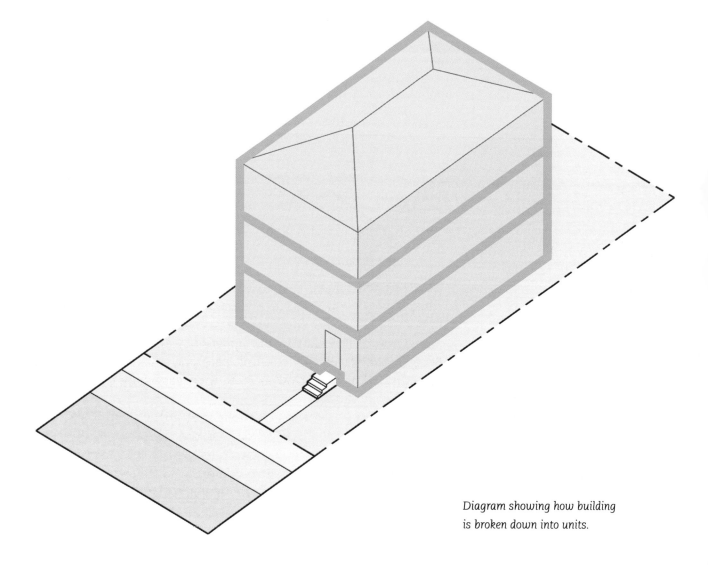

*Diagram showing how building
is broken down into units.*

STACKED
(TRIPLE DECKER)

This type has a small-to-medium-sized structure that consists of three dwelling units stacked on top of each other on consecutive floors. This type is basically a stacked duplex with a third unit added above. The stair to the upper-floor units is often shared. Because they have only one unit per floor, stacked triplexes can often fit on lots as narrow as 30 ft. wide, especially if the lot has an alley.

This type typically needs thoughtful application due to the third story. In more sensitive contexts, the third story of this type could be required to step back to keep the two-story appearance at the street. In less sensitive contexts, the third story can be expressed at the front of the building/lot at the street edge.

These types are prolific on the East Coast but also exist in West Coast cities such as San Francisco, Los Angeles, and Sacramento.

Design Characteristics

- Typically three stories
- House-scale width and depth (see examples and tables)
- Entries all typically face the street.
- One shared stoop/porch with one door entering directly into the ground floor unit and a second door entering into a stair shared by the units on the second and third floors.
- These types function best when there are front and/or rear porches that provide private outdoor space on the front and rear of the buildings. These porches were often referred to as piazzas in East Coast examples of this type.

(Photos, page 144–145) Examples of stacked triplexes.

How to Regulate This Type

- **Minimum lot width:** This type works well on 30 ft. wide lots or wider. Most zoning codes have much larger minimum lot sizes for a triplex. This is an important regulation to fix.
- **Maximum height:** Few multifamily zones regulate for a maximum three-story height, which is necessary to encourage this type.
- **Thoughtfully decide where to enable:** Because of this allowed third story, it should be integrated into single-family neighborhoods with a thoughtful decision that a desired degree of change is supported. Otherwise, it can be thoughtfully integrated and allowed in areas that transition from commercial corridors or main streets and higher-intensity areas into single-family neighborhoods.

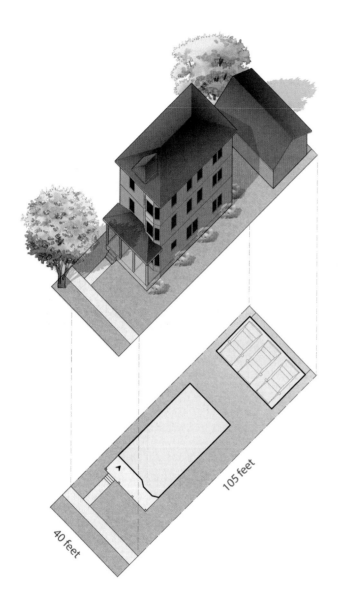

Table 5–10: Triplex: Stacked, Alley-Loaded

LOT	
Width	40 ft.
Depth	105 ft.
Area	4,200 sq. ft.
	0.096 acres
UNITS	
Number of Units	3
Typical Unit Size	1,008 sq. ft.
DENSITY	
Net Density	31 du/acre
Gross Density	23 du/acre
PARKING	
On-street Ratio	1.0 space per unit
On-street Spaces	2
Off-street Spaces	3
SETBACKS	
Front	15 ft.
Side	5 ft.
BUILDING	
Width	24 ft.
Depth	42 ft.
Height (to Eave)	30 ft.
Floors	3

Idealized alley-loaded axonometric drawing with data table.

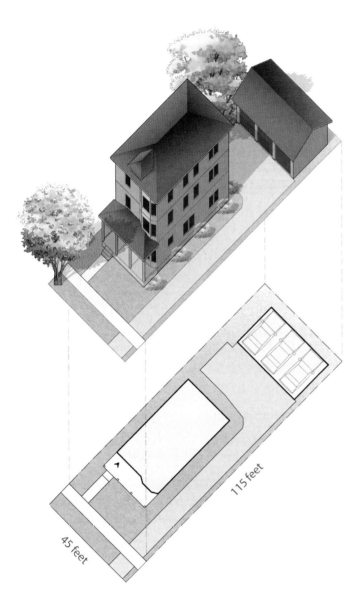

Table 5-11: Triplex: Stacked, Front-Loaded

LOT	
Width	45 ft.
Depth	115 ft.
Area	5,175 sq. ft.
	0.119 acres
UNITS	
Number of Units	3
Typical Unit Size	1,008 sq. ft.
DENSITY	
Net Density	25 du/acre
Gross Density	20 du/acre
PARKING	
Off-street Ratio	1.0 space per unit
On-street Spaces	1
Off-street Spaces	3
SETBACKS	
Front	15 ft.
Side	5 ft.
BUILDING	
Width	24 ft.
Depth	42 ft.
Height (to Eave)	30 ft.
Floors	3

Idealized front-loaded axonometric drawing with data table.

MULTIPLEX

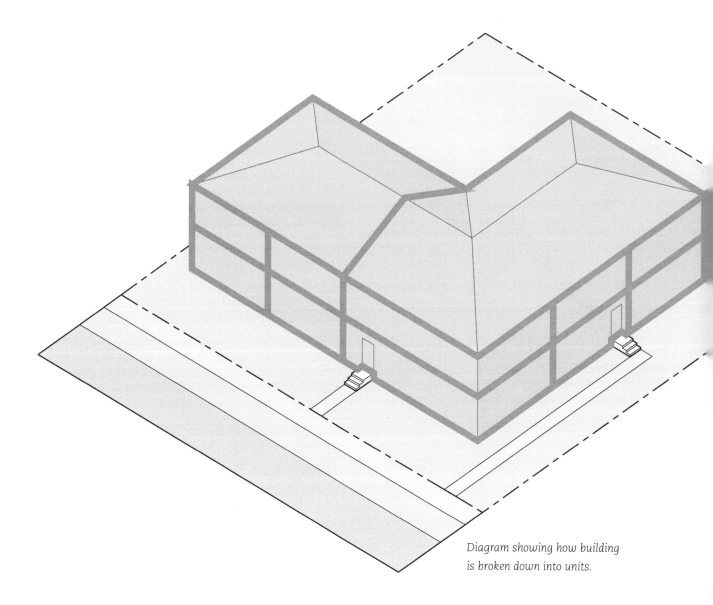

Diagram showing how building is broken down into units.

MEDIUM
(MANSION APARTMENT)

This type is a small-to-medium-sized structure that consists of five to twelve units stacked on top of each other on consecutive floors, often with a shared entry on the ground floor.

The names *multiplex: medium* and *mansion apartment* are interchangeable. Often *mansion apartment* is a more approachable name for these types.

Because of the accommodation of more units than many of the other types, this type often has the greatest variation in physical form.

Design Characteristics

- Maintains the form and scale of a large estate house.
- These types tend to be wider than they are deep. If the width gets closer to the upper end, or 75 ft., the depth is typically 45 ft. or less to compensate for the larger width.
- There are typically units facing the street and units facing the rear yard. The units facing the rear ideally share an entry from the street with the other units.

How to Regulate This Type

(Photos, pages 150–151) Examples of mansion apartments.

- **Regulate the size so the structures do not get too big.** Regulate a maximum building width of approximately 65–75 ft. and regulate the maximum building depth of 55–60 ft.
- **You could allow this type in a general Missing Middle zone or you could create an additional zone that allows the widths to go up to 75 ft.**

Table 5-12: **Multiplex: Medium, Alley-Loaded**

LOT	
Width	95 ft.
Depth	115 ft.
Area	10,925 sq. ft.
	0.251 acres
UNITS	
Number of Units	12
Typical Unit Size	765 sq. ft.
DENSITY	
Net Density	48 du/acre
Gross Density	35 du/acre
PARKING	
Off-street Ratio	0.75 spaces per unit
On-street Spaces	4
Off-street Spaces	9
SETBACKS	
Front	15 ft.
Side	5 ft.
BUILDING	
Width	75 ft.
Depth	65 ft.
Height (to Eave)	28 ft.
Floors	2.5

*Idealized alley-loaded axonometric
drawing with data table.*

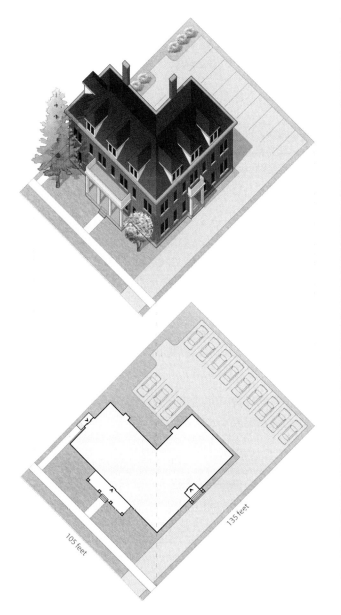

Table 5-13 Multiplex: Medium, Front-Loaded

LOT	
Width	105 ft.
Depth	135 ft.
Area	14,175 sq. ft.
	0.325 acres
UNITS	
Number of Units	12
Typical Unit Size	765 sq. ft.
DENSITY	
Net Density	37 du/acre
Gross Density	30 du/acre
PARKING	
Off-street Ratio	1.0 spaces per unit
On-street Spaces	4
Off-street Spaces	12
SETBACKS	
Front	15 ft.
Side	5 ft.
BUILDING	
Width	75 ft.
Depth	65 ft.
Height (to Eave)	28 ft.
Floors	2.5

Idealized front-loaded axonometric drawing with data table.

COURTYARD

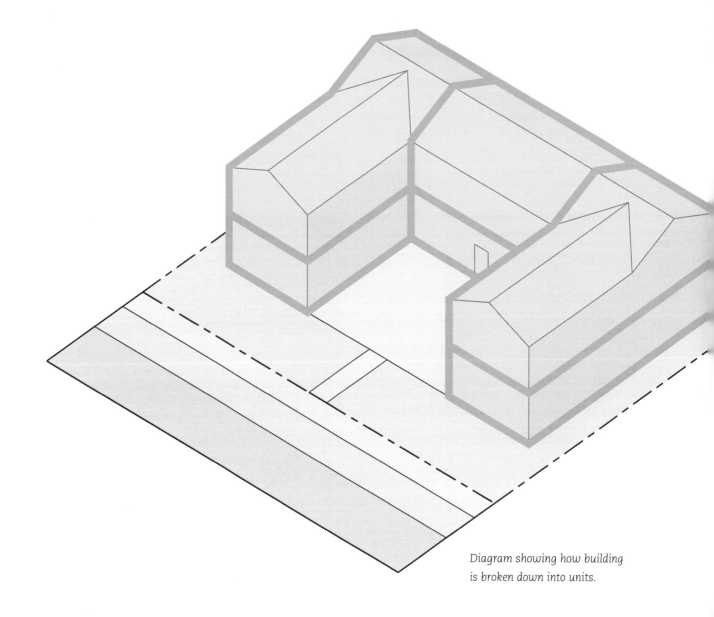

*Diagram showing how building
is broken down into units.*

BUILDING

This type is a medium-sized structure that consists of multiple side-by-side or stacked dwelling units oriented around a courtyard or series of courtyards. Each unit often has its own individual entry, or up to three units may share a common stoop, stair, or entry.

It is important to note that a building with a similar configuration, but with the units loaded with a shared internal corridor, does not deliver the same quality of living or foster the same sense of community within the courtyard, and thus does not fit within this classification.

There is a difference between a forecourt, often defined as a frontage, and a courtyard. The primary difference is if the depth of the space along the sidewalk edge is 20 ft. or less and is not defined by a privacy wall or element, it should be considered a forecourt. If it is larger than 20 ft. deep and/or defined by a privacy wall or element, then it should be considered a courtyard.

(Photos, pages 156–157) Examples of Courtyard Buildings.

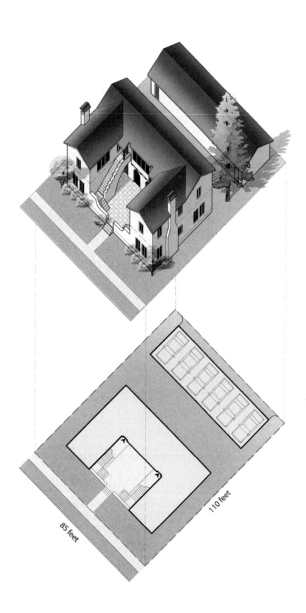

Table 5-14: Courtyard Apartments, Alley-Loaded

LOT	
Width	85 ft.
Depth	110 ft.
Area	9,350 sq. ft.
	0.215 acres
UNITS	
Number of Units	7
Typical Unit Size	667 sq. ft.
DENSITY	
Net Density	33 du/acre
Gross Density	24 du/acre
PARKING	
Off-street Ratio	0.85 spaces per unit
On-street Spaces	4
Off-street Spaces	6
SETBACKS	
Front	15 ft.
Side	5 ft.
BUILDING	
Width	67 ft.
Depth	47 ft.
Height (to Eave)	22 ft.
Floors	2

*Idealized alley-loaded axonometric
drawing with data table.*

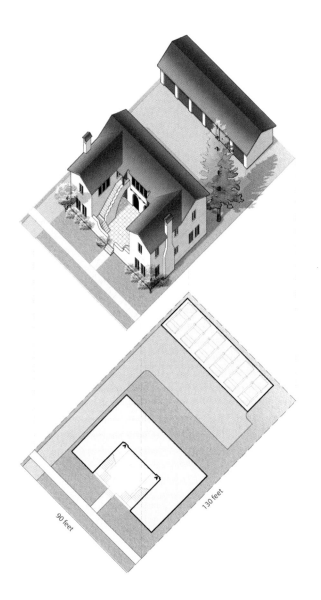

Table 5-15: Courtyard Apartments, Front-Loaded

LOT	
Width	90 ft.
Depth	130 ft.
Area	11,700 sq. ft.
	0.269 acres
UNITS	
Number of Units	7
Typical Unit Size	667 sq. ft.
DENSITY	
Net Density	26 du/acre
Gross Density	21 du/acre
PARKING	
Off-street Ratio	0.85 spaces per unit
On-street Spaces	3
Off-street Spaces	6
SETBACKS	
Front	15 ft.
Side	5 ft.
BUILDING	
Width	67 ft.
Depth	47 ft.
Height (to Eave)	22 ft.
Floors	2

Idealized front-loaded axonometric drawing with data table.

Design Characteristics

- The configuration and the size and shape of the courtyard will vary based on lot size.
- When the main building is wider than 70–75 ft. along the street, there are typically wings that project out perpendicular to the street that are no wider than 24 ft. wide and that visually break the scale down along the street.
- There are various configurations of a courtyard that include L-shaped, C-shaped, and O-shaped. L-shaped configurations are often used on corner lots.
- There are typically only a few short corridors to access the units.
- All ground floor units have direct access to a courtyard and a majority of upper-floor units have visual access to a courtyard.
- The width of street-facing wings of a C-shaped courtyard building is typically not wider than a house, thus making it feel compatible with houses.
- Due to the integration of a courtyard, these types often go deeper into a lot than other Missing Middle types. This should be considered when deciding where to allow these types.
- The width and depth of the courtyards should vary based on the local climate. In hot climates, small courtyards are preferred to provide comfortable shaded areas. In cooler climates or climates that vary, larger courtyards are better to allow sitting in either shaded or full-sun areas.
- If there are multiple courtyards, there are often passages through buildings into courtyards. In the Southwest and in Mexico this element traditionally was called a zaguan. This element was integrated historically to allow breezes and passive cooling within the courtyard while also allowing access to the courtyard without having to pass through anyone's dwelling.

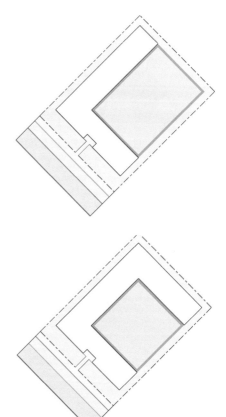

(Images, pages 160–161) Examples of the wide variety of courtyard configurations that can be used based on lot size.

- Seating and gathering areas should be provided within courtyards of multiunit buildings.
- These types, especially larger examples, often have varied massing, which means the building height varies in different parts of the building.

How to Regulate This Type

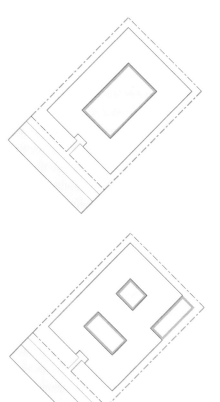

- **Regulate a minimum width and depth of the court:** This should be based on orientation and climate considerations. These minimum sizes (width and depth based on solar orientation) should be carefully studied and regulated.
- **Maximum units accessed from each stair:** Regulate so that no more than four units are accessed from each stoop, stair, or doorway.
- **Remove private-open-space requirements:** Due to the large amount of shared space provided, private open space is not necessary and should not be required in regulations.
- **Maximum wing width:** Require a maximum width of 35–40 ft. for wings on C-shaped configurations with court along the street.
- **Allow exceptions to height to encourage courtyard:** Cities may need to allow more height in a defined percentage of buildings to encourage this type because it has more unbuilt area and less development potential, due to the court space, compared to other types.

Box 5-2
Missing Middle Application to Tropical Climates and Developing Countries: Libreville, Gabon, Africa

Libreville is the capitol of Gabon, Africa, with a rapidly growing population. Opticos worked with Prince Charles's Community Building Foundation to implement a sustainable growth strategy for this ballooning metropolitan region. As part of the strategy created, our team designed a series of housing types that responded to the tropical climate and integrated Gabonese customs and culture in a way that maximized the livability of the units. Some of these housing types were more urban, but a core of these housing types were Missing Middle scale. Cresolus architects used their tropical-building-design expertise to make the types tropically appropriate.

Hot Air Release

Cross-Ventilation

Rain Protection & Shading

These graphics depict a few of the tropical design elements and approaches, such as ensuring cross-ventilation and providing screening from sun and rain for upper sashes to allow for windows to be open, even during heavy rain, to allow for cross-ventilation for passive cooling. (Source: Cresolus)

One of the adaptable tropical Missing Middle Housing types designed was the sideyard house. (Source: Cresolus)

One of these tropical Missing Middle types was the sideyard house shown in the adjacent graphics. Each of these types were designed to grow and evolve to meet the changing needs of families or owners, whether it be incubating a small business within the building or adding more space as a family grows or as space is needed for a relative or friend. These alternative designs also demonstrated how each building-type design could accommodate a broad range of uses and unit sizes. For example, the sideyard type shown, with its ancillary building included, could accommodate the following variations: six smaller units with two units on each floor of the main house and one unit on each floor of the ancillary building; three office spaces on the ground, with two in the main building and one in the ancillary building, and two units above, with one large unit on the second floor of the main building and one smaller unit on the second floor of the ancillary building; or, the building could function as one large, two-story villa in the main building with parking on the ground floor of the rear building with a small unit above it. This application demonstrates the ultimate flexibility of the types to allow the urbanism to evolve and for a limited range of types to accommodate a broad range of build-out options. The form of these types was carefully regulated in the very graphic, easy-to-understand form-based code that was written as the country's first zoning code.

Shared tropical building characteristics include:

- Deep overhangs or elements such as balconies or porches to allow windows to be open even during heavy rains to maximize natural lighting and cross ventilation

- Windows, interior features, and exterior elements that allow for maximum cross ventilation
- Termite-prevention elements and barriers
- Systems to drain water away from the buildings
- Elevated ground floors to allow cross ventilation below buildings
- Usable outdoor spaces, either private or shared, such as deep porches and courtyards to extend living outdoors
- Precast concrete building system developed by the team with modular unit sizes that can be standardized and fabricated locally. This also allows homeowners to infill the walls with whatever materials they have access to or can afford to enclose the building.

The-sideyard house design provides flexibility to accommodate a range of residential units and sizes as well as commercial uses within the same building footprint. This type can comprise multiple residential units on both floors, residential units on the upper floors and commercial spaces on the ground floor, or one large estate unit in the front and one smaller unit in the rear building. (Source: Cresolus)

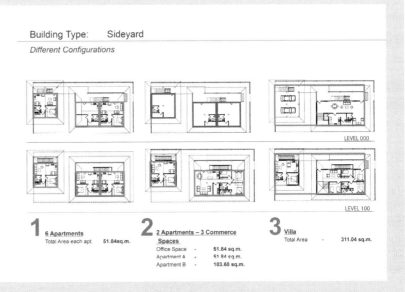

Building Type: Sideyard
Different Configurations

LEVEL 000

LEVEL 100

1 6 Apartments
Total Area each apt.   51.84sq.m.

2 2 Apartments – 3 Commerce
Spaces
Office Space   -   51.84 sq.m.
Apartment A   -   51.84 sq.m.
Apartment B   -   103.68 sq.m.

3 Villa
Total Area   -   311.04 sq.m.

LIVE-WORK

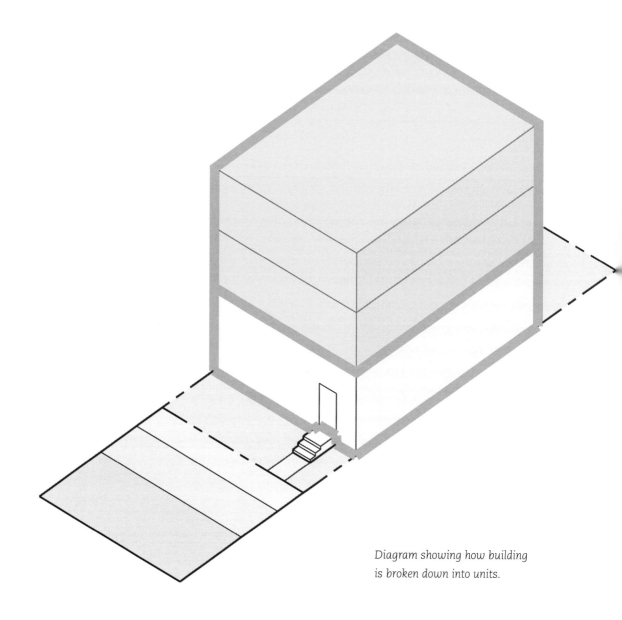

Diagram showing how building is broken down into units.

(FLEXHOUSE)

This building type integrates a unit as well as a separate flex space, accommodating a range of nonresidential uses. It is often three stories, which is an exception to the two-to-two-and-a-half-story height of most Missing Middle Housing types. It is included because it is a great type to incubate small businesses in a neighborhood. Flex houses enable an owner or renter to start a small business, use the space as an art studio, or rent it to another business to help pay the mortgage. This type should rarely be proposed or allowed within a residential block but rather should be treated as a transition type.

Cities do not typically have zoning to enable this type because it does not fit easily into either commercial or residential zones. It is best applied in areas where a city currently has zones for medium-density or multifamily residential.

The application of this type has been done very poorly in many examples, thus giving the concept a bad reputation in those places, but there are many good and successful examples to learn from across the country.

(Photos, pages 166–168) Examples of flex housing.

Box 5-3
Live-Work and the Missing Middle
By Thomas Dolan

Live-work types can play an integral role in creating vibrant, diverse, walkable neighborhoods and delivering a full range of housing choices. Careful consideration of proximity types, intensity types, and project types should be considered generally, but also within the context of Missing Middle Housing.

Proximity types define the physical relationship between the space designated for living and that designated for working. In a live-with configuration, there is a single space, including typically a kitchen located below a mezzanine or sleeping space, which looks out over a large contiguous working space. In a live-near (housing-over-retail town house) configuration, the work space is separated from the living space by a wall or a floor. In a live-near unit, the living portion may more closely resemble a typical apartment or town house. In a live-nearby configuration, a short walk separates the living portion and the work space—across a courtyard, to a converted garage or other accessory structure, or up or down an exterior staircase, for example.

Intensity types relate to the desired range of uses in the flex space, with consideration of the occupants and uses in adjoining units. This is a consideration that is often not carefully vetted and impacts the viability of the live-work project, especially if appropriate fire separations are not integrated for the full range of desired uses.

There are three intensity types to consider, which are home occupation, live-work, and work-live, but for Missing Middle Housing, the proximity types that make the most sense are home occupation and live-work. Within home occupation, employees and walk-in trade may or may not be permitted. Home occupation works best in a mixed-use or Missing Middle neighborhood, where opportunities for interaction exist on the street or in the courtyard. Within live-work, the predominant use for the unit is residence; work activity is secondary or, if separated, of comparable importance.

Different project types include the flex house, which is a "building that learns," with flexible spaces on ground floors of buildings laid out in town house modules with residential units above. It is often used initially in neighborhoods where retail is not yet viable, and it takes the form of housing-over-retail live-near units. A live-work courtyard community is a series of building elements that define a centralized, shared courtyard. This configuration maximizes a sense of community, with the courtyard providing a place for residents to cross paths and socialize, and also a presence on the street.

Find out more about live-work in *Live-Work Planning and Design: Zero Commute Housing* by Thomas Dolan (John Wiley and Sons, 2012) or visit www.live-work.com.

Design Characteristics

- It is best if this type is designed with a street entry into the flex space that is separate from the entry into the residential unit but also has lockable, direct, interior access from residential unit into the flex space.
- The flex space on the ground floor must have taller heights (10 ft. minimum and ideally 12 ft. floor to floor).
- The frontage of the flex space should feel like a shop front from the street edge or sidewalk.
- Fire separation must be provided to allow the desired range of nonresidential uses.
- A fairly unfinished interior space similar to a warehouse space is ideal for the flex space.

How to Regulate This Type

- **Be flexible with ground floor uses:** Allow the flex space to function as a separate unit if there is not viability for nonresidential uses.
- **Where to allow:** Allow this type in areas that transition from commercial corridors, main streets, or higher-intensity residential areas into single-family neighborhoods.
- **Ensuring a truly usable flex space:** Require two-hour fire separation between the flex space and the unit.
- **Limit required parking:** Do not require additional parking for the flex space.
- **Ground floor heights:** Require the floor-to-ceiling heights to be 10 ft. minimum.
- **Regulate good frontage:** Require a shop front frontage but allow for up to a 10 ft. front setback for a dooryard to provide a privacy transition if it is being used as an apartment.

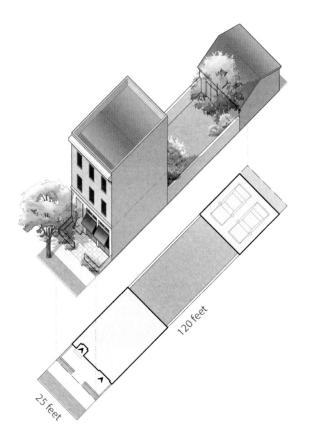

Idealized alley-loaded axonometric drawing with data table.

Table 5-16: Live-Work, Alley-Loaded

LOT	
Width	25 ft.
Depth	120 ft.
Area	3,000 sq. ft.
	0.069 acres
UNITS	
Number of Units	1
Typical Unit Size	1,750 sq. ft.
DENSITY	
Net Density	15 du/acre
Gross Density	11 du/acre
PARKING	
Off-street Ratio	1.0 space per unit
On-street Spaces	1
Off-street Spaces	2
SETBACKS	
Front	10 ft.
Side	0 ft.
BUILDING	
Width	25 ft.
Depth	35 ft.
Height (to Eave)	38 ft.
Floors	3

UPPER

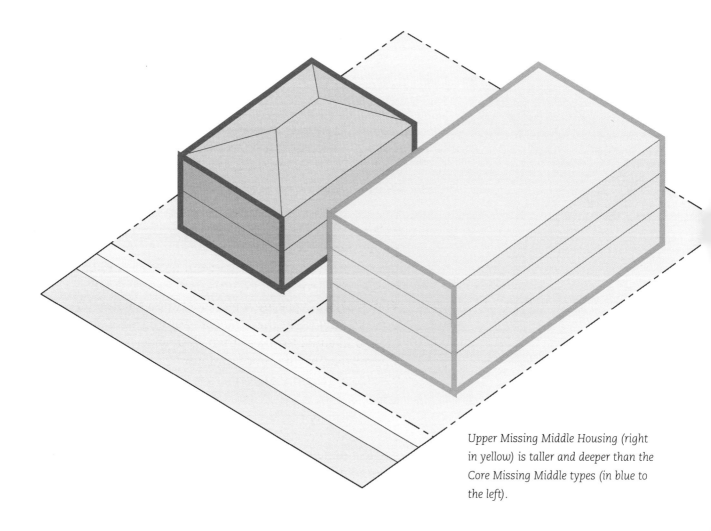

Upper Missing Middle Housing (right in yellow) is taller and deeper than the Core Missing Middle types (in blue to the left).

MISSING MIDDLE HOUSING TYPES

Upper Missing Middle should be treated as a separate category from Missing Middle. Compared to the Core Missing Middle types, the Upper Missing Middle types are:

- **Taller:** Mostly three to four stories, typically still walk-up. but sometimes up to five stories
- **Deeper:** These types often go from front setback to close-to-rear property line with little or no rear setback.
- **Wider:** These types are often wider than a house but not dramatically wider than the core Missing Middle types, often still equal to or less than 75 ft. wide.
- **Appropriate in different locations:** These types often provide an appropriate transition from corridor, main street, higher-intensity lots into single-family or lower-intensity neighborhoods, or are appropriate in residential areas that may currently have smaller buildings or single-family homes where policy and plans have a defined degree of change, evolution, or transformation for these areas.

OTHER

MISSING MIDDLE TYPE VARIATIONS

(Opposite) Missing Middle types are adaptable enough to accommodate commercial uses.

There are unlimited variations of multiunit housing types that can fit within the Missing Middle classification. They might include town houses over flats; the Mews Homes, which are highlighted as a case study in chapter 6; or types that mix town houses and flats in creative ways. The most important shared characteristic of these types is simply the house form and scale, but the design must not be compromised by the integration of parking (as we often see), and the types must also engage the street. But since housing type is not a common planning and zoning methodology and not a typical way to discuss housing, it is best to start with these basic configurations and then expand once community members, planners, local developers, and decision makers get comfortable with a types-based approach.

6.
CASE
STUDIES

THESE CASE STUDIES REPRESENT A BROAD SPECTRUM OF
RECENTLY BUILT OR RENOVATED MISSING MIDDLE HOUS-
ING APPLICATIONS SMALL AND LARGE, RANGING FROM
THE CONVERSION OF AN EXISTING SINGLE-FAMILY HOME

into a fourplex to the construction of a forty-acre Missing Middle Neighborhood. The examples differ based on the type and size of builder or developer that built them, as well as the geography and size of town they were built in. In some instances, the Missing Middle project represents the first project for a newly converted builder; in other instances, the project is being built by a seasoned, large-scale production builder. All scales of Missing Middle projects and the delivery of Missing Middle by builders big and small is needed to effectively address the enormous demand for Missing Middle Housing across the country. These case studies differ from those presented at the end of chapter 7, which are specifically focused on zoning policy and regulatory changes.

DEKUM/CHARLES FOURPLEX:
Converting a Single-Family Home into a Fourplex with For-Sale Units

PORTLAND, OREGON
Within the spectrum of Missing Middle projects, among the most enticing for policy makers is the conversion of single-family homes into multiplexes. Increasing the amount of housing and providing more choices in this way seems to have the most potential to preserve the visual status quo of a community, thus resulting in the least amount of pushback. Moreover, because single-family homes make up the majority of the housing stock in most American cities, conversions seem to offer a solution that can be effectively scaled and provide much-needed housing in walkable neighborhoods in high-demand markets. Some of these types of conversions were done historically for rental units in low-value neighborhoods or often near university campuses, where zoning allowed it, but few conversions have happened that deliver for-sale units as an alternative to owning a home. Presumably, they also offer higher profit potential for the developer as well.

At 6817 NE Seventh Avenue in Portland, Oregon, Garlynn Woodsong, who is an urban planner turned builder and broker in the state of Oregon, wanted to illustrate the feasibility of such a project and show how it could deliver more affordable for-sale units to the market in small, Missing Middle–scale buildings. The story of this project is a great case study that shows how this type of conversion is physically possible, but it also illustrates the challenges and

A single-family home before renovations, in a fairly run down and unmaintained condition. (Source: Garlynn Woodsong)

barriers developers and policy makers should consider in relation to enabling and delivering these types of projects.

Situated on a 5,000 sq. ft. lot, 50 ft. wide and 100 ft. deep, in Portland's highly desirable Woodlawn neighborhood, approximately a twelve-minute drive or thirty-minute bus ride into downtown Portland, this conversion project began in 2015 with the purchase of the property for $255,000. The lot was zoned for commercial uses (CM) with an allowed 45 ft. height limit and a 2:1 allowed FAR. While this allowed for significant density on the site, Woodsong chose to rehab the existing structure and integrate units within it with the hope that this would be more cost effective, for environmental reasons, knowing that the embodied energy of the initial construction of this house has already been amortized fully over its current 125-year lifespan and that the character of the 1890s building could not be replicated today. The old-growth timbers used for the structure's framing are of a size not even available today; it was constructed entirely with handmade square iron nails, produced in the late nineteenth century by local blacksmiths; and the Victorian details were somewhat intact.

But the Queen Ann Victorian style, four-bedroom, three-bath, 1,819 sq. ft. home had deteriorated from its original splendor and required a complete gut renovation. Woodsong aimed to convert the home into a fourplex by digging out a basement, creating an English basement unit, adding additional square footage deeper into the lot, and converting the attic into a livable space. The result was a fourplex much like the ones built one hundred years earlier—essentially a New England triple-decker with one unit on each floor but with an added basement to accommodate a fourth unit. The units themselves ranged in size from 875 to 966 sq. ft. Each unit contains two to three bedrooms and one to one and a half bathrooms.

The entitlements process proved to be a challenge even for Woodsong, who has a long career as a professional planner. An anticipated monthlong process took six months due to the inexperience of the city's planning staff in assessing this type of project. The delay cost him his general contractor and pushed the beginning of construction into January, the rainy season in the Pacific Northwest, which made moving dirt far more difficult.

Rehabbing the structure itself presented three major challenges: First of all, the aging building had to be brought back into a square shape and needed major work to meet shear-wall requirements. Secondly, because the structure had more than two units it had to be built up to commercial building code versus a duplex or single-family home, which only need to meet residential building code standards. This adds quite a bit of cost to a smaller project because it triggers a whole host of required improvements, including: new structural walls and floors with fifty decibels of sound reduction; brand-new hardwood and tile floors; new sheetrock walls and ceilings; all-new plumbing, electrical, fire alarm, and fire sprinkler systems; and a new foundation; Lastly, the project triggered Fair Housing Act requirements, so at least one of the units had to be fully accessible, which wound up meaning a new wheelchair-grade ramp to the basement.

The thoughtful conversion in progress, with some of the historic details having been uncovered in demolition. (Source: Garlynn Woodsong)

The completed conversion of the single-family home into a fourplex, having maintained much of the original character during the process. (Source: Garlynn Woodsong)

While the project successfully saved some of the original Victorian details, such as wooden acorns at the bottom of hanging balustrades, gingerbread details at the top of the gable end facing the street, and the original solid-wood front-porch columns, the benefits did not measure up to the costs and challenges of such an undertaking. Woodsong jokes that he preserved some "extravagantly expensive two-by-fours" that you can't see on the inside of the walls.

The final product came to the market in 2016 with two-to-three-bedroom condos selling between $360,000 and $395,000. At the time, a comparable three-bedroom single-family home in the area would have cost about $430,000–$550,000, thus enabling Woodsong to achieve the goal of delivering more attainable housing choices in this neighborhood. On the pro forma side, Woodsong's total income for the project amounted to $1.507 million. All in, costs came out to $1.501 million. Thus, the

(Opposite) Interior of one of the units showing very livable, high-quality spaces created by this thoughtful conversion.
(Source: Garlynn Woodsong)

endeavor's value was more as an immersive education into the challenges of Missing Middle renovation than as an actual profit-making enterprise. In hindsight, building a new multiplex from scratch, configured with six to eight units, would have made the project more feasible and created revenue to help fund the next project, but Woodsong did enjoy the challenge. He likes to share the lessons learned on this project with other builders or potential builders so they can successfully navigate this type of small but important project type to deliver Missing Middle Housing.

BASEMENT PLAN
Unit A: 966 sq. ft.

FIRST FLOOR PLAN
Unit B: 875 sq. ft.

SECOND FLOOR PLAN
Unit C: 915 sq. ft.

THIRD FLOOR PLAN
Unit D: 844 sq. ft.

Unit plans for each of the four units on separate floors.
(Source: Garlynn Woodsong)

Dekum Charles	
Program Summary	
Site Area	0.11 acres
Context	Preexisting Walkable Neighborhood
Dwelling Units	4
Unit A: 2 bed, 1 bath	966 sq. ft.
Unit B: 2 bed, 1.5 bath	875 sq. ft.
Unit C: 3 bed, 1.5 bath	915 sq. ft.
Unit D: 2 bed, 1 bath	844 sq. ft.
Density (Net)	35 du/acre
Parking	
Off-Street (Surface)	1
On-Street	2
Ratio w/o On-Street Parking	0.25 spaces per unit
Ratio w/ On-Street Parking	0.75 spaces per unit
Development Process	
Entitlements	6 months
Construction	19 months
Listing and Sale Period	5–6 months
Development Cost Information	
Site Acquisition Cost	$255,000
Construction Costs	$875,000
Soft Costs	$371,000
Total Development Costs	**$1,501,000**

Source: Garlynn Woodsong

KEY FACTS

Financial Structure: Set up as an LLC, with 60–80 percent debt with the remainder as equity. Construction loan had four-year term with an original interest rate of 12 percent (eventually adjusted down to 9 percent). Debt financing was obtained through a variety of private sources. In general, lenders were less willing to finance a renovation compared to new construction.

THE LIBRARY COTTAGES:
Renovating Two ADUs on a Single Lot

HEALDSBURG, CALIFORNIA

This case study highlights the benefits of allowing multiple units, often in addition to a main house, in small buildings on small-to-medium-sized lots located within established walkable neighborhoods. This project is located in a neighborhood adjacent to downtown Healdsburg, California, and adjoins the city's only library. The Library Cottages consist of two 625 sq. ft. cottages with a shared wall at the rear of a lot and a 1,050 sq. ft. original main house built in the Italianate style in 1911. The two attached rear units were added to the lot by a previous owner. The developer, Jim Heid, purchased the property in 2010 with his wife in hope of quickly renovating the cottages and using the rental income to finance a remodel of the historic main house.

The initial work required clearing trees that had overtaken the yard, threatened the foundation, and put the entire house in constant shade, accelerating rot. Because of the landlocked backyard, a crane was needed to take the trees out piece by piece.

Another dramatic change was leveling the carport that masked the units from the street and added to their derelict appearance. With the carport and its accompanying Rube Goldberg collection of awnings, covered walkways, and "laundry shack" gone, the cottages regained visibility.

The existing property was nonconforming, which meant the city's zoning code would not allow this number of units to be built on the site today. Luckily the City of Healdsburg has a classification of an "existing nonconforming use," so the renovations to the property did not require a zoning change as long as they did not add additional square footage. However, with the

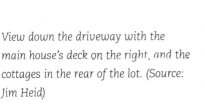

View down the driveway with the main house's deck on the right, and the cottages in the rear of the lot. (Source: Jim Heid)

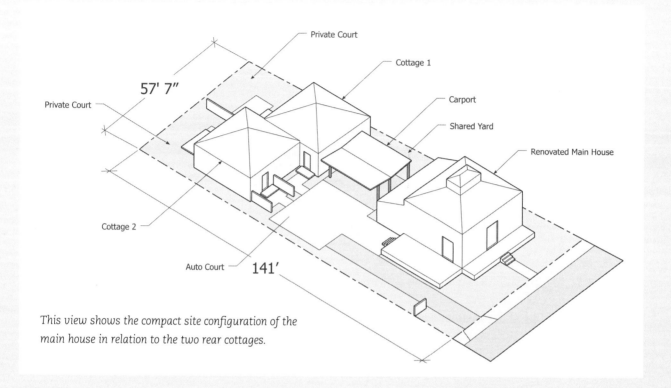

This view shows the compact site configuration of the main house in relation to the two rear cottages.

upgrades to the property, the City did require it to meet current parking standards for multifamily properties. Those standards require one covered parking space and one half-uncovered space per unit, adding up to three covered spaces and two uncovered ones. Meeting this high parking requirement was challenging, and it would have been enough to stop many similar projects due to physical constraints on smaller lots. But some creative design was able to solve the problem. The Heids had just enough space to rework their site plan to create a layered car court with the covered portion behind the main house while simultaneously bringing the cottages and their entries into view of the street.

With the site work completed, the couple turned their attention to the cottages. Bathrooms and kitchens were completely redone, creatively using cost-effective materials (Martha Stewart cabinets from Home Depot, IKEA closet systems, engineered maple flooring) to create a fresh and open feel. Exterior decks were added to the rear of each cottage unit that extend living outdoors into a private court space. This is a common approach for small units on lots that have the space for it. All in, the renovation of the backyard and two cottages took nine months at a total cost of $150,000.

The 1,400 sq. ft. main house proved to be more of a challenge. To increase the usable square footage by adding a basement, they utilized hydraulic jacks to get enough clearance for an excavator to get in and remove 100 cu. yds. of earth. Other notable elements included moving the foundation and adding a newly framed roof and cupola. All in, the process took another sixteen months.

In terms of financials, the project benefited immensely from market timing. The developer acquired the property in 2009 out of foreclosure for $410,000. After investing $150,000 in rehab-

(Below) Entries to the two rear cottages off the parking court.
(Source: Jim Heid)

bing the cottages, the property was reappraised at $800,000, which was used as collateral to finance the main-house renovation. Critically, this valuation categorizes the property as a single-family home with ADUs, not as a three-unit apartment complex, which would command a lower valuation. These values are hard for many in other markets to relate to, but the important lesson learned from this case study is that three units were thoughtfully and compatibly integrated onto a lot that was initially plotted for one house. Returns on similar projects in other regions of the country will likely not be as

Views of the renovated main house with glimpses of the barely visible cottages to the rear. (Source: Jim Heid)

A shared space between the main house
and the cottages provides a welcoming
place that enables activities to spill out
into the space. (Source: Jim Heid)

high, but, if done thoughtfully, they will generate returns and will go a long way in increasing housing supply in a thoughtful manner and delivering smaller, more attainable housing choices.

In 2016, California passed statewide ADU reform, which has been modified since then several times to remove further barriers, which resulted in 3,818 ADU permits in Los Angeles in 2017 versus 299 in 2015[1] prior to the bill passing. Even smaller cities like Asheville, North Carolina, have passed similar local regulations to enable ADUs.[2] As more cities across the country face housing shortages and unattainable rents and purchase prices, this project serves as a model of how cities should change zoning and parking standards to enable this type of thoughtful small-scale infill, even in single-family neighborhoods, and how developers/builders can thoughtfully tackle similar opportunities to provide more housing where it is allowed. This type of neighborhood within walking distance to a downtown is a perfect application of this approach.

Healdsburg Library Cottages	
Program Summary	
Site Area	0.21 acres
Context	Pre-Existing Walkable Neighborhood
Dwelling Units	3
Number of Different Building Types	2 (renovated main house; new cottages)
Unit A: Renovated main house (2Bd/1Ba)	1,400 sq. ft. (inclusive of basement)
Unit B: Cottage (1Bd/1Ba)	625 sq. ft.
Unit C: Cottage (1Bd/1Ba)	625 sq. ft.
Net Density	14 du/acre
Parking	
Off Street (Surface)	2
Off Street (Carport)	3
On Street	2
Total	7

Ratio w/o On-Street Parking	1.0 space per unit	
Ratio w/ On-Street Parking	1.67 spaces per unit	
Development Cost Information		
Acquisition Cost	$410,000	
Construction Costs (Cottages Renovation)	$150,000	
Construction Costs (Main House Renovation)	$350,000	
Soft Costs	$50,000	
Total Development Costs	$960,000	
Appraised Value (after cottage renovations only, 2012)	$585,000	
Appraised Value (after cottage and home renovation, 2012)	$1,350,00	This allowed Jim to take all of his equity out and basically finance the full project with an $840,000 I/O loan, which the cottages funded 85% of.
Appraised Value (2019)	$2,550,000	This allowed Jim to pull out additional equity via a $1,200,000 fully amortizing loan, which he used to fund his next development, a coworking space. He is able to cover 85% of that cost with his rental income.
Project Timing		
2010	Purchased out of foreclosure	
August 2011	Cottage completed	
May 2012	Renovation of main house begins	
September 2013	Move into main house	
Source: Jim Heid		

GOOD SPACE:
Renovating Small, Historic Missing Middle Buildings in a Walkable Neighborhood

DALLAS, TEXAS

With small-scale blocks and streets lined with cottages, brick storefronts, and a mix of two-story walk-up apartments and single-family homes, the Kidd Springs Neighborhood in southern Dallas, renamed Bishop Arts, stands out in this sprawling Sunbelt metropolis. Largely built before the heyday of the automobile, the neighborhood was the site of the city's busiest trolley stop in the 1930s and was one of the few streetcar neighborhoods in Dallas that was not torn down as part of urban renewal. While the streetcars are long gone, the walkable, human-scale neighborhoods they promulgated are once again highly desirable.

The beginnings of this neighborhood's revival are in the 1990s, when an enterprising community-development specialist, David Spence, fell

The Bishop Gate building was originally a hotel that was converted into eight one-bedroom apartments. It is a house-scale building with a density of over 60 du/acre. (Source: Good Space)

The Bishop Green apartments is a group of Missing Middle buildings oriented around a shared yard. (Source: Good Space)

Bishop Terrace's hardwood floors, wavy-glass windows, and plaster walls were painstakingly restored by Good Space to deliver sixteen one-bedroom apartments to the neighborhood within walking distance to a neighborhood main street. (Source: Good Space)

in love with the area while working for a community-development corporation (CDC) and moved to nearby Oak Cliff and started renovating a bungalow with his wife. After losing his job, and since his work experience had been with CDCs working in Dallas, his first impulse was to create a community-development non-profit, but on the advice of urban redeveloper Bennett Miller, he started his own development company, Good Space, focused on revitalizing the Bishop Ars Arts neighborhood one Missing Middle building at a time. At the time, there was little interest from banks or investors in taking part in his projects, but entry into ownership of these buildings was cheap at $4 per sq. ft., which was necessary for a small developer without a lot of equity.[3]

Good Space's first project was Bishop Terrace, a once-inspiring two-story, brick, sixteen-unit apartment building with terra-cotta details built in 1929 that had been condemned. It was financed entirely out of Spence's life savings.

Having little construction or development experience, he was mentored by Trey Bartosh, an architect and business partner. Buy, thoughtfully renovate, and hold was his business plan. Because of this long-term hold strategy, Good Space took pains to save worn hardwood floors, wavy-glass windows, built-ins, and plaster walls while integrating new systems. After spending $50,000 to acquire the property in 1996 and another $500,000 to rehab it, the property was worth only $300,000. While quixotic by conventional metrics, the on-the-ground reality told a different story. Spence immediately noticed the effect of his renovation on the other side of the property line. Soon after he completed Bishop Terrace, his neighbors across the street started making repairs. The apartment building continues to provide attainable housing in this walkable neighborhood. While the project today is worth $2.5 million, rents are still affordable: a one-bedroom unit in Bishop Terrace starts at $850 a month, which is affordable for a single person making 65 percent of the area median income.

Spence was able to use the income from Bishop Terrace to fund his second project, Bishop Green. The Bishop Green has twelve units in multiple buildings oriented around a shared communal space. "At one point in time, these apartments were mostly occupied by landscape architects, who were attracted to the native landscaping, communal gardening area, and at least two 'outdoor rooms' with each apartment," says Spence. The rents started at $.75 per sq. ft. in 1995 and are now $1.50 per sq. ft. for two of his properties and $2.00 per sq. ft. for Bishop Gate. In comparison, newly constructed mid-rise buildings in the same neighborhood rent for $2.00–$2.20 per sq. ft. Bishop Gate was a hotel that Spence renovated into eight small one-bedroom apartments that are each 495 sq. ft. One interesting aspect of this building is that it has eight units in the same footprint and lot size as a fourplex building that sits right next to it, and because of the small units, it generates a density of nearly 80 du/acre. Spence used the equity in these buildings to get a $1 million construction loan at 2 percent against the buildings to fund a new project. The cap rate on these properties is now 7 percent.

Unlike other real estate investors who see geographic diversification as a key strategy, Spence prefers to keep investing in Bishop Arts. He considers it a different way of mitigating risk. As he puts it, instead of spreading out, you should saturate a market so you can be vigilant about your properties, nursing them along "like a mother hen." This singular focus on the neighborhood includes a philanthropic and civic component. Spence estimates that a third of his time is spent on non-business endeavors, such as volunteering in the local schools and serving on boards and commissions. Spence serves as a great role model for a Missing Middle developer who wants to have an impact and play a civic role in a community.

THE MEWS HOMES:
Rethinking the Conventional Town House to Deliver High-Quality, Attainable Homes

SOUTH JORDAN, UTAH

This case study is an example of how home builders large and small can use Missing Middle Housing to broaden their portfolio of housing types beyond single-family homes, to differentiate their housing from competitors, and to achieve price points attainable to more buyers. Utah-based Holmes Homes found developing new homes, even town houses, at an attainable price point to be a challenge. They also were exploring a business strategy to move away from their traditional single-family product type

to respond to shifting demand. Holmes Homes approached Opticos Design, wondering if Missing Middle Housing could help them achieve these goals. And the Utah home builder had an enigmatic site that could be a proving ground for innovation.

The 3.2-acre site was within the master planned community of Daybreak, in South Jordan, Utah. The site is only a seven-to-ten-minute walk to a light-rail station with service to

(Below) A view down the mews toward a small, shared community plaza where the north–south and east–west mews intersect. The three-story unit was included for variation in height and thoughtfully placed within the site plan.

Two-story living spaces with lots of natural light makes the small units very livable and makes them feel larger than they actually are.

downtown Salt Lake City in approximately forty to forty-five minutes. The Daybreak master developer had done an excellent job of delivering a broad range of housing types throughout the community, and their entitlement gave the builders great flexibility to explore new housing types. The 3.2 acres purchased by Holmes Homes were planned as two deep blocks that were ill-suited for traditional townhomes. Opticos responded to this challenge with the Mews Homes, a concept for an intimate collection of attached homes situated along a central pedestrian-only walkway that is evocative of the carriage-house side streets of eighteenth-century Europe. The site plan elegantly splits the two large blocks into four microscale blocks with the pedestrian-only street or mews that provides a high-quality address for the internal units, promotes a sense of community, provides a comfortable pedestrian connection to a nearby school, and delivers a small shared courtyard at the middle of the block where the north–south and east–west paseos come together. The mews was

(Above) The Mews Homes site is located within the larger Daybreak Master Planned Community and within a seven-minute walk to a light-rail station that goes directly to downtown Salt Lake City.

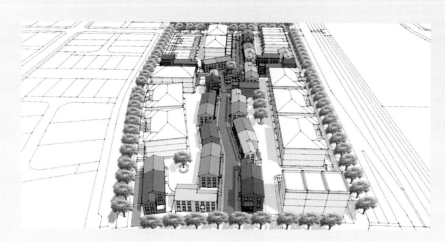

3-D diagram showing the site-plan layout of the Mews Homes and the mix of unit types, each represented by a different color.

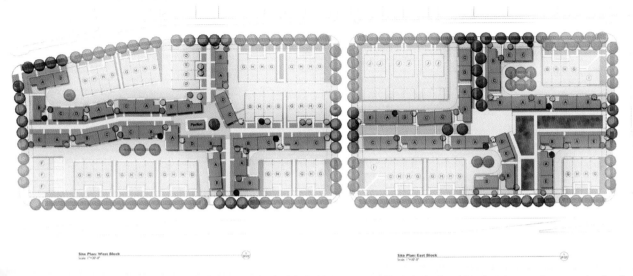

Site Plan: West Block
Scale: 1" = 30'-0"

Site Plan: East Block
Scale: 1" = 30'-0"

(Above) The 3.2-acre site was split into four smaller blocks with the introduction of an east–west and a north–south pedestrian-only mews that allowed interior Mews Homes units to have an address on the mews and external town houses to have an address on the street.

(Below) Unit plans for the Mews units range in size from 968 sq. ft. to 1,400 sq. ft., which is small for this market. This size made them attractive to single-women households and empty nesters.

MEWS II
1255 sq. ft.

MEWS III
1170 sq. ft.

MEWS IV
975 sq. ft.

purposefully made slightly irregular to frame interesting vistas as you traverse the mews.

The key to the efficient resolution of the site-plan design was a compact plan that had alley-loaded units that were 26 ft. deep and 26–50 ft. wide. This was achieved by flipping a conventional town house on its side, orienting each home's long facade to the mews. This move also maximized natural light in the units and increased privacy by reducing potential noise from neighbors because there was only a short wall attached to the neighboring unit. The units are on the smaller side of what was being built in Daybreak, ranging from 968 to 1,416 sq. ft., which was another aspect that enabled Holmes to deliver lower price points, differentiate themselves from their competitors, and yield 20 du/acre. Unlike comparable conventional town houses, each unit comes with a small private yard. Another important aspect of the design was the flex garage spaces with mews-facing entryways, which can incubate small business, home offices, or function as maker spaces. An alternative shop front facing the mews was designed for these spaces. Unfortunately, because the entitlement for this area within the master plan was only for residential uses, this aspect of these types was not allowed in this phase of the project.

The architects challenged themselves to keep the buildings simple, as opposed to the typical overly articulated massing on many suburban homes that also adds cost. These simple forms kept construction costs low—they were $99 per sq. ft. in phase one, with thoughtful attention to where and when to add more detail. The quality of the interior spaces makes the units highly livable, with two-story living spaces in all of the units and breakfast nooks in some of them. Simple and elegant were the overarching goals for the design. The simple and easy-to-construct massing and details have allowed delivery at affordable prices.

Sales of new units were brisk, with sales prices in the first phase ranging from $180,000 to $220,000. These prices were approximately $20,000 below Holmes's previous entry-level price to purchase a home and were affordable for a family of four making 80 percent of Salt Lake County's area median income. But at the same time, these Mews Homes have achieved the highest per-square-foot sales prices of any attached homes in the Daybreak master planned community. The primary buyers in the first round of sales were single women.

Jason Nageli of Holmes Homes said, "I think the big difference in the mews versus single-family homes is the starting price point. We are able to introduce a lower price point to fit more people's needs. Our single-family homes start in the high $300s. The mews is in the mid $200s."

Mews Homes
Program Summary

Site Area	3.2 acres
Context	Newly Developed Walkable Master Planned Community
Density	20 du/acre
Dwelling Units	65
Number of Different Unit Types	5
Unit A: 2 bed, 2.5 bath	1,435 sq. ft.
Unit B: 2 bed, 2.5 bath	1,255 sq. ft.
Unit C: 2 bed, 2.5 bath	1,170 sq. ft.
Unit D: 1 bed, 1.5 bath	975 sq. ft.
Unit E: 1 bed, 1.5 bath	1,205 sq. ft.
Density (Gross)	20 du/acre
Parking	
Off-Street Spaces (Garage)*	1–2 per unit

* Garages designed to function as flex/maker spaces if owner chooses to use them for a range of nonresidential uses.

Development Cost and Revenue Information

Construction Costs	
Cost per Square Foot (phase 1)	$89–$104
Cost per Square Foot (phase 2)	$106–$130
Sales Revenue*	
Sales Price per Square Foot (phase 1)	$145–$184
Sales Price per Square Foot (phase 2)	$175–$218
Sales Price per Unit (phase 1)	$169k–$209k
Sales Price per Unit (phase 2)	$224k–$264k
Gross Margin	24%
Time on Market	Majority of the units were sold before construction was completed. None of the units was on the market for more than 30 days.

* 2.5 years between these phases. Costs increased, but due to demand for this product, their margins increased in phase 2.
  Source: Mews Homes

CULLY GROVE:
Incubating a Community within a Pocket Neighborhood

PORTLAND, OREGON

This case study highlights a successful strategy for building Missing Middle on infill sites that are larger than an individual lot or two but not larger than five acres. The project is situated on a nearly two-acre site in Northeast Portland's Cully neighborhood, a highly diverse, major-ity-low-income neighborhood. Cully's unique combination of rural features, sparse commercial development, and relatively low household incomes have made it somewhat deficient in the commercial and recreational opportunities that characterize the rapidly developing inner neighborhoods of Portland.[4]

This pocket neighborhood includes sixteen homes oriented around a shared green space, with a primary goal of fostering a strong sense of community. The project includes a host of communal features, such as a 1,068 sq. ft. common house with a kitchen, a living/dining area, and two guest bedrooms as well as a community garden and shared green space. Eli Spevak and Zach Parrish, two small-scale local builders, developed the project as a partnership after competing to purchase the site in 2009. Once they realized they had similar visions for the property, they combined their expertise and resources to bring it to fruition.

While there was a mix of neighborhood support and opposition, the project was consistent with the City of Portland's zoning allowances and priorities and thus enjoyed a smooth entitlement

(Photos, pages 202–203) The welcoming nature of this project is reinforced by a great site plan, beautiful landscaping, and thoughtful building design. Units engage the shared green space. (Source: Eli Spevak)

Their approach for the site plan centered the development around shared community spaces for residents of the project. A common house with guest bedrooms stands in the center—dividing the community spaces into two distinct areas: To the south a large lawn for unprogrammed activity, which preserved a magnificent 47 ft. oak tree. To the north, a space was created for a variety of shared uses, including a children's play area and a community garden. With the primacy of these communal assets established, other necessary amenities, such as storage sheds, bike parking, and carports (twenty-two parking spaces for residents with another two for guests), shifted to the site's periphery. The desire to preserve community space at the center of the development impacted the design of the homes. While building sixteen large single-family homes on the site would have maximized their return, it would have crowded out the communal uses Spevak and Parrish envisioned. Instead, the site includes some single-family homes along with duplexes and triplexes built as townhomes. While stacked flats were considered, the developers thought townhomes would be more palatable to buyers in this largely single-family-home neighborhood. The floor plans are a mix of two , three- and four-bedrooms, ranging from 1,000 to 1,800 sq. ft.

Each unit has at least some private outdoor space for the residents, allowing some level of personalization. Under the provisions of the condo homeowners association, residents own their backyard and front yard. Shared spaces are maintained through monthly HOA fees, as is typical for this kind of structure.

process with no required zoning changes. The site's residential (R5) zoning allowed for sixteen homes on one large lot—one unit per 5,000 sq. ft. of lot area—as part of a discretionary "Planned Development" that Eli and Zach opted for.

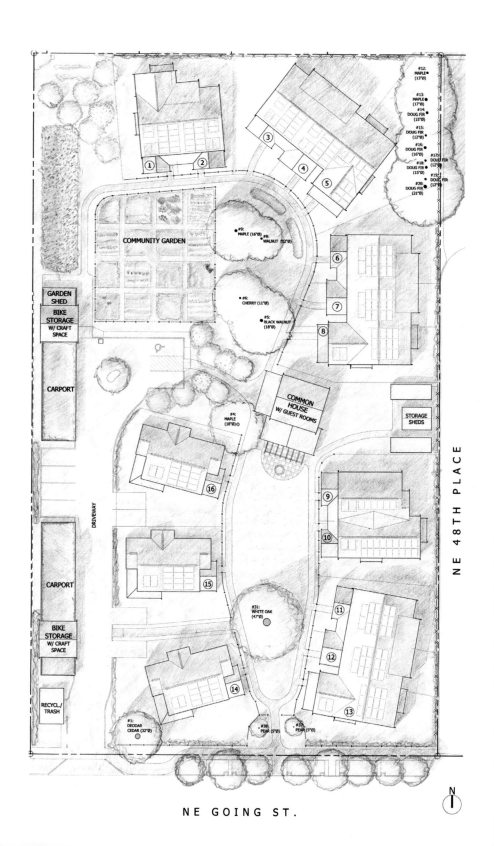

#12:
MAPLE
(13"∅)

#13:
MAPLE
(17"∅)
#14:
DOUG FIR
(15"∅)

#15:
DOUG FIR
(12"∅)
#16:
DOUG FIR
(16"∅)
#17:
DOUG FIR
(12"∅)
#18:
DOUG FIR
(15"∅)
#19:
DOUG FIR
(12"∅)
#20:
DOUG FIR
(21"∅)

1

2

3

4

5

COMMUNITY GARDEN

#9:
MAPLE (16"∅)
#8:
WALNUT (12"∅)

6

#6:
CHERRY (11"∅)

7

#5:
BLACK WALNUT
(18"∅)

8

GARDEN
SHED

BIKE
STORAGE
W/ CRAFT
SPACE

CARPORT

#4:
MAPLE
(18"∅)

COMMON
HOUSE
W/ GUEST ROOMS

STORAGE
SHEDS

16

9

10

15

CARPORT

#31:
WHITE OAK
(47"∅)

11

12

BIKE
STORAGE
W/ CRAFT
SPACE

DRIVEWAY

14

13

RECYCL./
TRASH

#1:
DEODAR
CEDAR (32"∅)

#38:
PEAR (5"∅)

#37:
PEAR (5"∅)

N E   4 8 T H   P L A C E

N E   G O I N G   S T .

N

(Left) There is a strong community aspect of this project that is sought after by residents. The large community spaces enable a wide range of activities and formal and informal interaction among residents. (Source: Eli Spevak)

Another overarching goal of the project was to provide a wider range of housing choices. The homes, which were completed in 2013, sold at a price point of $350,000–$450,000 in 2013. The homes themselves are designed with sustainability in mind and include a number of green features, such as high-efficiency heat, low-flow toilets, iron bathtubs, insulation, and solar-ready roofs. One of the challenges with projects like this is that there is great demand and little supply, so prices often escalate. Some of the Cully Grove homes resold at higher prices—one 1,500 sq. ft. townhome (three bedrooms, two baths) sold for $616,000 in 2018.

One complex aspect of this condo development was funding, particularly as the city was emerging out of the Great Recession. The developers' construction loan lender required that they presell thirteen of the sixteen condos on the site, thus locking in a lower price point given the low point in the market cycle. Another effect of preselling the condos was the buyers having input on the interior design at multiple stages during the construction process. For example, the project incorporated a number of artistic features, including a metal structural element at the peak of the gable rooftops of the buildings. Resident feedback helped determine what shapes these structures took: a grasshopper, an octopus, a sundial, a big curvy fish, and so on. While this was a logistical hurdle, it required Spevak and Parrish to truth test their decisions in real time and ultimately made Cully Grove a better project. That said, there are some things they will do differently on future projects, namely locking home buyers into design decisions up front and allowing for the price to adjust accordingly with the market. Buyers would still get a right of first refusal.

Ultimately, Cully Grove is a project driven by and for residents desiring a more communal neighborhood than the cookie-cutter cul-de-sacs that our current zoning codes incentivize. By that measure, the project has been an unambiguous success. The residents regularly gather for organized events, such as shared gardening, musical concerts, and shared dinners. Parents with school-age children take turns cooking breakfast. And once a month, all the residents take part in a work party where they help maintain the property (Cully Grove does not have a maintenance team). Spevak lives on-site with his family and is currently planning another pocket neighborhood, Cully Green, across the street. "A lot of families want to live in a tight-knit community," he says, "but they're aren't very many options like Cully Grove."

KEY INFORMATION

- **Deal Structure:** A private lender provided a $4.7 million construction loan with a valuation of $6.3 million and an LTV ratio of 75 percent. The remainder of the financing came from equity and a developer fee.

Cully Grove

Program Summary

Site Area	1.87 acres
Dwelling Units	16
Number of Different Building Types	3 (single-family detached, town houses, flats)
Unit Sizes	1,000–1,800 sq. ft.
Density (Gross)	9 du/acre
Parking	
Off Street (Covered)	12
Off Street (Uncovered)	8
Guest Parking (Uncovered)	2
On Street	8
TOTAL	30
Ratio w/o On-Street Parking	1.38 spaces per unit
Ratio w/ On-Street Parking	1.88 spaces per unit
Other Program Elements	
Common House	1,068 sq. ft.
Covered Bike Storage	
Storage Sheds	
Community Garden	

Development Process

Entitlements	8 months land-use approval; 5 months permitting
Construction	15 months
Sales Period	All sales complete before construction as a condition of debt financing

Development Cost and Revenue Information

Costs	
Site Acquisition Cost	$800,000
Construction Costs	$3,765,000
Soft Costs	$975,000
Total Development Costs	$5,540,000
Sales Revenue	
Sale Price per Square Foot	$236
Sale Price per Unit	$350k–$450k
Rate of Return for Equity Partners	6%

Deal structure: A private lender provided a $4.7 million construction loan with a valuation of $6.3 million, and an LTV ratio of 75%. The remainder of the financing came from equity and a developer fee.

Source: Orange Splot

Buildings max out at two stories. Some buildings are single-family homes and others have multiple units. (Source: Union Studio Architecture & Community Design)

COTTAGES ON GREENE:
Delivering Housing Choices in a Small Town with Thoughtful Infill

EAST GREENWICH, RHODE ISLAND
Located in the waterfront "main street" town of East Greenwich, a town of approximately thirteen thousand people, on a 0.85-acre lot, fifteen units of mixed-income condominiums have been organized into a compact cottage court development. These two-bedroom, 1,000 sq. ft. cottages are a mix of building types consisting of freestanding single units, duplexes, and a three-unit town house structure.

Despite nine of the units being attached, the overall neighborhood appears as a cluster of freestanding one-and-a-half-story cottages organized around a linear court and gardens. Bioswales and rain gardens have been used not only as stormwater management but also as the landscape theme of the neighborhood. Small bridges and boardwalks cross and recross the spillways, creating a defining image of the landscape. The common spaces are anchored by community gardens (well contained behind white picket fences) and a more formal sod linear court that provides a setting for neighborhood gatherings as well as a fittingly formal address on the public street. The front-porch community offers a unique alternative for home buyers looking for a safe, walkable neighborhood with shared upkeep.

Cottages on Greene

Program Summary

Site Area	0.85 acres
Dwelling Units	15
Number of Different Building Types	3 (single-family detached, duplex, town house)
Unit Size (2Bd)	855–1,094 sq. ft.
Net Density	18 du/acre
Parking	
Off-Street (Surface)	24
On-Street	-
Total	24
Ratio w/o On-Street Parking	1.6 spaces per unit
Ratio w/On-Street Parking	1.6 spaces per unit
Other Program Elements	
Community Garden Plots	960 sq. ft.

Development Process

Entitlements	9 months land-use approval
Construction	13 months

Development Cost

Costs	
Site Acquisition Cost	$531,000
Construction Costs	$1,619,945
Soft Costs	$251,328
Closing Costs	$39,700
Cost Contingency	$100,000
Bank Loan Debt Service	$27,101
Total Development Costs	$2,939,150
Sales Information	
Sale Price per Unit	$165,00k–$299k

Notes:

Project was conventionally financed

Project was permitted through a specialized process called the comprehensive permit, which relaxes zoning and empowers the planning board to make broader determinations of suitability in return for the inclusion of 25% affordable housing

75% of buyers were single women of all ages

Source: Union Studio

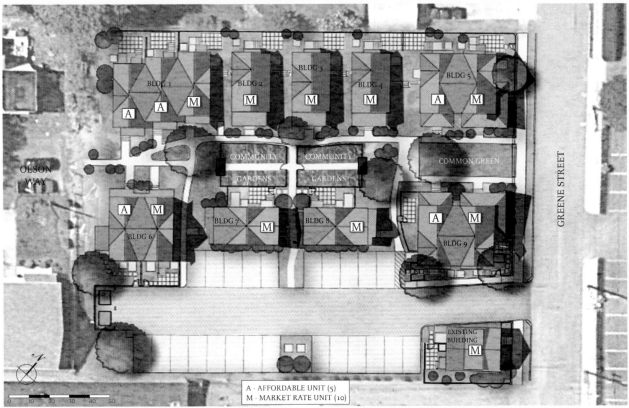

OLSON WAY

GREENE STREET

BLDG 1 · A A M
BLDG 2 · M M
BLDG 3 · M
BLDG 4 · M
BLDG 5 · A M

COMMUNITY GARDENS · COMMUNITY GARDENS · COMMON GREEN

BLDG 6 · A M
BLDG 7 · M
BLDG 8 · M
BLDG 9 · A M

EXISTING BUILDING · M

A - AFFORDABLE UNIT (5)
M - MARKET RATE UNIT (10)

0 10 20 30 40 50

The site plan reinforces the organization around the green spine that integrates community gardens and a common green. The parking is screened from the street and clustered in one location, providing opportunities for residents to informally interact on their way to and from their cars.

PRAIRIE QUEEN:
Delivering a Missing Middle Neighborhood to Fill the Gap for High-Quality Rental Living

PAPILLION, NEBRASKA

As is the case in most metropolitan regions, Omaha builders had been giving renters few choices beyond the standard garden apartment projects. A growing, sophisticated group of renters was not being delivered choices. With this in mind, one developer decided to use his unique experience of renovating historic Missing Middle buildings in Midtown Omaha and developing a few conventional suburban garden apartments, to develop a new kind of neighborhood. The end result is the new, walkable Prairie Queen neighborhood in Papillion, Nebraska, just outside of Omaha, developed by Jerry Reimer of Urban Village.

The live-work units and town houses along the edge of the project provide a gateway into the project. The live-work units have a ground-floor flex space that can incubate small local businesses and commercial amenities. (Source: Jennifer Settle)

Reimer had a background in business and had moved back to his hometown of Omaha after years of working in cities around the world. His parents had owned rental property, and he always had an interest in owning them as well. After returning to Omaha, he saw an opportunity in a down-and-out neighborhood called Midtown. He loved the beautiful historic brick multiunit buildings and could see beyond the disrepair and blight that plagued these neighborhoods. He ended up acquiring over three hundred scattered units in this neighborhood within a 1.2-mile radius, completely renovated them, and had great success in renting them to the market that was not being given good urban-housing choices.

After this success, Reimer decided to take a break from renovating buildings and to use his experience in multifamily development to jump into the development of suburban apartment complexes. He successfully delivered several hundred units in these projects but found this work devoid of interest compared to his experience renovating historic buildings in Midtown. As he was exploring what to develop next, Reimer realized that the small historic apartment buildings he was so passionate about had a name: Missing Middle Housing. He wondered if he could utilize his experience renovating and managing scattered units, and knowing what that type of renter was looking for in term of walkability, and his knowledge of the economic aspect of multifamily development, and deliver something new to the market. Reimer acquired a forty-acre site in a greenfield context at the edge of the Omaha metro in the town of Papillion. He approached Opticos with this challenge.

The foundation for the project approach was creating a catalogue of units plans that shared a module so that they could be stacked and combined in different ways.

The units plans were combined in different ways to create multiple Missing Middle Housing types that were thoughtfully distributed in a network of streets and blocks to create a neighborhood.

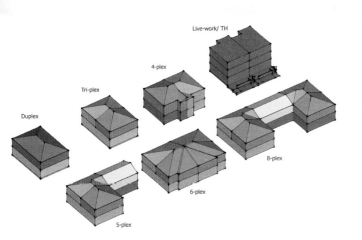

What we came up with as an approach was the creation of the country's first Missing Middle Neighborhood and the Missing Middle Neighborhood System™ that can be used to deliver similar neighborhoods efficiently in other cities across the country.

The foundation of the Missing Middle Neighborhood System™ was created utilizing eight different unit plans that were carefully vetted by Reimer based on his knowledge of the market. The plans were combined in various ways to create seven different Missing Middle Housing types, including triplex, fourplex, fiveplex, sixplex, and mansion apartments. Jerry felt that the efficiencies delivered by repeating the same units in different building configurations could partly make up for additional costs of building more, smaller buildings. The architecture reflects a simplified traditional range of styles inherent in Omaha's historic neighborhoods, but done in a thoughtful way that is economically feasible.

Unlike a conventional suburban apartment project, the plan is broken down into a series of streets and blocks with units facing onto the narrow, tree-lined streets that will ultimately accommodate 542 units on forty acres. A greenway leads from the high point on the site toward the lake, thus capturing valuable view corridors and maximizing connectivity for pedestrians to and from the lake. Another innovation in the plan and approach, as well as being a budget-saving strategy, was that there are no large parking lots, but rather each units had one space off street, either parking in a garage or parking space off of the alley, and the second space for each unit is provided on the street.

This is the range of Missing Middle types that were designed for this project to provide a variety of sizes, roof forms, and character.

The walkability of the plan is maximized with the integration of one block of live-work units with a flex space at the ground floor. This was seen as an opportunity for Urban Village to incubate a coffee shop or provide a shared coworking space, the type of amenity renters are looking for in place of a seldom-used pool and clubhouse. Ideally this space can function as an incubator for a small business, but if the commercial uses do not show up, the space can be rented as a small one-bedroom apartment.

The units are pretty large by Missing Middle standards, ranging from 864 sq. ft. one bedrooms and 1,500 sq. ft. two bedrooms with double-story living spaces to 2,500 sq. ft. three-bedroom town houses, but Reimer wanted them to be comparable with competing apartments nearby, knowing he could reduce the size as needed in later phases.

The site plan creates a walkable neighborhood that is organized around a network of pedestrian-scaled streets and blocks. Each block has a variety of Missing Middle types. In the southwest corner is a neighborhood Main Street that had a pizza shop and yoga studio as initial tenants.

Streetscape view showing the fiveplex and fourplex along a street edge.

Streetscape with varied types and massing creates a neighborhood.

Parking is loaded off of alleys to the rear of the buildings. Granny flats/ADUs are built over many of the garages.

These mansion apartments, which are seven units in a
building that looks like a large mansion, will create a high-
profile address along the Lake Drive.

Urban Village used a mixed-use development agreement, which included a new set of simple form-based zoning and street standards for this entitlement that also challenged many city standards, such as minimum widths for street and alley design.

As of August 2019, the first phase of the project has been successfully completed and leased. Because the project is so unique and different from the multifamily competitors in the area, rents attained in this first phase are at the upper end of the rental market and range from $1,000 for a one-bedroom flat to $3,000 per month for the three-bedroom town house, all mixed within the same block. This three-to-one ratio of rental ranges is rare for a rental project but provides amazing economic diversity within the neighborhood. It is also seen as a huge success by the City of Papillion: the mayor likes the project so much that he is using it as a case study for city departments, encouraging them to reconsider changing engineering standards and development regulations to allow narrower streets and alleys with on-street parking, fewer off-street parking spaces, and a different approach to lighting and utility hookup requirements so that this type of development can be entitled by right in the future.

Prairie Queen *Program Summary*		
Site Area	50 acres	
Context	Suburban	
Dwelling Units	742	
Density (Gross)	14.8 du/acre	
Number of Building Types (with Units Per Building)	Number of units	Times used in overall plan
Building 1: Carriage House	1 unit over garage	53 total
Building 2: Town House	1 unit	82 total
Building 3: Live-Work	1 unit + flex space	25 total
Building 4: Duplex	2 units	7 total
Building 5: Triplex	3 units	7 total
Building 6: Fourplex	4 units	8 total
Building 7: Fiveplex	5 units	6 total
Building 8: Sixplex	6 units	21 total
Building 9: Forecourt Building	8 units	7 total
Unit Size (Gross)		
Unit A: 1 bedroom, 1 bath	738 sq. ft.	
Unit B: 1 bedroom, 1 bath	813 sq. ft.	
Unit C: 1 bedroom, 1 bath	963 sq. ft.	
Unit D: 2 bedroom, 2 bath	1,156 sq. ft.	
Unit E: 2 bedroom, 2 bath	1,407 sq. ft.	
Unit F: 2 bedroom, 2 bath	1,659 sq. ft.	
Unit G: 3 bedroom, 2 bath	1,487 sq. ft.	
Unit H: 3 bedroom, 2.5 bath	2,440 sq. ft.	
Parking		
Off Street	1 space per unit	
On Street	1 space per unit	
Ratio w/ On-Street Parking	2.0+ spaces per unit	

Nonresidential Space		
Live-Work Units	32 units	
Live-Work Flex Space per Unit	860 sq. ft.	
Total Flex Space	27,520 sq. ft.	
Parks and Open Space*	20.1 acres	

*Adjacent to regional park and trail system

Development Process

Entitlements	Approx. 6 months
Construction (phase I)	Ongoing, 2 years from start of site grading to opening of phase 1

Development Cost

Costs	
Site Acquisition Cost	$1,591,000
Construction Costs	$21,000,000
Soft Costs	$545,000
Closing and Financing Cost	$493,000
GC Fee	$1,200,000
Interest Carry	$309,000
Operating Reserve	$40,000
Total Development Costs	**$25,178,000**
Rental Information	$1,000–$3,000/unit

Key Deal Assumptions

10-year treasury=1.9%

10-year fixed non-recourse at perm financing. Projected interest rate = 4%

Expected cap rate for local market=6% over ten-year fixed borrowing cost

Yield to cost target=100 to 125 bps over cap rate

Notes

Buildings were designed to be 100% efficient. Zero nonrentable square feet.

Project was permitted through a specialized process called the mixed-use development plan

There is a big demand from baby boomers for one-story, ground-level, large two-bedroom units

For additional information visit UrbanWaters.com and BungalowsOnTheLake.com

Source: Urban Village

Scale 1" = 100'

0   100'   200'   N

(Left) The fine-grain nature of the master plan is possible because cars did not have to be incorporated into the project for residential units. The desert-responsive urbanism will be unlike any other place built in the past two hundred years in the United States and will provide high-quality urban living.

CULDESAC TEMPE:
Using Technology, Urbanism, and Missing Middle Housing to Deliver a Post-Car Community

TEMPE, ARIZONA

This project, which is being developed by the post-car development company Culdesac, responds to the unmet demand for car-free living and exemplifies the future of Missing Middle Housing as an excellent tool to deliver it. When completed, this project will be the largest newly constructed car-free community in the United States. The site is a seventeen-acre infill site in Tempe, Arizona, located along the light-rail line that traverses Apache Boulevard in eastern Tempe.

Not only is this community car-free, but mobility choices are expanded, as items that would typically have to be picked up using a car, such as groceries or takeout, are being delivered with assistance from technology.

The community will be 100 percent rental, thus also providing a different approach to multifamily development, and it will be a model for larger future applications.

Culdesac selected Opticos to lead the master planning and housing-type design and to be the overall design director and adviser for the project. From the very start, they challenged Opticos to propose a project that from a planning, architecture, and housing-type perspective had never been built before. Opticos coordinated the multidisciplinary team, including a civil engineer, landscape architect, lighting consultant, commercial/food and beverage consultant, and architect of record.

There is a light-rail station at the northern edge of the project. This corner will be activated by a restaurant, a coffee shop, coworking space, a small market, and a food hall.

The housing types are all courtyard types that generate a series of large and small shared courtyard spaces within each block that are defined and activated by the buildings.

There is a main plaza that serves as a focal point for residents and visitors. This will be activated by the food hall, a bar, and a community building.

Each of the blocks are created using multiple two-to-three-story building types. Intimate, irregular paseos connect pedestrians through the project and provide a sense of discovery.

THE MASTER PLAN:
Delivering Desert Urbanism at a Village Scale

Since the project does not have to accommodate cars, the design focus shifted to great urbanism and place making. It is more in character with a Greek, Italian, or French historic village with irregular, narrow, meandering paseos; a hierarchy of public spaces; and thoughtfully placed buildings and building elements that deliver a sense of discovery as you make your way through the project. It will be unlike anything built in the United States in the past 150 years and unlike anything ever built in the Phoenix region because this region's urban patterns have always been dominated by the accommodation of the automobile.

There is a major east–west paseo that serves as an organizing element through the project. Retail spaces with unique local businesses, restaurants, a coffee shop, and a coworking space activate the plaza that serves as the northwest entry into the project. A large mural by a local artist also roots the project in its context. As you move east along the spine, you come across the primary plaza, which serves as the social focal point for the community and visitors. This compact, shaded space is surrounded by a market hall and bar and provides informal seating around a cooling water feature that becomes the focus of the space, just like the fountains in European plazas. Halfway through the project along this "spine" is a maker space and community pool. At the eastern end of this paseo, an amenity building with ground floor flex space anchors the eastern end of the project and provides a gateway from that edge.

There is an informal and irregular pattern of blocks and narrow pedestrian-only paseos that define the urban form. The blocks, called pods, are defined at their edges with buildings and deliver a network of internal, semiprivate courtyard spaces accessible to residents.

THE ARCHITECTURE:
Restrained Character with a Focus on Courtyards

The architecture is simple, elegant, and purposefully restrained, allowing the buildings to play their role as "fabric buildings" defining and activating the public realm of the project. The seven residential building types are a series of two- and three-story walk-up buildings that are clustered to create and define paseos and courtyard spaces that are perfect for the desert climate and that serve the goal of fostering a strong sense of community among the residents. They provide direct entries off the courtyards and no long, placeless corridors. Across the project there is a hierarchy of architectural character between the residential, mixed-use, and amenity buildings. As mentioned above, the residential buildings are simple; the mixed-use buildings still retain a restrained desert feel but introduce a broader palette of materials, elements, and window types; and the amenity buildings, which serve as the public/civic buildings within the project, take on a much more complex desert-modernism palette of materials, massing, and details.

On the residential buildings there are a series of elements or a kit of parts, including stairs, bay windows, shutters, chimneys, and various levels of shading devices that provide variety and hierarchy while responding to solar orientation.

The project went through a rezoning and a rigorous design-review process with the City of Tempe. The project is scheduled to break ground in late spring of 2020.

Culdesac Tempe
Program Summary

Site Area	15.5 acres	
Dwelling Units	638	
Density (Gross)	41 du/acre	
Number of Different Building Types	Units/Building Type	Times Used in Plan
Building Type 1	1 units	7 total
Building Type 2	2 units	7 total
Building Type 3	2 units	11 total
Building Type 4	3 units	24 total
Building Type 5	3 units	15 total
Building Type 6	5 units	52 total
Building Type 7	6 units	13 total
Building Type 8	8 units	8 total
Unit Sizes (Gross)	570–1,200 sq. ft.	Times Used in Plan
Unit 1	684 sq. ft.	38 total
Unit 2	648 sq. ft.	8 total
Unit 3	570 sq. ft.	7 total
Unit 4	788 sq. ft.	4 total
Unit 5	900 sq. ft.	2 total
Unit 6	1,080 sq. ft.	19 total
Unit 7	1,195 sq. ft.	4 total
Parking		
Off-Street Spaces	152 spaces	
Resident Parking	0 spaces	
Guest Parking	64 spaces	
Commercial Uses	55 spaces	
On-Street Spaces	45 spaces	

Ride-Share Parking	14 spaces	
Car-Share Parking	19 spaces	
Commercial Uses	12 spaces	
Bike Parking Ratios	**627 spaces**	
Residential Bicycle Parking Ratio	0.75 spaces per 1-2 bed units & L/W units	606 total
	1.0 spaces per 3-4 bed units	
Nonresidential Bicycle Parking Ratio	1.0 space per 500–750 sq. ft.	21 total
Program		
Office/Retail/Commercial/Nonresidential Space	20,000 sq. ft.	
Restaurant/Café/Office/Retail	9,650 sq. ft.	
Bar/Restaurant/Café	1,800 sq. ft.	
Maker Space	3,400 sq. ft	
Community Pool	3,200 sq. ft	
Rentable Community Space	9,200 sq. ft	
Bar	1,200 sq. ft.	
Public Space		
Apache Plaza	7,600 sq. ft.	
Center Plaza	11,700 sq. ft.	
Main Park	21,300 sq. ft.	
River Drive Park	2,600 sq. ft.	
Public Paseos	172,400 sq. ft.	
Semipublic (internal to pods)	125,300 sq. ft.	
Development Process		
Entitlements (Planning approval based on previously approved plan)	Approx. 6 months	
Construction (phase 1)	Starting summer of 2020	
Source: Opticos Design		

IMPLEMENTING MISSING MIDDLE HOUSING

Overcoming Planning and Regulatory Barriers

(with case studies)

IT IS CRITICAL FOR JURISDICTIONS IN CITIES LARGE AND
SMALL AND CONTEXTS RURAL AND URBAN TO UNDERSTAND
HOW TO ENABLE MISSING MIDDLE HOUSING TO MEET
THEIR HOUSING NEEDS. THE CONVENTIONAL APPROACH

to creating plans, zoning, policies, and strategies related to delivering housing needs to be rethought to effectively deliver Missing Middle Housing. Many cities have attempted to remove these barriers and fix their zoning, often with well-intended multiple area plans, zoning overlays, or design guidelines that have been less than effective. It is important to understand how to effectively introduce Missing Middle Housing into your community and then recommend changes to plans, policies, and zoning. The steps in this chapter will help you to effectively frame the Missing Middle conversation in a community, determine where Missing Middle application should be prioritized, identify barriers, and identify specific policy and zoning changes that are needed to deliver results. The chapter also offers specific zoning approaches, from simple to complex, that can be considered to overcome barriers to Missing Middle Housing.

INTRODUCE THE IDEA OF MISSING MIDDLE HOUSING INTO YOUR COMMUNITY

Creating a solid foundation for a planning process related to housing has become more and more challenging. It is important

Unattractive residential infill (dingbat apartment), which represents what most community members envision when the terms density, upzoning, or multifamily are heard.

TIPS:

. Identify and document existing Missing Middle types in a community to see what types of densities they output, how much parking is provided, and other basic form parameters to use as a foundation for a Missing Middle conversation.

. Think about an allowed range of Missing Middle building types, rather than density, as the starting point of zoning. Ask yourself the question: What range of Missing Middle types (predictable form) should be allowed in a particular neighborhood rather than what density (unpredictable form) should be allowed.

. Tip for council members: Ask staff to verify if a density-based planning and zoning system is required by state planning law. If it is not, ask them to provide alternative approaches.

. Address the misconception about households that rent directly. The number of households that rent is growing, even among upper-income and white households that have historically chosen to buy.[1]

to build support early to increase the likelihood of a successful process.

Framing the Housing Conversation

Framing the conversation about a community's housing needs is very important but rarely done effectively. Before launching into a discussion related to a planning or policy effort focused on delivering a broader range of housing choices, it is important to understand a community's needs and to think very carefully about how to frame or message the project to establish a solid, attack-resistant, support-building armature.

The housing conversation is often framed around needing more density or more multifamily housing, or even needing to upzone neighborhoods to deliver more housing. It is very difficult to build support for an effort framed in this way because of widespread negative perceptions associated with these terms, often due to undesirable results from past efforts. Therefore, the terms *density*, *multifamily*, and *upzoning* should be avoided altogether when framing the conversation or intent of a planning process.

Using the term *Missing Middle Housing* and the names of the types, such as *duplex*, *town house*, *courtyard apartment*, *cottage court*, and so on is an effective way to get people to think about a form and scale of buildings. Convey that Missing Middle is primarily about form and scale (house scale) and secondarily about middle income. Not vice versa. Reinforce that it doesn't matter whether these types are for sale or for rent. A single-family house, whether it is rented or owned, is still a single-family house.

Instead of using the terms *density*, *multifamily*, and *upzoning*, use these terms in framing the housing conversation:

- Missing Middle Housing (focus on form, scale, and type)
- Duplex, fourplex, cottage court, courtyard building, mansion apartment
- House-form or house-scale buildings that just happen to have multiple units within them

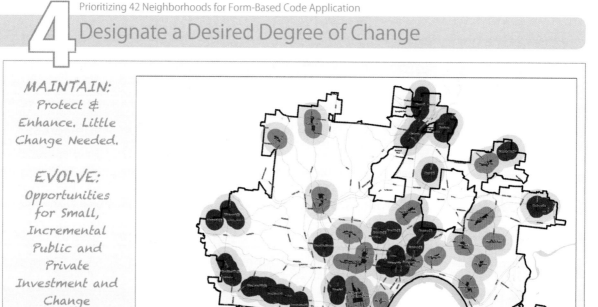

4 Designate a Desired Degree of Change

MAINTAIN: Protect & Enhance. Little Change Needed.

EVOLVE: Opportunities for Small, Incremental Public and Private Investment and Change

TRANSFORM: Desire and Opportunities for Major Improvements

Degree of Change Key
- Evolve
- Maintain
- Transform

Desired Degree of Change

- Housing choice
- Attainability (where will the good teachers, firefighters, police, and so on live in your community? Where will your children live?)
- House-scale buildings with multiple units within them
- Broad range of housing types

This map from Cincinnati's award-winning comprehensive plan labels each identified walkable urban place type with a desired degree of change, thus establishing a form-based policy.

Clarify the Desired Degree of Change

When framing a housing conversation in your community, be clear about the desired degree of change as identified in the com-

Sample of a poster that gives a good visual overview of Missing Middle types by category and is an invaluable resource in building support for Missing Middle Housing.

Building Types

Cincinnati, Ohio
April 28, 2012

prehensive plan or in the small-area plan or for each sub area or neighborhood of a city. The desired degree of change in each area should be based on thorough analysis, input from the community, clearly defined goals and objectives, and, ideally, a detailed vision. The reason this is important is that most community members typically envision the transformative approach with widespread and dramatic change everywhere, but the reality is that many planning efforts are really targeted for more incremental change.

Use the Following Degrees of Change

1. *Maintain:* Smaller, more incremental changes, mostly reinforcing the existing scale of an area
2. *Evolve:* Opportunities for small-to-medium-sized public and private investments or projects. Minor changes in scale. Opportunity sites should be targeted.
3. *Transform:* Opportunities for larger-scale changes, such as a significant increase in scale and possibly mix of uses. The changes are more likely to be widespread and not on focused sites.

The reason this is important in framing is that most community members typically envision the transformative approach with widespread and dramatic change everywhere, but the reality is that many planning efforts are really targeted for the evolve degree of change, that sensitively allow for smaller changes, especially if Missing Middle Housing is the focus or priority.

Gather Local Examples of Missing Middle Housing

In this preliminary analysis phase, collect photographs of local examples of Missing Middle types. If local examples are not available, use regional examples. Typically local planners, community members, or historians know where these examples exist. If not, local examples can be found using Google Maps (see box 7-1), GIS data, or data from your county assessor's office to create a preliminarily set of maps that illustrate the number of units per lot for targeted neighborhoods. These photos ideally would be arranged

Walking tours are often part of the programming for a series of events to effectively introduce Missing Middle Housing to a community.

as posters or in an online database organized by housing type and referenced and utilized frequently throughout the process. This step seems rudimentary, but it should not be skipped. Photos reinforce the shift away from density to a conversation about housing type, scale, form, and who is going to live in these homes. In addition, some community members will refer back to these photos throughout the process, even as more detailed information is produced, because they can relate to these local photo examples more easily. The website MissingMiddleHousing.com presents a large palette of photographic examples of each Missing Middle type for this purpose.

Host an Introductory Missing Middle Housing Presentation or Event

A presentation is an important tool for explaining Missing Middle Housing. In this early phase, presentations are typically focused on the general public or local or regional planning groups and are supplemented with meetings with decision makers such as the city manager, mayor, council members, or planning commissioners. Focused discussions and short presentations are also hosted for groups such as the local development community and affordable-housing advocates.

A guided Missing Middle walking tour will ideally supplement the introduction of Missing Middle Housing to a community. This allows people to see how existing examples function and to build a better understanding of their form and scale and is an effective step in building support from community members. The tour should be led by a Missing Middle expert, with additional guides who know the local zoning, as well as longtime community members who know the history of the neighborhood.

The intent is to build an initial understanding and value of Missing Middle Housing and lay the foundation for a positive discussion and begin to build support from local leadership.

Sometimes this effort is funded by a jurisdiction; other times it may be partially or completely funded by local stakeholder groups that are interested in moving the housing conversation along. For

This cottage court was designed for a city-owned infill site as part of the award-winning Richmond Livable Corridors project in Richmond, California, as part of a strategy to deliver more affordable, high-quality housing choices to existing residents.

example, in Bend, Oregon, the process was initiated by Building a Better Bend. In Arlington County, Maryland, an initial presentation was sponsored by Alliance for Housing Solutions. In Greenville County and the City of Greenville, South Carolina, a group of realtors and members of the development industry called Impact Greenville found funding for the entire process. In other instances organizations like AARP have initiated the Missing Middle conversation in communities, hosting a road tour through Southern Oregon.

DETERMINING WHERE TO APPLY MISSING MIDDLE HOUSING

Regardless of the size of a city or county, there is always a hierarchy of walkable urban places that can be considered for Missing Middle application. The following are context types to be considered.

Small, Individual Lot Infill

This approach tends to make the most sense in pre-1940s neighborhoods that are already walkable, mostly built out, and often have a mix of Missing Middle types. Start by identifying where these types exist and the barriers to building these types in your current parking and engineering standards, and then revise or refine your zoning and other regulations to enable these types. Often existing Missing Middle types would not be allowed to be constructed again according to current regulations. This could be part of a small-area planning effort as well.

Secondary Corridors

Many cities have zoned miles of corridors for commercial uses, and many of these corridors are trapped in a state of disinvestment as the commercial uses move farther out of the city or back into the downtown cores. These corridors, which are often abutted by single-family or mixed-type neighborhoods, are great opportunities to enable Missing Middle Housing. These are typically secondary corridors or corridors with shallower lots that could not easily accommodate larger mixed-use or higher-density housing but are ideal for lower-intensity Missing Middle types.

Transitions from Higher-Intensity Corridors

Many cities over the past couple decades have introduced strategies, policies, and zoning to allow higher-intensity development, often transit oriented, along their major corridors. The result has

Secondary corridors with vacant and underutilized properties are prime opportunities for Missing Middle–scale infill projects.

The scale of Missing Middle types makes them perfect for providing transitions from higher-intensity corridors into single-family or lower-intensity neighborhoods.

Proposal for North Berkeley BART with four-to-seven-story buildings in the center and Missing Middle types at the edges to transition in scale into adjacent single-family neighborhoods while still achieving an average density over the targeted 75 du/acre.

often been awkward, with five-plus-story buildings abutting single-family homes, which usually results in an outcry from adjacent neighborhoods. Applying Missing Middle Housing is a great strategy to transition from these corridors into lower-scale neighborhoods.

Thoughtful Transit-Oriented Development (TOD)

The application of Missing Middle Housing around new or existing transit stations is a good strategy where the lots are smaller or constrained, making larger buildings difficult, or where single-family homes abut the stations. Missing Middle Housing should be considered in some transit-rich locations as an alternative or as a transition from the larger buildings directly adjacent to stations into neighborhoods. Not all transit-oriented development needs to be five-plus stories.

Interface of Greyfield Sites with Adjacent Neighborhoods

Rapid change in retail has left many mall sites, including medium to large strip malls, vacant in cities across the country. These are prime opportunities to develop new walkable communities, which

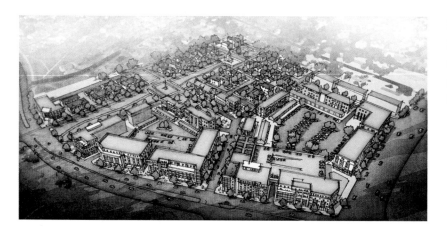

Blocks composed of Missing Middle types provide great transitions in scale at the edge of larger, redeveloping greyfield sites that also have higher-intensity buildings along the corridors.

may have larger, mixed-use buildings as a component along the corridors, but an effective strategy can also integrate Missing Middle Housing within blocks at the edges of the site to transition into adjacent neighborhoods.

Downtown Transitions (Small-to-Mid-Sized Cities)
The edges of most downtowns suffer from poor planning and ineffective zoning. Many of these areas had a great mix of Missing Middle Housing types that were torn down for freeways, parking, or suburban-style development such as drive-through banks.

New Growth Areas at the Edge of Cities
Many cities and counties have targeted undeveloped areas to accommodate growth and new development. If they enable or require compact, walkable urban development as part of their long-term planning, Missing Middle Housing will be a critical component. As construction costs have risen, builders are finding that Missing Middle Housing types can deliver housing at better price points than single-family housing, especially for entry-level buyers.

Single-Family Neighborhoods
This is the most challenging application politically, but this is an area where we are seeing change, such as the sweeping legisla-

Many buildings on lots adjacent to downtowns in most small- and medium-sized towns were torn down and are now parking lots or one-story suburban buildings that make these sites prime opportunities for Missing Middle infill within a one-block walk to downtown amenities.

tion in the City of Minneapolis to ban single-family zoning. The changes are in response to the extreme level of the housing crisis in some areas and the fact that a majority of land has been zoned for single family in many cities. Cities are thoughtfully considering allowing Missing Middle types to deliver more housing choices and achieve a higher level of affordability.

IDENTIFY BARRIERS

The following steps will help to develop a solid foundation for future planning efforts, specifically a comprehensive plan or general plan update and detailed, targeted zoning fixes to enable Missing Middle Housing.

Review the Comprehensive Plans (City, County, or Both)

Review the comprehensive plan to identify policies that present barriers or limits to achieving Missing Middle Housing. This is most often done at a citywide scale, but in regions where there is a lot of growth in the surrounding county or counties, it often makes sense to analyze both the city and the county comprehensive plans. This process should assess where the multiunit land-use classification is designated, if it is proposed in logical locations, and if the defined geographic area is large enough to accommodate non-single-family housing choices if the barriers were removed. The review should focus on the future land-use categories and their location and parameters, such as allowed densities and lot sizes. Then policies should be identified and assessed related to delivering more housing choices. This analysis can help jurisdictions to make targeted changes in future land uses and where they are mapped. It can also guide the refinement or addition of polices to remove these barriers rather than taking on the time-consuming work of a complete comprehensive-plan update.

Comparison illustrating the gap between the low densities allowed by existing future-land-use categories and higher densities required to enable Missing Middle Housing by type in Greenville County, South Carolina.

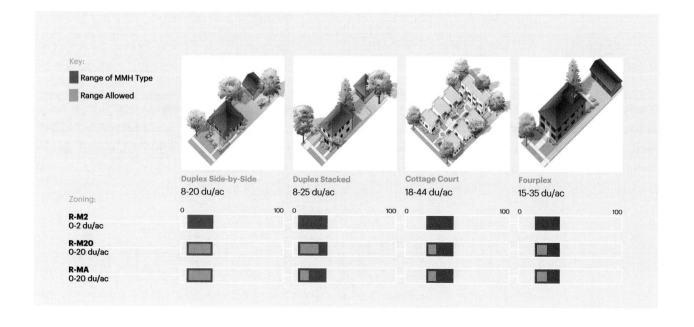

Barriers for MMH in Greenville County

Barriers to MMH	Imagine Greenville Comp Plan	Berea Plan	Brandon Plan	Conestee Plan	Monaghan Mill Plan*	Cherrydale Plan	City View Plan	Dublin Road Plan	Dunean Plan	East Woodruff Plan	Fountain Inn Plan
Max. Density Allowed: Too Low	Barrier	Barrier	?	?	Barrier	Not a Barrier	Barrier	Not a Barrier	?	Barrier	Barrier
Min. Lot Area: Too High	Not a Barrier	Barrier	Barrier	Not a Barrier	Barrier	Not a Barrier	Not a Barrier	Not a Barrier	Not a Barrier	Barrier	Barrier
MMH Types Identified[1]	Not a Barrier	2	2	2	2	2	2	2	2	2	2
Content is Supportive of MMH	Not a Barrier	Not a Barrier	Not a Barrier	Not a Barrier	Barrier	Barrier	Not a Barrier	Not a Barrier	Not a Barrier	Not a Barrier	Not a Barrier

Notes:

[1] Only reference to duplex, townhouses and multifamily.

[2] Plan update proposes down-zoning from multifamily to single-family, and down-zoning R-7.5 to R-10.

[3] Policy direction to limit "apartment" style of multifamily housing leaves it unclear if MMH is intended or not.

[4] Majority of area is zoned for single-family.

[5] The future land use map includes a TND category that allows mixed residential types within a maximum overall density of 1.7 units per acre for the master planned area.

[6] In R-M and R-MA, multifamily requires a min. of 2-acre site size and 12,000 sq. ft. size respectively.

[7] In R-M, once 2-acre site is provided, no individual lot minimum.

[8] Duplexes through Fourplexes mentioned but majority of R-M Zoning being changed to Single-Family Zoning.

* In Progress version reviewed

The PD and FRD are not shown because it is unclear what they allow given that each project is reviewed on a case-by-case basis.

Key: ● Barrier   ? Unclear   ○ Not a Barrier

This table summarizes the analysis of the twelve small-area plans that the City of Greenville has completed in recent years, including the clarity of intent related to delivering Missing Middle Housing and if they remove zoning barriers.

Review the Small-Area Plans

Cities often have plans for smaller geographic areas within their jurisdictions, such as neighborhoods, corridors, transit areas, or downtowns. Unfortunately, they are not always clear on the intent, often not getting beyond general policies, such as "allowing a broader range of housing choices," without clarifying the scale or type of housing allowed for that specific area. In addition, these plans often do not identify zoning changes that need to be made to deliver the plan's intent, and sometimes introduce design guidelines or design parameters that are conflicting or inconsistent with the existing zoning. This step assesses these plans and identifies the specific gaps and barriers within them that prevent the effective delivery of Missing Middle in the planning areas.

For example, Greenville, South Carolina, has completed twelve small-area plans over the course of fifteen to twenty years, and only a few of the most recent efforts were clear in their ultimate intent beyond "deliver more housing choices." Of these twelve plans, only two of the more recently completed plans, which were implemented with form-based codes, had clear intent and had truly eliminated the zoning barriers. Unfortunately, this type of disconnect between intent and application is fairly common. The form-based codes that were created were all one-offs, created specifically to be applied to a limited area rather than being part of a comprehensive strategy for zoning changes that is typically recommended. But they do provide a model for future coordinated changes.

Review Zoning

A targeted group of residential zoning districts, focusing on medium-density or multifamily zones, should be analyzed to assess if they can effectively deliver Missing Middle Housing. In the preliminary assessment, identify the top barriers and communicate them in a clear, graphic form.

Zones that truly enable Missing Middle are often missing entirely from a zoning code. Does the city have a zone that allows a minimum of 35 and ideally up to 75 du/acre residential uses but also caps the height at two to two and a half stories? If so, does it regulate a maximum width of building to 45–60 ft.? The zoning codes for 99 percent of cities across the country do not have a single zone that meets all of these requirements and thus truly enables Missing Middle Housing. Typically the biggest barriers are allowed building envelopes much larger than Missing Middle (height, width, depth), densities that are too low, minimum lot sizes that are too high, and parking requirements that are too high. Often there are single-family zones that enable duplexes, often as single family attached, and then the medium-density/multifamily zones immediately jump up to allowing a 45–50 ft. tall building with unlimited width as long as it meets the density limitations.

TIP

A good supplemental test is to pick a neighborhood, map the number of units per lot, then verify conformity or whether the existing development on these lots meets the existing minimum lot–size requirements, maximum density, or maximum square footage required per lot using a system similar to the micro-scale analysis process.

MAP PRIORITY AREAS FOR MISSING MIDDLE HOUSING APPLICATION

The areas for Missing Middle Housing may have been identified generally at the very beginning of the process. Now is the time to identify and map the specific areas where Missing Middle Housing application should be prioritized. It is recommended that this step be completed before starting a comprehensive plan update to better inform that process.

Examples include the areas within or surrounding a downtown core, downtown transition areas (a prime opportunity for Missing Middle), neighborhood main streets, areas near parks and open space, and other areas that deliver walkability. These areas are typically identified through careful analysis of proximity to schools, parks, commercial services, transit, and other amenities and should be represented on a map using the five-minute-walk or pedestrian shed. It is very important to focus the discussion in the short and long term about where it makes the most sense to enable Missing Middle Housing within a jurisdiction and to establish this foundation for future planning efforts.

The map that is generated from the analysis can function as the foundation for comprehensive-planning updates, in particular for a future, place-based land-use map, transit or other mobility-network improvements, and prioritization of other city investments in these areas.

The areas that are suitable for Missing Middle Housing may represent a small or a large percentage of the jurisdiction overall. If it is a large percentage of the area, the challenge can be priori-

Box 7-1

Where and How to Find Missing Middle in Your Community Using Google Maps

The following steps can be followed to use Google Maps to help identify existing Missing Middle Housing in a community. This can supplement the mapping and the walking tour.

Step 1: Open Google Maps for the city you are analyzing and turn the Map View option on (Satellite View off).

Step 2: Find neighborhood commercial areas/main streets: Start in areas around pre-1940 commercial districts, which were often neighborhood main streets. With Map View on, these areas will show up highlighted in yellow. You may want to use a zoning map to see where smaller geographic areas are zoned commercial to understand where to start or test.

Step 3: Search adjacent neighborhoods for Missing Middle types: Turn on the Satellite View and then zoom in on one of the areas that is adjacent to the neighborhood commercial district. Look for multiple rooftops, courtyard configurations, or building outlines that are slightly bigger than others that likely will be Missing Middle

types. This is the challenging part that will take some time and training.

Step 4: Zoom in and out and use 3-D View and Street View to verify potential types: When you have found a building you think is a Missing Middle type, click on the 3-D View button next to the + – Zoom tool to confirm whether or not the lot and type you have chosen is a Missing Middle type. Sometimes you may need to drop into Street View and look for multiple doors, mailboxes, doorbells, etc. to confirm this.

Step 5: Take a screen shot of the street view for your records and be sure to include the address at the top left corner. These screen shots will be your catalog of potential Missing Middle types to visit. They can also be compiled into one document to serve as an initial overview of existing types in a community that will ultimately be replaced with better photos.

Step 6: Create a map in My Maps and pinpoint each of the types you find for future reference.

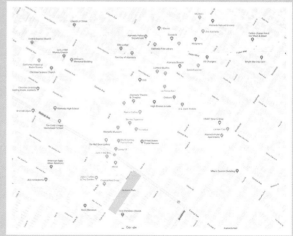

(Opposite left) Google map of Alameda, California, with map view turned on, which highlights the commercial area/main street in yellow which is a logical area to begin to look for existing Missing Middle Housing.

(Opposite right) When you zoom in on this area, building footprints begin to show up that show the size and lot configuration of adjacent residential buildings.

(Top) When you turn the satellite option of the map on, you can begin to look for slightly larger buildings or courtyard configurations. This takes some time to train yourself to find these variations and Missing Middle Housing.

(Center) This search for Missing Middle buildings is often easier in 3-D view, which can be turned on by clicking the 3-D button in the lower right of the view.

(Bottom) When you find a building that has a footprint that looks slightly larger than a single-family home or appears to be a courtyard, you can go into street view to verify by placing the yellow person in the lower right onto the map to see if the building has multiple units. This unit has two doors, thus having at least two units. You can go back and forth between the aerial, 3-D view, and street view to find Missing Middle types.

Where are Greenville's walkable centers?

The map identifies walkable environments in the City of Greenville focused around a variety of walkable centers identified through this analysis. The walkable environments shown represent approximately 2.15% of Greenville.

Interstate 385

Downtown

Interstate 85

Key

Identified Walkable Centers
- Downtown Core
- Urban Center/ Downtown Transition
- Neighborhood Main Street
- Medical/Institutional

Amenities
- Parks/Open Space

Walkable Environments
- ▪ ▪ 5 min walking distance from Centers
- ▪ ▪ 5 min walking distance from Bus Stops

Zoning Districts
- Residential Districts
- Commercial Districts

This map defines walkable contexts that are priorities for Missing Middle Housing application. This map can be used to inform the comprehensive and small-area planning and to prioritize city investment in mobility improvements and other city expenditures for these areas.

tizing the opportunities to enable Missing Middle. If it is a limited geography defined that is appropriate for Missing Middle, then the challenge is often how to transform additional targeted areas to improve walkability and enable Missing Middle Housing to have enough impact. The latter is more likely the case in a jurisdiction that developed mostly or completely after the 1940s.

RECOMMEND CHANGES TO PLANS, POLICIES, AND ZONING

The intent of this step is to utilize the previously completed analysis of policies, planning, and zoning to complete another level of deeper analysis to inform specific recommended changes to policy, plans, and zoning.

Graphically Test Existing Zoning to Inform Specific Changes

Using the map created in the previous step, select a series of small-to-medium-sized lots within the areas identified as priorities for Missing Middle Housing. The lots selected should represent a range of typical conditions such as lot size, adjacencies, alley-loaded or not, and so on. They are used to test the existing development standards (zoning) and design guidelines on these lots. The goal is to create a detailed, hypothetical, three-dimensional build-out on a variety of lot sizes that clearly illustrates the issues identified in the regulations on a variety of different lot sizes and conditions. For example, such a 3-D graphic often shows how limiting parking requirements are for delivering multiple units, that large side setbacks discourage any development, and that compatible-scaled buildings can deliver much higher densities than the zoning regulations allow on small lots. This hypothetical development scenario analysis informs the recommended changes and refinements in the zoning, area plans, and comprehensive plan policies to effectively enable Missing Middle Housing.

R-M2 Zone - Development Standards

Max. Envelope per Existing Standards

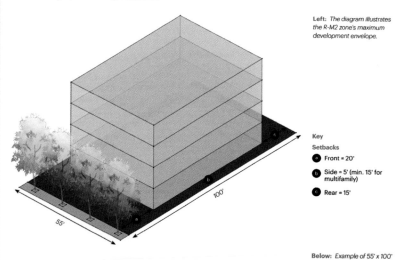

Left: *The diagram illustrates the R-M2 zone's maximum development envelope.*

100'

55'

Key

Setbacks

Ⓐ Front = 20'

Ⓑ Side = 5' (min. 15' for multifamily)

Ⓒ Rear = 15'

Below: *Example of 55' x 100' lot and existing development.*

R-M2 Zone, 55' x 100' Lot Size Max. Envelope per Existing Standards	
Building Form	
Lot Area	5,500 sf
Max. Height	40'
Max. Lot Coverage	40%
Parking	
Min. Parking Spaces	2 per unit for single family; 1.5 per unit for multifamily
Density	
Max. Allowed Density	20 du/ acre

(Images, pages 246–247)
Graphic analysis of R-M2 zone on a 55 x 110 ft. deep infill lot.

Existing zoning standards hypothetically allow up to a maximum of 40 ft. of height and 20 du/acre.

Even though it is in a multiunit zoning district, the on-site parking requirement of 1.5 spaces per multifamily unit and the low density cap of 20 du/acre encourage the site to be built out with one large single-family home that generates a density of 8 du/acre, thus not achieving the intent of the multiunit zone.

R-M2 Zone - Allowed

Max. Potential Development per Existing Standards

Right: *The diagram illustrates what type of development and form are possible after applying all standards.*
***Note:** After applying the minimum side setbacks for multifamily buildings, the resulting building is 25' wide, significantly limiting the development of the site to essentially a townhouse.*

Key

Setbacks

a Front = 36'

b Side = 5' (min. 15' for multifamily)

c Rear = 15'

Note: *Although the building complies with the zone standards, the resulting building is out of scale with the neighboring buildings and does not contribute to a streetscape of building facades.*

R-M2 Zone, 55' x 100' Lot Size Allowable Development per Existing Standards	
Building Form	
Resultant Footprint	2,200 sf
Resultant Height/ Stories	35'/ 3
Resultant Lot Coverage	40%
Parking	
Min. Spaces Required	2
Density	
Number of Units	1*
Resultant Density	8 du/ acre

R-M2 Zone - Missing Middle

Option 01 - Fourplex

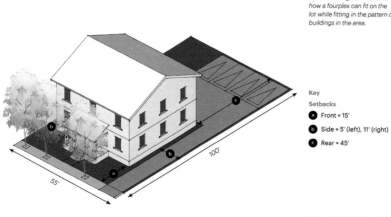

Left: *The diagram illustrates how a fourplex can fit on the lot while fitting in the pattern of buildings in the area.*

Key

Setbacks

a Front = 15'

b Side = 5' (left), 11' (right)

c Rear = 45'

Below: *The fourplex provides a small front yard and a building footprint smaller than what the R-M2 zone allows.*

R-M2 Zone, 55' x 100' Lot Size Missing Middle Option 01	
Building Form	
Resultant Footprint	1,560 sf
Resultant Height/ Stories	32'/ 2
Resultant Lot Coverage	28%
Parking	
Spaces Required	4
Density	
Number of Units	4
Resultant Density	32 du/ acre

A hypothetical build-out of the same lot of a two-story fourplex, which maxes out the realistic Missing Middle–scale development potential on the site using a requirement of one parking space per unit on-site. It generates a density of 32 du/acre. This build-out scenario is used to recommend adjustments in the current zoning to encourage Missing Middle Housing infill including decreasing parking requirements to one space per unit and increasing density to 32 du/acre. Note this build-out has one and a half times the density of what the current zone district allows, but it only needs to utilize two of the four stories allowed, and 28 percent of the allowed 40 percent lot coverage, to achieve this density. This is an indicator that the development standards are ineffective.

Inform Comprehensive Plan and Small-Area Plan Land Use and Policy

The addition of this detailed lot testing and the analysis done previously can inform specific changes to comprehensive plans and small-area plans to effectively deliver Missing Middle Housing. The following is a list of typical policy changes:

- Define walkable environments and create a map that identifies them as priorities for Missing Middle Housing application and differentiates them for other policy applications as well, such as reduced parking.
- Define a specific intended physical form and character for these areas.
- Define Missing Middle Housing as house-scale buildings with multiple units within these plans.
- Clarify the intent of Missing Middle Housing to be both for small-lot infill and within new communities.
- Introduce the full range of Missing Middle types and their characteristics, ideally using photographs of local examples.
- Be clear that Missing Middle Housing is different than conventional multifamily development.
- When promoting housing choices, be clear on the scale, form, and type of housing that is desired in certain areas.
- Define a desired degree of change (maintain, evolve, transform) for each neighborhood/sub area and clearly articulate how that informs Missing Middle application as well as future land use and zoning. For example, is the intent to completely transform a single-family neighborhood into a neighborhood with a mix of Missing Middle Housing or to allow a neighborhood already zoned for multifamily to evolve in a more incremental manner?
- Create land-use categories that specifically identify the desired intent of Missing Middle Housing that allows higher densities but requires smaller buildings.

- Option 1: Future Land Uses
  - High density: house scale
  - Medium density: house scale
- Option 2: Future Land Uses
  - Missing Middle Housing
  - Upper Missing Middle Housing

ZONING FIXES

As one of the major barriers to the delivery of Missing Middle Housing, zoning needs to be thoughtfully fixed and in some instances replaced. Several strategies, both targeted and comprehensive, are summarized in this section.

Address Nonconformities of Existing Missing Middle Buildings

Many good examples of existing Missing Middle Housing types are nonconforming, which means the existing zoning regulations—often setbacks, lot size, density, or parking requirements—would not allow you to build them today. This often makes it hard for an owner to maintain the building without having to comply with the newer regulations. This compliance with regulations is typically financially infeasible so the buildings are often left in a state of disrepair because the owner has been put in an impossible position.

First, identify these nonconformities in existing Missing Middle types as legal nonconforming buildings, lots, and uses. Ensure that there is a section in your code that enables the owners of these nonconforming buildings to make improvements, to any dollar amount, as long as they do not add square footage to a building, without having to comply with current size, use, density, parking, or form standards. This will enable (but not require) the owner to more easily maintain the Missing Middle buildings so they are a welcome part of a community and not the eyesore.

Targeted Missing Middle Housing Zoning Fixes

The following are quick, targeted changes and refinements that can be made to your zoning that will not typically get a lot of pushback so you can immediately remove barriers for the delivery of Missing Middle Housing.

1. Regulate maximum building width and depth (keep the scale small).
2. Increase maximum allowed density or reduce minimum required square footage of lot per unit.
3. Adjust maximum allowed heights to be no more than two and a half stories.
4. Reduce minimum-lot-size requirements and replace with minimum lot width.
5. Reduce or remove parking requirements.
6. Remove open-space requirements.
7. Map the zones that allow these types more broadly.
8. Do not allow multiple single-family homes on a lot or tuck-under town houses.

Regulate Maximum Width of Building to Be Approximately 45–60 Ft.

Why is this important? This ensures that if a lot size gets bigger, or if someone aggregates a couple of lots, the building does not get larger than what is desired, but rather two, appropriately scaled buildings get built. When lot sizes vary, or lot aggregation occurs, it is often when a density-based system falls apart and delivers out-of-scale buildings. This regulation of maximum building width assures community members that buildings that get built, even if density is increased, will be house scale.

> **TIP:**
> You may have one zone that regulates a maximum building width of 45 ft. so that the form is more compatible with single-family homes, and then another zone that allows the same range of types but regulates a maximum building width of 65 ft. and is more thoughtfully mapped along evolving corridors or as transitions from corridors into neighborhoods. This is a nuanced, form-based approach to allowing Missing Middle types.

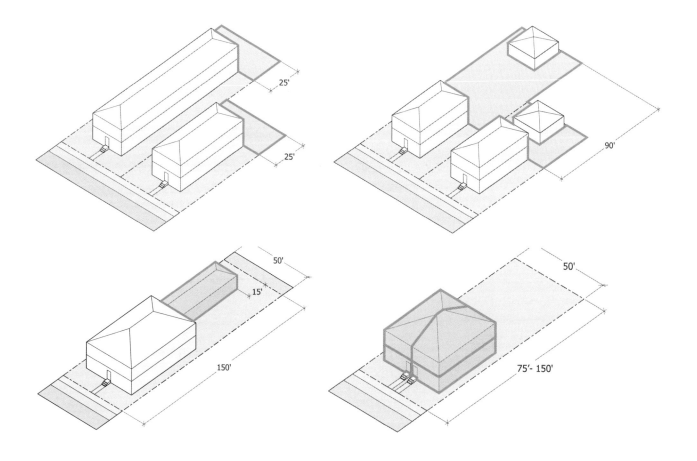

Regulate Maximum Depth of Approximately 45–60 Ft. Deep

Regulating a maximum depth of building is critical for Missing Middle Housing types. Unfortunately, depth is rarely regulated. It is a more direct and effective way to regulate a predictable form than relying on rear setbacks. The problem with a rear setback is if a lot gets deeper than the one adjacent to it (which often happens in pre-1940s neighborhoods that have irregular lot patterns) then the scale and form of a building is allowed that is not compatible with the one adjacent to it. A one-story wing is sometimes allowed to project farther into the rear yard if it is thoughtfully regulated, as per the figure above.

(Top left) Rear setbacks are ineffective in defining a compatible built form. If lot depths change on adjacent lots, a much larger, incompatible form is allowed.

(Top right) Maximum building-depth regulations effectively regulate a house-scale form, even when lot depths change. This is also why floor-to-area ratio (FAR) regulations are ineffective with varying lot sizes.

Opposite:

(Bottom Left) Some communities are okay with a building going deeper into a lot, as long as the element or wing of the house that goes deeper is only one story.

(Bottom right) This is a fourplex building form that represents the maximum scale that should be allowed in a Missing Middle zoning district. The exact same fourplex building form generates a broad range of densities, FAR, and lot coverage percentages when applied to different lot sizes, thus illustrating the need for a form-first approach to zoning rather than using these numeric parameters to enable predictable results and to remove barriers.

Ensure House-Scale Buildings with Medium to High Densities

The most basic strategy related to effective zoning for Missing Middle Housing is to ensure that zoning has development standards (within one or more zones, as defined below) allowing medium to high densities but requiring house-scale buildings/forms. It is this regulated form/building envelope—not density, FAR (floor-area ratio), or other numeric parameters—that delivers predictable built results. This has been done in jurisdictions across the country, including Flagstaff, Arizona; Cincinnati, Ohio; Iowa City, Iowa; and Kauai County, Hawaii.

Increase Maximum Allowed Density or Reduce Minimum Required Square Footage of Lot Per Unit (If You Must Use Density Requirements)

It is unnecessary to regulate density if you carefully regulate the building form/allowed envelope. But if a density requirement is politically necessary, make sure the maximum allowed density is high enough: at a minimum, 35–45 du/acre and as high as 75 du/acre to truly encourage smaller units. Use the tables in chapter 5 provided for each of the types to understand the range of densities each generates on typical lot sizes.

> **TIP:**
> If you need to keep density requirements, start thinking about density as output (what a specific type on a specific-size lot generates) versus the input or primary controlling factor. You can compare the typical densities that the Missing Middle types generate to the densities allowed by your current zoning districts.

Adjust Maximum Allowed Heights to Allow No More Than Two and a Half Stories

This is the component/regulation that is often missed but is critical to delivering house-scale buildings. The difference between two and three stories in terms of perception is big. The upper end of Missing Middle is often three to four stories, and cities should have another zone that enables these taller, Upper Missing Middle buildings, but a zone that regulates the core of Missing Middle should not allow buildings taller than two to two and a half stories. It is important to note that this three to four stories only pertains to certain types, not all of the Missing Middle types. If more height is allowed within a zone, it also often overinflates land prices, thus making it impossible to build, even if a builder wants to deliver Missing Middle.

Box 7-2
Create a Walkable Neighborhood or Missing Middle Housing Overlay

If you can't add new zones and need to tweak existing zones, you can apply the new standards and densities to the existing zone through a targeted walkable neighborhood overlay district. To implement the walkable neighborhood overlay, define areas on the zoning map where you want the new regulations to override the existing ones, then define the new regulations, such as density, heights, parking, building width and depth, that replace the existing regulations. This enables the new standards to be used in certain walkable areas while not changing zoning elsewhere. Overlays should typically be avoided because multiple overlays are often hard to understand and administer, and they are often used as the easy fix, when a more comprehensive one is what is actually needed for long-term effectiveness. That being said, a thoughtfully created overlay can be a good code hack to enable Missing Middle. You need to be sure the new standards do not conflict with existing standards by clearly stating that these new regulations trump preexisting ones. Make sure the overlay exists on your zoning map and can be found easily within your zoning document.

This photo shows the dramatic difference in perceived scale between a two-story and a three-story building. This is why most Missing Middle types max out at two to two and a half stories.

TIP:

If a zone currently allows more than two to two and a half stories, you need to be careful not to downzone or reduce development potential without careful consideration or policy direction. This is not done very often, and we do not typically recommend it. You will need to find areas that are not already zoned for larger-scale buildings, often meaning selecting targeted areas currently zoned for single family or converting areas zoned for commercial to all Missing Middle.

Reduce Minimum-Lot-Size Requirements and Replace with Minimum Lot Width

Make sure Missing Middle types are enabled on one existing, typical lot width. Zoning codes typically regulate a minimum lot size. A more effective way to regulate for Missing Middle and more

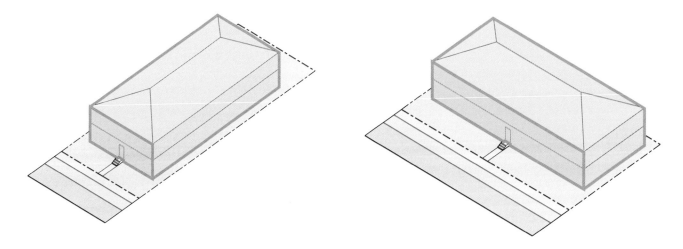

generally a predictable, desired form, is to regulate minimum lot widths for each of the Missing Middle types. See examples of minimum lot sizes for each of the types in chapter 5.

Assess the typical lot widths in pre-1940s neighborhoods and ensure that these types are allowed on one typical lot, in areas that have been identified as having Missing Middle Housing potential. Do not require a developer to aggregate two lots, which is typically not economically feasible.

Remove Open-Space Requirements

Open-space requirements are well intended but are very suburban in their intent, and such requirements often prohibit good urban-housing types. They also are the primary reason one sees really bad balconies added to multifamily projects. This is typically done to meet the open-space requirements for each unit. The recommended approach is to completely remove open-space requirements. This is possible in walkable urban places because the high-quality public realm takes the place of these private open spaces.

Map the Zoning District That Allow These Types More Broadly

If effective zoned districts are in place or have been tweaked to enable Missing Middle Housing, these areas may only be mapped in a small geographic area or are not in ideal locations. The loca-

Both lots are 6,000 sq. ft., but due to the different width along the street, different housing types or forms are appropriate for each. This is why minimum lot width is more important to regulate than lot size.

tions may be isolated, auto-dependent areas that are not very good areas for application of Missing Middle Housing. If this is a problem, identify walkable urban areas or intended walkable urban areas and prioritize them for application of Missing Middle Housing. This may mean converting additional single-family or commercially zoned areas to allow Missing Middle Housing. This may seem like a radical step for some jurisdictions, but, as further explained below, the City of Minneapolis and the State of Oregon have both taken dramatic steps to remove single-family zoning altogether, on a citywide and statewide basis, to enable Missing Middle Housing more broadly and directly.

These analysis maps of Medford, Oregon, done as part of strategic zoning analysis and changes, reinforces the disconnect between where multifamily zones were mapped (in red) and where walkable contexts (black dashed lines), which are the ideal locations for Missing Middle Housing, exist.

Do Not Allow Multiple Single-Family Homes on a Lot or Tuck-Under Town Houses

Be careful what is enabled. In existing medium-density zones, or when converting single-family zones to allow more than one unit per lot, unless it is specifically not allowed by the regulations builders will often build multiple single-family detached houses forced onto one lot or three-story, tuck-under town houses, without a strong relationship to the street. Why does this happen?

MFR-30

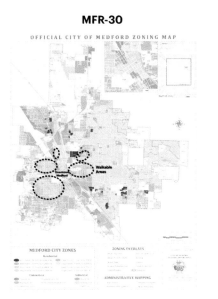

MFR-20

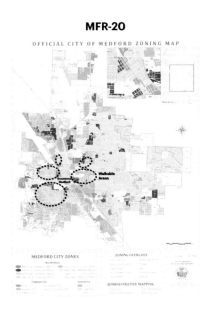

MFR-15

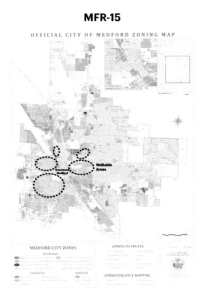

Developers like these housing types because they can be sold as fee-simple units, meaning the buyer owns the land that the unit sits on rather than sharing ownership of the land as in a condominium with stacked units; they eliminate or reduce construction defect liability, and there is an actual or sometimes perceived premium for these types. The problem is that these types are unlikely to deliver the range of affordability and attainability desired because they primarily deliver large units. They are also bad urban form, with one major flaw being that the three-story massing of the buildings is often pushed right up against the rear property line, impacting privacy of neighbors.

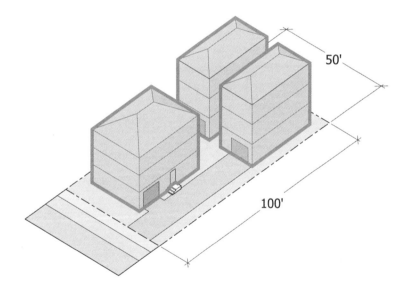

In most cities, developers will build high-end tuck-under town houses or single family homes on lots zoned for multiunit buildings unless they are not allowed. To deliver a broader range of affordability and better urban form this should not be allowed.

CREATE NEW MISSING MIDDLE HOUSING ZONES

As a start, tweaking existing zones is often an easier fix, but does not achieve the level of predictability that creating new zones will, so the tweaks should be seen as a temporary fix or test, with the zone replacements as a longer-term goal. With this in mind, every zoning code should have a minimum of two zones to enable Missing Middle Housing: one to enable the lower and middle range of housing types from the Missing Middle spectrum, such as duplexes, cottage courts, and fourplexes (mostly two to two and a half stories maximum) and another to enable the upper end of the Missing Middle spectrum, which are slightly bigger buildings, such as courtyard apartments and multiplex: medium, with three to four stories and deeper buildings being allowed or encouraged. It is not always necessary but can be ideal to have a third zone at the upper end of what are now a city's single-family zones that enable the smaller-scale Missing Middle types, such as duplexes and cottage courts, along with single-family homes.

With housing affordability being a growing issue across the country, more and more cities are discussing the replacement of single-family zones with zones that allow a range of Missing Middle types that will be compatible in scale with single-family houses. For this approach, it is recommended that the "Parameters for Zone 1: Missing Middle Housing Zone" below be followed

This zone-intent illustration from Cincinnati, Ohio's Form-Based Code illustrates the intended house-scale Missing Middle forms.

in creating that new zone, unless a higher degree of change or transformation has been determined in policies to completely change the form and scale of a neighborhood. In that instance only, the scale for "Zone 2: The Upper Missing Middle Housing Zone" defined below should be considered.

Whichever approach you take, here are some parameters for the zones you need to create and end up with after adjustments to your existing zones. Ideally a fair amount of documentation of existing conditions or local examples is completed to inform any adjustments that are needed to these numeric parameters.

Parameters for Zone 1: Missing Middle Housing Zone

- **Maximum building width:** 45–60 ft.
- **Maximum building depth:** 45–60 ft.
- **Maximum height:** two to two and a half stories
- **Max Density:** Ideally would not be used. If using density, 35 du/acre as a minimum threshold, ideally 65–70 du/acres maximum to truly enable a full range of attainable Missing Middle Housing units.
- **Allowed types:** Duplex: stacked, duplex: side-by-side, bungalow court, fourplex, courtyard apartment, multiplex: small, carriage house, town houses (be careful about how many in a row you allow without a break)
- **Minimum lot sizes for each type:** See table for each type for general parameters that should be calibrated based on existing local conditions. Most of the Missing Middle types should be allowed on a 50 ft. wide lot, the bungalow court on a 100 ft. wide lot.
- **Ideally no off-street parking requirements:** Maximum 0.5 spaces per unit for one bedroom and larger, 0.25 spaces for a studio or unit under 650 sq. ft.
- Additional form regulations will be needed for bungalow courts to ensure good form.

This zone-intent illustration from Cincinnati, Ohio's Form-Based Code illustrates the intended Upper Missing Middle Housing forms, which are taller and wider than the Core Missing Middle Housing forms.

TIP:

This zone should allow fourplexes on a 50 ft. wide lot and a cottage court with an unlimited number of one-story, 650 sq. ft. or smaller, cottages on a 100 ft. wide lot in a bungalow court format.

Parameters for Zone 2: Upper Missing Middle Housing Zone

- **Maximum width:** 65–85 ft. This is wider than Missing Middle zone, but not that much wider.
- **Maximum depth:** 5–10 ft. rear setback. Allows the building to go deeper into the lot than Missing Middle zones. This is one of the primary differences between Missing Middle and Upper Missing Middle.

T4 Neighborhood Small Footprint (T4N.SF)

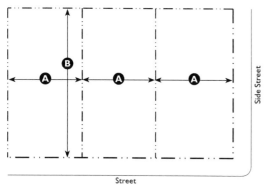

Street

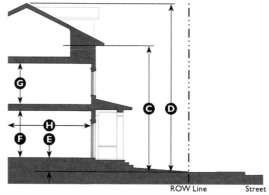

ROW Line   Street

Key

---- ROW / Lot Line

Key

---- ROW Line

C. Allowed Building Types			
Building Type	Lot		Standards
	Width Ⓐ	Depth Ⓑ	
Carriage House	n/a	n/a	1703-3.40
Detached House: Compact	30' min.; 50' max.	75' min.	1703-3.60
Cottage Court	75' min.; 100' max.	100' min.	1703-3.70
Duplex	40' min.; 75' max.	100' min.	1703-3.80
Rowhouse	18' min.; 35' max.	80' min.	1703-3.90
Multi-Plex: Small	50' min.; 100' max.	100' min.	1703-3.100
Live/Work	18' min.; 35' max.	80' min.	1703-3.130

D. Building Form		
Height		
Main Building		
Stories	2½ stories max.	
To Eave/Parapet	24' max.	Ⓒ
Overall	35' max.	Ⓓ
Accessory Structure(s)		
Accessory Dwellings	2 stories max.	
Other	1 story max.	
Ground Floor Finish Level above Sidewalk	18" min.	Ⓔ
Ground Floor Ceiling		Ⓕ
Service or Retail	12' min.	
Upper Floor(s) Ceiling	8' min.	Ⓖ
Ground floor lobbies and common areas in multi-unit buildings may have a 0" to 6" ground floor finish level.		
Footprint		
Depth, Ground-Floor Space	24' min.	Ⓗ
Accessory Structure(s)		
Width	24' max.	
Depth	32' max.	
Miscellaneous		

Loading docks, overhead doors, and other service entries shall be screened and not be located on primary street facades.

- **Height:** Three to four stories maximum
- **Allowed types:** courtyard apartments, multiplex: medium, multiplex: large
- **Minimum lot sizes for each type:** See table for each type for general parameters that should be calibrated based on existing local conditions.

USING A FORM-BASED VERSUS DENSITY-BASED APPROACH

If cities are taking the previous steps, with more thoughtful attention given to allowed scale/form/building envelope, your zoning/approach will automatically fall under a more form-based approach. A form-based approach is where the zoning more prescriptively defines a desired built form or allowed building envelope rather than primarily regulating with numeric parameters, such as density and FAR, within a larger allowed building envelope and allowing a broader range of built results within that allowed building envelope.

Most form-based codes do not regulate a density directly but still have a potential density output (which is calculated using a maximum number of units allowed within each housing type and minimum allowed lot sizes for each type), but the form intent, the building width, depth, height, and location on a lot, is regulated first and most importantly.

Integrate Allowed Missing Middle Types for Each Zone

Not all form-based codes do this, but some take the regulations for Missing Middle Housing to the next level and directly enable an allowed range of building-type forms (not uses) within each new zone. This has been done in cities large and small, urban and rural, all across the country.

In this approach, each of the building types has a set of supplemental form standards that are often in a separate section of the zoning code, because each of the types apply to and are allowed in multiple zones. Clear referencing between these sections is important for usability. So the basic form parameters such as setbacks, heights, maximum building footprints, and locations

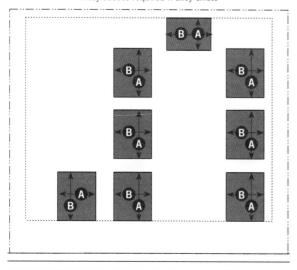

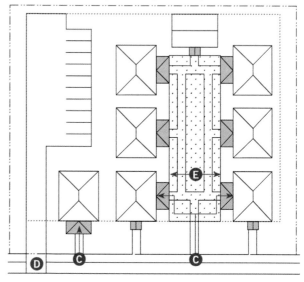

Front Street

Front Street

Key

–··– ROW / Building Site Line   ■ Building

····· Setback Line

Key

–··– ROW / Building site Line   ■ Frontage

····· Setback Line   ⠿ Common Open Space

3. Building Size and Massing

Height	N-S	N-M
Max. Number of Stories	1	1
Max. Height to Highest Top Plate	14'	18'
Main Body		
Width	32' max.	Ⓐ
Depth	24' max.	Ⓑ

Facades on a street or civic space shall be designed in compliance with Section 40.14.080 (Specific to Massing, Facades and Architectural Elements).

4. Allowed Frontage Types

Porch: Projecting	40.14.090.D
Stoop	40.14.090.F
Dooryard	40.14.090.G

5. Pedestrian Access

Shared court shall be accessible from front street. Ⓒ

Main entrance location to units from shared court.

Units on a corner may enter from the side street.

Pedestrian connections shall link all buildings to the public ROW, shared court, and parking areas.

6. Vehicle Access and Parking

Driveway and parking location shall comply   Ⓓ
with standards in Subsection F (Parking) of the applicable zone.

Spaces may be individually accessible by the units and/or a common parking area located at the rear or side of the building site.

7. Common Open Space

Width	20' min.	Ⓔ
Depth	30' mins. (3 Units);	
	40' min. (5 to 9 Units)	

Required street setbacks and driveways shall not be included in the common open space area calculation.

(Opposite) An example of supplemental form standards needed to effectively regulate the cottage court type. Some cities do this through a Cottage Court Ordinance rather than a zoning district.

of parking are still established by the zone. Then supplemental form standards specific to a type reside in the "Building Type Standards" section. These standards sometimes trump the standards in the base zone standards. For example, a bungalow court might be allowed in a zone whose base standards allow two and a half stories. The bungalow-court standards typically trump that and set a height limit within a bungalow-court type at one and a half stories. Taking this height away is possible without discouraging development of this type because you are allowing developers to build more units on the lots. At first this may seem complex, but having these supplemental form standards by housing type is no different than having supplemental use standards like almost every zoning code does.

A word of warning: many recent codes that have attempted to take this approach of integrating housing types have failed because the numeric parameters are still not correct, or they still have a category called multifamily that is a catchall for all Missing Middle types and treat them more as a *use* rather than a *desired form*. Ultimately, it is the thoughtful metrics that are needed to enable Missing Middle, not just adding text about types into an otherwise conventional zoning code.

TIPS for Effectively Integrating Building Types into Your Zoning:

- If you take this approach, staff—especially staff at the front desk doing project review—will need some supplemental training about Missing Middle types. This approach is very different than they are used to because it takes the ability to understand physical form and housing types in a way and within a system they have not used.
- If your code integrates allowed building types, one of them should not be multifamily. If it is, it is not truly enabling Missing Middle types partly because it is treating them all as one use (might as well call this medium-density residential) rather than a range of forms.

ENABLE MISSING MIDDLE BY REDUCING OFF-STREET PARKING REQUIREMENTS

The sad reality is that most cities of all sizes have done a better job housing cars than housing people. If the parking issue is not addressed by substantially reducing or removing off-street parking requirements, then Missing Middle will not be enabled effectively. Consider that, at a minimum, a wood-constructed garage adds approximately $15,000 to $20,000 to the cost of a unit, which can easily put the price out of reach for many buyers. If a city requires more than one off-street parking space for each unit, it is likely that it is not enabling Missing Middle Housing. In some higher-priced markets this requirement drops to 0.5 spaces per unit and often even zero spaces per unit.

The Best Parking Approaches

- Option 1: Ideally cities would remove all off-street parking requirements for residential uses, particularly in defined walkable urban contexts. In addition, cities would not require off-street parking for guests in either in these locations.
- Option 2: Remove parking requirements for residential buildings of less than eight units in walkable urban contexts.
- General note for best approaches: Allow on-street parking adjacent to a lot to count toward off-street parking requirements.

Backup Approaches (far less desirable)

- Regulate parking requirements by unit size or number of bedrooms so smaller units are not disincentivized. For example:
  - 0.5 spaces per studio or units under 650 sq. ft.
  - 1 space for one-bedroom units or units under 750 sq. ft.
  - 1.5 spaces per two bedrooms
  - 2.5–3 spaces per three bedroom and 1 space for every additional bedroom or
- Regulate by unit size as per above, and in this approach you could allow the inclusion of on-street parking adjacent to the site toward off-street parking requirements. This incentivizes Missing Middle on corner lots because of the extra curb space for corner lots.
- Pick a pilot-project area that requires no off-street parking for residential projects for up to fifteen units and then determine a set amount of time or number of built units after which it will be evaluated.

CASE STUDIES

HOW MISSING MIDDLE HOUSING IS BEING USED BY JURISDICTIONS, STATES, AND REGIONAL PLANNING AGENCIES

The following is a brief summary of some of the many and diverse types of Missing Middle applications that have been completed or are in process by cities, counties, and states across the country and around the world.

PORTLAND, OREGON

A Thoughtful, Effective Zoning-Reform Strategy

The City of Portland has one of the most well-thought-out and well-communicated (graphically, in text, and verbally) strategies in the country for removing zoning barriers for Missing Middle Housing, and it should be carefully studied. This effort was split into two tasks: task 1 was called the Residential Infill Project. This phase was intended to allow a broader range of Missing Middle types at the lower end of the Missing Middle spectrum, including small multiplexes, in areas previously zoned for single family; and, task 2 was called Better Housing by Design, which directly addresses the multi-dwelling zones (R3, R2, R1 and RH) outside the central city to allow a broader range of Missing Middle and Upper Missing Middle Housing types.

These efforts were started to address three concerns: 1. The rising cost of housing; 2. Increasing teardowns in neighborhoods; and, 3. The scale of additions and new buildings within neighborhoods.

Strategies for the Residential Infill Project were: 1. To limit the size of structures. This was to not allow further spread of oversized single-family homes; 2. Allow a broader range of hous-

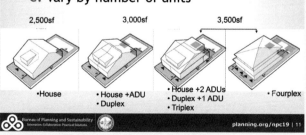

In Portland, Oregon, new regulations allow more FAR for multiunit buildings than for single-family homes to encourage Missing Middle Housing.

ing types; 3. Thoughtfully increase the allowed FAR as the number of units increases. This was important to incentivize the construction of multiplexes on individual lots and disincentivize or not allow out-of-scale single-family rebuild or additions; and, 4. Improve the design of infill.

The City also conducted an economic feasibility analysis, which showed that with the introduction of new limits on structure size paired with allowing for more units in those structures, average rents were projected to decrease by more than half. In addition, as part of this comprehensive effort, the City completed a displacement impact risk analysis to inform the conversation about how these changes would impact different communities. This study demonstrated that the Residential Infill Project, if implemented, could substantially reduce displacement compared to a scenario where the Residential Infill Project was not implemented.

The goal of the Better Housing by Design is to establish development and design standards in Portland's multi-dwelling zones (R3, R2, R1 and RH) outside the central city to allow a broader range of Missing Middle and Upper Missing Middle Housing types and buildings that are larger than what would typically be classified as Missing Middle. The project will update the zoning code and align with the 2035 comprehensive plan to improve building design and development. This project is reviewing the zones on a citywide basis but also includes a special focus on East Portland to foster good new development that reflects the area's distinct characteristics and the needs of community members. These multi-dwelling zones are intended to accommo-

date up to twenty-three thousand new units by 2035 or approximately 20 percent of the growth.[2]

As part of the Better Housing by Design project, staff analyzed pre–World War II multifamily housing, such as courtyard apartment buildings, and found that most historic examples could not be built today in Portland's low-rise multi-dwelling zones because they exceed maximum density regulations. Proposed code amendments will regulate primarily by building scale, with more flexibility for numbers of units and new options intended to facilitate courtyard housing.

THE STATE OF OREGON

Statewide Enabling Legislation
In July 2019, Oregon's legislators passed the first state bill of its kind, Housing Bill 2001, which effectively eliminated single-family zoning statewide and enabled a range of Missing Middle Housing types everywhere to address its affordable-housing issues. The bill allows up to two housing units on all residential lots located within cities that have at least ten thousand residents. For cities of twenty-five thousand residents and up, the bill allows up to four units per lot, including row houses and cottage clusters. The bill will go into effect starting in 2020.

THE TWIN CITIES

Metro-wide Missing Middle Housing Policies
Over the past couple years, the Twin Cities metro area has become a leader in the discussion and application of progressive Missing Middle Housing policies, strategies, and zoning.

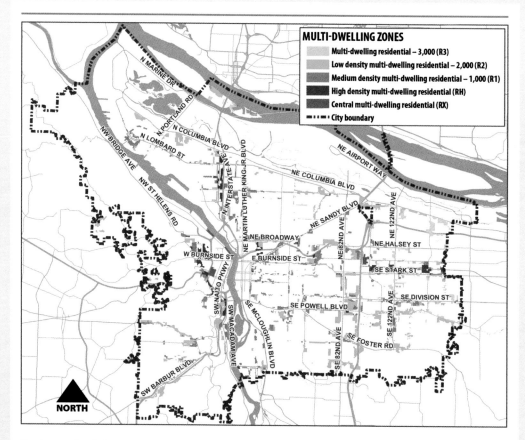

MULTI-DWELLING ZONES

- Multi-dwelling residential – 3,000 (R3)
- Low density multi-dwelling residential – 2,000 (R2)
- Medium density multi-dwelling residential – 1,000 (R1)
- High density multi-dwelling residential (RH)
- Central multi-dwelling residential (RX)
- ▪ ▪ ▪ City boundary

Project schedule

Phase	Public Involvement – Comments/Testimony
1: Fall 2016 Research and Assessment	Existing Conditions Assessment Report available for public review end of December 2016 • Initial meetings and walks with community groups
2: Winter – Spring 2017 Concept Development	Public workshops on design concepts and preferred development outcomes. • Stakeholder working group meetings • Public open house on Concept Plan
3: Summer 2017 Code Development	Public review of Discussion Draft code amendments • Public open house • Stakeholder working group meetings
4: Fall 2017 – Winter 2018 Public Hearings / Adoption	Proposed Draft and Recommended Draft of code amendments available for public review • Public hearings at Planning and Sustainability Commission and at City Council

Better Housing by Design – February 2017

code-dev_better-housing 02/14/17

Map of Portland's multi-dwelling zones that illustrates
how little of the city's geographic area allows multi-dwelling
buildings.

Following is a summary of what has been done and is in progress.

MINNEAPOLIS

In 2019, the City of Minneapolis, Minnesota, took the lead in progressive Missing Middle Housing policies within its comprehensive plan. One of the overarching concepts reinforced by the plan's policy is "Affordable and Accessible Housing," which was reinforced by the goal that, "In 2040, all Minneapolis residents will be able to afford and access quality housing throughout the city." The plan states,

> *The loss of affordable housing units and changes in household income have resulted in a greater number of cost-burdened households—households in which more than 30 percent of household income goes toward mortgage or rental payments. Forty-nine percent of all households in Minneapolis are cost-burdened, but this is not equal across racial groups. Over 50 percent of black households and over 45 percent of American Indian and Hispanic households in Minneapolis are cost-burdened, whereas 1 in 3 white households are cost-burdened.*

One of the steps taken to enable the City to achieve this goal within the plan was creating and approving "Policy 1—Access to Housing: Increase the Supply of Housing and Its Diversity of Location and Type." This policy allows up to three units (Missing Middle–scale housing) on any lot in the city, even those currently zoned for single-family housing in "neighborhood inte-

riors farthest from downtown" and in "neighborhood interiors that contain a mix of housing types from single-family homes to apartments, increase housing choice and supply by allowing new housing within that existing range." This aggressive policy to remove single-family land use, and ultimately single-family zoning, from the entire city was groundbreaking and noticed across the country by policy makers, developers, planners, and community members.

After approving a comprehensive plan policy to allow up to three units on any lot previously zoned for single-family homes, the City of Minneapolis Community Planning and Economic Development department (CPED), in partnership with Minnesota Housing and Land Bank Twin Cities, initiated a pilot program to help fund Missing Middle–scale projects up to twenty units on city-owned lots. The City committed $500,000 to the first phase of this program. Total financing for ownership and rental projects is up to $70,000 per affordable unit, and projects that demonstrate a compelling basis for deeper subsidy, such as including lower AMI restrictions, larger units, or longer-term affordability, may be eligible for up to $95,000 per affordable unit. In addition, Land Bank Twin Cities offers interim construction financing to Minneapolis home developers subject to underwriting and approval. The City released an RFP for potential projects.

SAINT PAUL

Saint Paul, Minnesota, followed the lead of its sister city and in 2019 adopted a comprehensive plan that had Missing Middle Housing policy as a

Capitol Area Baselines

Baseline 1: The Capitol Area's Current Mix

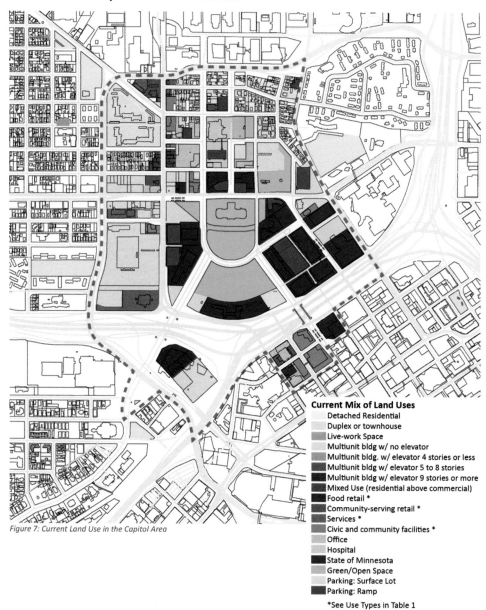

Current Mix of Land Uses

- Detached Residential
- Duplex or townhouse
- Live-work Space
- Multiunit bldg w/ no elevator
- Multiunit bldg. w/ elevator 4 stories or less
- Multiunit bldg w/ elevator 5 to 8 stories
- Multiunit bldg w/ elevator 9 stories or more
- Mixed Use (residential above commercial)
- Food retail *
- Community-serving retail *
- Services *
- Civic and community facilities *
- Office
- Hospital
- State of Minnesota
- Green/Open Space
- Parking: Surface Lot
- Parking: Ramp

*See Use Types in Table 1

Figure 7: Current Land Use in the Capitol Area

(Opposite) Minnesota's state capitol building is surrounded by neighborhoods filled with Missing Middle Housing types that are thoughtfully identified in the Capitol Area Plan document.

driver to address its current and future housing needs. Under "Goal 7: Strong neighborhoods that support lifelong housing needs," one of the policies that directly supports Missing Middle Housing is Policy H-48. It expands permitted housing types in urban neighborhoods (as defined in the land-use chapter) to include duplexes, triplexes, townhomes, small-scale multifamily, and accessory dwelling units to allow for neighborhood-scale density increases, broadened housing choices, and intergenerational living.

THE CAPITOL AREA PLAN

Even the Capitol Area Plan, led by the Capitol Area Architectural and Planning Board, which has authority over the geographic area surrounding the Minnesota state capitol, states, "Housing remains a key component of neighborhoods close to the Capitol, and a diversity in housing types, ownership, and residents will enrich the character of each residential neighborhood." It then goes on to introduce Missing Middle Housing and states, "The existing low-rise range of housing types in Capitol and along Sherburne and Charles Avenues should be preserved and enhanced over time by the sensitive addition of new single-family homes and 'missing middle' types. As most of the structures in these areas are over 100 years old, a careful balance between redevelopment and restoration, renovation and rehabilitation

will be required." It then introduces policies and development standards to implement this objective and vision.

STATE OF MICHIGAN

Using Missing Middle as One Tool to Implement the State's Place-Based Economic Development Strategy

The State of Michigan has advanced over the course of the past five to seven years from introducing the concept of Missing Middle Housing in its toolbox to inform strategic planning to targeting Missing Middle as a project priority in its redevelopment incentive programs. "MIplace" is a place-based economic development strategy initiated in 2012 by the State. With an intensive academic literature/practitioner environmental scan, MIplace developed and operated a full-curriculum education component from 2013 to 2015, started the programming phase from 2015 to 2017, and since 2017 has integrated the principles within and as part of its community-development readiness certification.

According to Jim Tischler, now with the State's Land Bank Authority, the primary goal of their work with Missing Middle Housing was not just to inform about the range of housing products but to create a paradigm shift within which local jurisdictions play an active role in the development process. The State, very smartly, realized that this was important because it meant that local jurisdictions did not need to wait around for big developers to deliver results but rather could rely on incremental development and small builders to deliver much-needed housing.

Section through Courtyard looking North

West Garage Elevation

Courtyard

Aerial View

This award-winning scheme in the State of Michigan's Missing Middle Housing Design Competition, submitted by Brian and Jennifer Settle, thoughtfully integrates courtyard housing behind a small mixed-use building.

The State's development-readiness standards, marketed as "Redevelopment-Ready Communities," require locals to demonstrate inclusion and priority of Missing Middle in their policies, plans, and review processes to achieve certification and have priority status for State program investments.

In addition, the concept of Missing Middle has been adopted by the affordable-housing community statewide and is intrinsically linked to deliver workforce housing between 110 percent and 80 percent AMI and below, the latter being where federal subsidies come into play. Tischler stated, "The concept of Missing Middle Housing was a philosophical and a paradigm shift statewide that allows us to move toward production with socioeconomic integration of housing types at neighborhood scale. This would not have happened unless Dan had created this concept and given his keynote presentation at the state APA conference. That planted the seeds of this effort."

To promote the concept, in 2015 the State of Michigan also sponsored the first-ever Missing Middle design competition that looks at opportunity sites in various contexts around the state.

As part of the effort to enable Missing Middle, the State promoted the completion of a target-market analysis (TMA), a unique approach to residential-market analysis that specifically identifies the demand for each of the Missing Middle Housing types based on the lifestyle characteristics of migrating households. This is in contrast to a conventional residential-market analysis that identifies the demand for more general classifications of single family or multifamily and looks mostly in the rearview mirror at what types of housing have been built in the recent past.

This conventional approach to market analysis does not work to identify the demand for Missing Middle because none or little has been built in the recent past, thus making it easy to say it is not viable. According to Tischler, the primary goal for this effort was to cost-share with local jurisdictions to get this work done. This got them to commit and contribute to the effort, and then the TMA would provide them with data defining the need for these housing types in their specific jurisdictions. Tischler said, "this was especially important in the smaller, not-so-hot markets, where the government needs to assume a role in development to make it happen." The State preapproved consultants for the target-market analysis and required one of these preapproved consultants to be used by local jurisdictions in order for this cost sharing to happen. The State cost-shared sixty-five TMAs, which seeded widespread adoption of the approach, and now over two hundred jurisdictions that have completed these TMAs.

What comes next? Tischler states, "Missing Middle Housing is so desperately needed in small towns, rural contexts, and larger cities, and the opportunities exist along corridors and in nodes as defined by the TMAs completed. We are pioneering use of parcel-specific 'micro-

Target-market analysis by the Incremental Development Alliance for the State of Michigan shows the gap between supply and demand for Missing Middle types and the oversupply of single-family homes.

Michigan's Missing Housing - Here's the Scoop

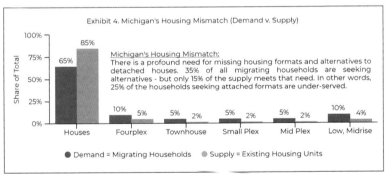

Exhibit 4. Michigan's Housing Mismatch (Demand v. Supply)

Michigan's Housing Mismatch:
There is a profound need for missing housing formats and alternatives to detached houses. 35% of all migrating households are seeking alternatives - but only 15% of the supply meets that need. In other words, 25% of the households seeking attached formats are under-served.

● Demand = Migrating Households   ● Supply = Existing Housing Units

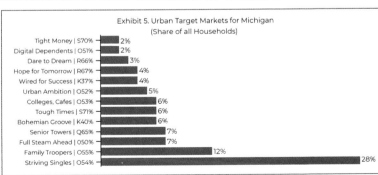

Exhibit 5. Urban Target Markets for Michigan
(Share of all Households)

TIFs' for extraordinary-cost coverage, including purchase and rent subsidies, to accelerate production of Missing Middle units at incremental, neighborhood scale. The delivery of Missing Middle Housing can drive the economic and social change that needs to happen across our state." There is much to learn from this case study.

ATLANTA, GEORGIA

The Missing Middle conversation has been percolating in the Atlanta region for several years now. In 2016, the Georgia Conservancy hosted a series of Missing Middle presentations that informed this conversation and seems to have brought the need for these housing choices to the forefront of conversations about the future of the Atlanta region.

The City of Atlanta has made enabling Missing Middle Housing a priority within its citywide zoning-code update. Early in this process, the City's "Zoning Ordinance Diagnostic" document defined Missing Middle Housing as a priority, identified barriers and issues within existing zoning for the delivery of Missing Middle, and recommended strategies to remedy these barriers. Note that the City's communication was very effective, focusing on "ensuring housing diversity" and not focusing on density at all. The following is a list of the thoughtful recommendations included.

- Recommendation 5.4: **Building Types.** Define Missing Middle Housing building types during the update to the zoning ordinance. Types should include those historically found in Atlanta, such as duplexes and small apartment buildings, as well as those not traditionally found that serve current housing needs, such as town houses, cottage housing, and live-work units.
- Recommendation 5.5: **Integration into Existing Districts.** Allow Missing Middle Housing types within the appropriate existing or new zoning districts. Within existing districts this will require incorporation of the recommended building types and updated lot metrics. It will also require either increases to the permitted FAR or the complete elimination of FAR as a tool for controlling bulk.
- Recommendation 5.6: **R5 Amendment.** Amend R5 to require duplexes to resemble a single house. Typically, this will mean that the units must be stacked vertically or horizontally within a single building mass.
- Recommendation 5.7: **Land-Use Map.** Update the 15-Year Future Land Use Map to allow Missing Middle Housing in every medium-density residential (or equivalent) classification.

In January 2019, Atlanta's zoning changes were approved. These changes removed barriers for ADUs, made targeted changes to the metrics of the zoning to better enable Missing Middle, and created a new zoning category called Multi-Unit Housing (MR-MU) that was specifically created to enable Missing Middle Housing.

TENNESSEE

NASHVILLE

Under the leadership of former director Rick Bernhardt, Nashville was an early adopter of the concept of a Missing Middle Housing. Their comprehensive plan, adopted in June 2015 has a housing element that identified Missing Middle Housing as a "key idea." This policy continues to inform their small-area planning and form-based code applications that are implementing the plan. The plan states,

> *Missing middle housing can achieve multiple goals in Nashville's housing market. It can be used to create transitions—in height, scale and density—between higher density centers and corridors and single family neighborhoods. When located by prominent corridors or commercial centers, missing middle housing allows more residents near transit, services, retail, and other amenities. Finally, missing middle housing can provide new housing options and meet the market demand for smaller units with less maintenance in walkable settings. . . . Changes to the zoning code to address transitions, contextual design, and ideal locations to permit the development of missing middle housing will aid in including this housing type in Nashville's supply.*

As part of its focused area-planning efforts, the City of Nashville continues to focus on enabling Missing Middle Housing. The City even named one of its efforts "The Missing Middle: Retrofitting the Centers and Corridors of Nashville." This effort focused on defined focal points or centers as prime opportunities to enable more Missing Middle Housing to locate people closer to amenities such as transit and services. The effort will change zoning regulations, including height and bulk, to produce these house-scale Missing Middle types that will provide an area of transition between centers or corridors and the existing neighborhoods.

CHATTANOOGA

In Chattanooga, the Chattanooga Neighborhood Enterprise, with support from the Lyndhurst Foundation, led an effort to enable Missing Middle within the city's downtown-adjacent neighborhoods. These efforts included a design charette, a developer's boot camp, and the creation of a document that summarized a range of locally appropriate Missing Middle types, all created by the Incremental Development Alliance.

STATE OF CALIFORNIA

Local and State Efforts to Deliver the Much-Needed Housing in the State

California is one of the places that needs Missing Middle Housing the most, but local jurisdictions have lagged behind in their application of the concept. AARP's California chapter took the lead in providing information about Missing Middle Housing in California as part of its age friendly/livable community efforts by releasing a three-part series of Missing Middle Housing videos. Enabling the Missing Middle types was also an objective of many early form-based

All Nashvillians need housing that is affordable ...

In recent years, people making less than 120 percent of Nashville Median Family Income (MFI) have felt the pinch of higher housing costs. This includes seniors and veterans on fixed incomes, those in the hospitality and retail industries, teachers and public safety providers, as well as nurses and technicians in the healthcare profession. Housing is considered affordable when a household spends less than 30 percent of their gross income on housing. Housing affordability leads to economic stability for individuals, families, and our community as a whole.

Extremely Low Income	Very Low Income	Low Income	Moderate Income
< 30 % MFI	30–50 % MFI	50–80 % MFI	80–120 % MFI

81% of individuals with income make less than $56,280

65% of families with income make less than $80,280

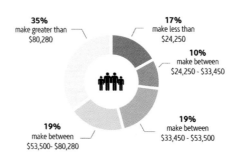

Individuals:
- 19% make greater than $56,280
- 17% make between $37,450 - $56,280
- 20% make between $23,450 - $37,450
- 17% make between $14,050 - $23,450
- 27% make less than $14,050

Families:
- 35% make greater than $80,280
- 17% make less than $24,250
- 10% make between $24,250 - $33,450
- 19% make between $33,450 - $53,500
- 19% make between $53,500- $80,280

Sources:

Tennessee Department of Labor and Workforce Development, Labor Market Information, June 2014. Web Access April 2 2015.
https://www.jobs4tn.gov/vosnet/Default.aspx

Notes:

All data are derived from 2013 American Community Survey 1-Year Estimates for Davidson County TN and HUD FYI 2015 Income Limits.
Family income limits in this case assume 1 Person (Individuals) and 4 Persons in a Family. HUD FY 2015 Nashville Median Family Income is
reported at $66,900.

In Nashville, households making less than 120 percent of median family income have been housing-cost burdened due to rising housing prices. The Nashville Comprehensive Plan uses Missing Middle Housing as one tool to deliver housing to these households.

codes adopted in California cities, a few of which include Grass Valley, Ventura, Livermore, Petaluma, Hercules, Benicia, and Paso Robles.

There is a large list of housing-related bills recently passed or working their way through approvals. Some of these are quite progressive, such as the bill that started as SB827 and was brought back in a new iteration as SB50, both led by State Senator Scott Weiner, that would remove barriers for housing delivery by reducing local regulatory control, in particular to areas close to transit and jobs, by eliminating setbacks, density caps, and parking requirements and establishing much higher allowed height limits. Another, SB2, The Building Homes and Jobs Act, passed in 2017 as part of a fifteen-bill housing package aimed at addressing the state's housing shortage and high housing costs. The California Department of Housing and Community Development released $123 million with approval of the Senate Bill 2 (SB 2, 2017) Planning Grants Program (PGP) to local jurisdictions to comply with the Objective Design Standards criteria defined in this bill. In addition, California's Department of Housing and Community Development (HCD) has substantially increased Regional Housing Needs Allocations (RHNA) for all jurisdictions, which will require local jurisdictions to think more creatively about delivering more housing, including Missing Middle scale. None of these efforts specifically address Missing Middle, but Missing Middle Housing will need to be one of the tools in every jurisdiction's housing toolbox to address these housing needs.

The following is a brief highlight of planning efforts that are directly utilizing Missing Middle Housing in the State of California.

THE GRAND BOULEVARD INITIATIVE

This effort facilitated the design of multimodal streetscape improvements for two case study locations on El Camino Real in Redwood City, California, and Palo Alto, California. The effort began in summer of 2017. As part of its "Policies and Programs" information this effort introduced and defined Missing Middle Housing and states, "Missing Middle Housing is a housing and urban design concept focused on moderate-density housing types that provide more housing choices while working within the scale and form of walkable neighborhoods."

THE CITY OF BERKELEY

The City of Berkeley's city council has approved funding to direct City staff to have a Missing Middle Housing study completed.

THE SACRAMENTO REGION

The Sacramento Area Council of Government's (SACOG) staff released a "Housing Policy Toolkit" that introduced the concept of Missing Middle Housing and included "Expand Missing Middle Zoning," as one of the recommended strategies for its jurisdictions. This is very relevant to this region as staff concluded through research that 90 percent of the land zoned for residential development in the region did not allow enough density to enable Missing Middle. As the State of California adjusts its Regional Housing Needs

Allocations (RHNA), every jurisdiction is asked to accommodate more housing to address the state's housing crisis, Missing Middle is sure to play a role in enabling small, rural, suburban, and urban cities and counties to meet these required allocations/number of units.

COUNTY OF SAN DIEGO AFFORDABLE-HOUSING STRATEGY

The County of San Diego has been using the concept of Missing Middle Housing in its toolbox to deliver affordable-housing options.

In 2018 California passed AB 1637, also known as the Missing Middle Act. According to assembly member Todd Gloria, who introduced the bill, "AB 1637 authorizes the housing authorities in the City of San Diego and Santa Clara County to provide gap financing for middle-income housing projects—meaning, projects with at least 40 percent of units affordable to persons of low-income and 10 percent of units affordable to persons of middle-income. Currently, housing authorities can only assist with the low-income units of a project. With the Governor's signature, AB 1637 went into effect in 2018 and will operate as a pilot program with a four year sunset."[3]

This legislation focuses more on the affordability side rather than form and scale, but it is an interesting and important application.

Leadership Groups Promoting the Need in Regional Strategies

CASA was a group created by the San Francisco Bay Area Metropolitan Transportation Commission and Association of Bay Area Governments to help direct housing policy in the Bay Area to address the dire need for more affordable-housing solutions across the regions. This group comprised major employers, for-profit and nonprofit housing developers, labor and environmental leaders, public policy and affordable-housing advocates, transportation experts, charitable foundations, and elected officials. In late 2018 the twenty-one-member CASA Steering Committee finalized a ten-point set of policy recommendations known as the CASA Compact. One of the seven core principles defined in this document was "Promote 'Missing Middle' housing types." And one of the proposals was for minimum zoning near transit. According to the document, "This policy would create an inclusive mix of homes near transit and jobs, consistent with the goals of Plan Bay Area. It would spur the development of 'missing middle' housing types that are within reach of working families and blend into existing neighborhoods."

The one major mistake this document makes is that it refers to Missing Middle primarily as an income level rather than as house-scale buildings that can deliver affordability to middle-income households.

KAUAI COUNTY

Adapting and Applying Missing Middle for Rural Contexts

Hawaii's Kauai County (the island of Kauai) has been working on several fronts to create more

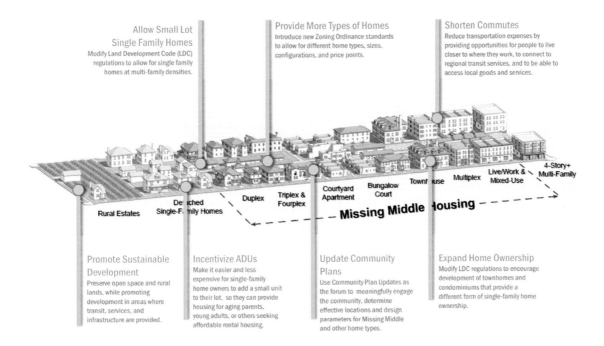

Strategies for Housing Affordability

Allow Small Lot Single Family Homes
Modify Land Development Code (LDC) regulations to allow for single family homes at multi-family densities.

Provide More Types of Homes
Introduce new Zoning Ordinance standards to allow for different home types, sizes, configurations, and price points.

Shorten Commutes
Reduce transportation expenses by providing opportunities for people to live closer to where they work, to connect to regional transit services, and to be able to access local goods and services.

Rural Estates

Detached Single-Family Homes

Duplex

Triplex & Fourplex

Courtyard Apartment

Bungalow Court

Townhouse

Multiplex

Live/Work & Mixed-Use

4-Story+ Multi-Family

Missing Middle Housing

Promote Sustainable Development
Preserve open space and rural lands, while promoting development in areas where transit, services, and infrastructure are provided.

Incentivize ADUs
Make it easier and less expensive for single-family home owners to add a small unit to their lot, so they can provide housing for aging parents, young adults, or others seeking affordable rental housing.

Update Community Plans
Use Community Plan Updates as the forum to meaningfully engage the community, determine effective locations and design parameters for Missing Middle and other home types.

Expand Home Ownership
Modify LDC regulations to encourage development of townhomes and condominiums that provide a different form of single-family home ownership.

San Diego County in California is utilizing Missing Middle Housing as an affordable housing strategy.

walkable, bikeable, and transit-friendly communities on the island and to expand housing choices, including Missing Middle Housing, under Mayor Bernard P. Carvalho's Holo Holo 2020 sustainability initiative. This work included the adoption of a countywide multimodal land-transportation plan, a countywide comprehen-

sive plan update, which won a National APA Burnham Award, and work on community plans for Līhu'e and South Kauai, that were implemented with a form-based code.

A straw poll conducted by the County in June 2014 identified walkability and affordable housing as key concerns among county residents. The poll found that 37 percent of community members felt unsafe when walking in their community and 27 percent said housing is too expensive—only a quarter of the island's residents can afford most of

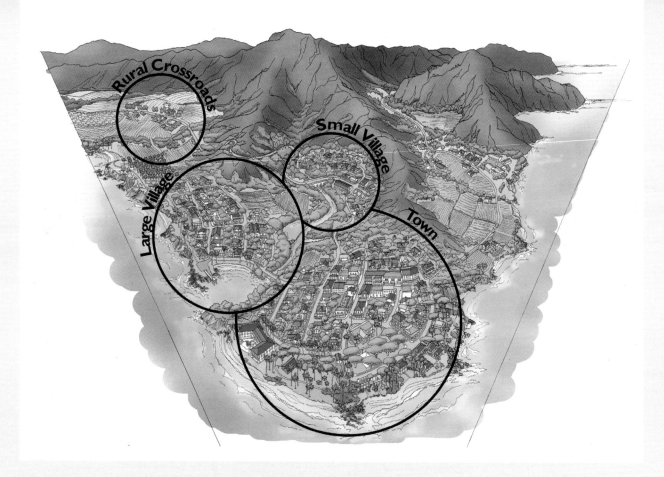

(Above) The award-winning Kauai General Plan used a place-type approach that had Missing Middle Housing types as building blocks for these context-appropriate place types.

(Below) Cincinnati's strong history of Missing Middle Housing provided a solid foundation for their form-based code and comprehensive plan.

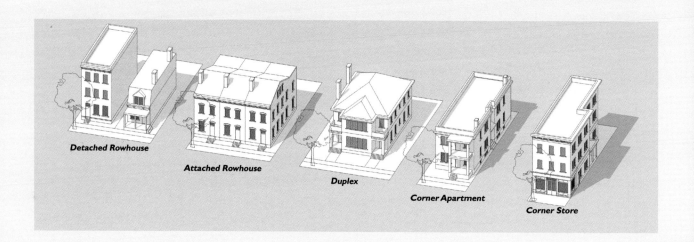

Detached Rowhouse

Attached Rowhouse

Duplex

Corner Apartment

Corner Store

the housing inventory available. The South Kauai Form-Based Code was seen as a "pilot" to ensure development patterns can improve walkability and increase affordable-housing stock while preserving the county's rural character.

"Our area's beauty and natural setting attracts worldwide interest, which is reflected in its high housing costs and resort-style development proposals," said Marie Williams, long-range planner with the Kauai County Planning Department. "The South Kauai Form-Based Code will encourage appropriately scaled infill development and ensure new greenfield development provides a variety of housing types. We hope this will translate to workforce housing adjacent to Kauai's largest resort center."

Within the comprehensive plan's "Actions by Sector," the plan defines infill housing as a priority. It then goes on to discuss supporting infill development and Missing Middle Housing and states.

> Infill development is an important opportunity to diversify Kauai's housing stock through 'Missing Middle' housing in walkable town centers. 'Missing Middle' housing is characterized by small-scale, multi-unit housing types such as duplexes, fourplexes, bungalow courts, and mansion apartments that are not bigger than a large house, often integrated into blocks with single-family homes. Enabling this environment means creating or adapting planning and zoning requirements in a manner that will stimulate private investment in new or renovated structures.

The plan then goes on to establish a policy within the "Permitting Actions and Code Changes" section that states island housing officials will "substantially increase the amount of market rate multi-family and 'missing middle' housing on Kaua'i by requiring housing type diversity in all new subdivisions."

The larger-scale framework for enabling this infill and walkability was a place-types-based land-use framework in the island-wide comprehensive plan within which building types become the building blocks of the spectrum of walkable places defined.

CINCINNATI, OHIO

Building Upon a Long History of Missing Middle Housing Types to Promote Urban Revitalization

Cincinnati was also an early adopter of the concept of Missing Middle Housing, with a citywide form-based code that played an instrumental role in the framing of the concept of Missing Middle. Cincinnati has a tremendous opportunity. In its urban neighborhoods they already have what other cities want and are trying to build: a variety of urban housing types, including some of the best Missing Middle Housing in the country; a network of neighborhood main streets ready to be revitalized; a rich, diverse, and well-built collection of historic architecture; and easily accessible open-space networks created by the topography weaving throughout these neighborhoods.

The Queen City positioned itself to capture this demand and put a strategy in place to make these neighborhoods complete places with everything urban neighborhoods have to offer. A comprehensive plan update, a citywide form-based code, and a completed streets document were created to enable the city to achieve these goals. A Sustainable Communities Challenge Grant from the Department of Housing and Urban Development funded the form-based code project. The Cincinnati Form-Based Code was adopted in 2013 and applied to four pilot neighborhoods, which were four of the forty-two defined walkable urban neighborhoods in the comprehensive plan that are all targeted locations for future application of the form-based code. These efforts were championed by Roxanne Qualls, the former mayor and vice mayor and city council member at the time.

AUSTRALIA

Spreading the Missing Middle Application Internationally

To deal with rapid growth and rapidly rising house prices, various jurisdictions in Australia have implemented the concept of Missing Middle Housing, including the Cities of Brisbane and Adelaide, and the States of New South Wales and Queensland to help them provide a more diverse range of housing choices at attainable price points.

NEW SOUTH WALES
"The Low Rise Medium Density Housing Code"

A report titled A *Place for Everyone*, created by PricewaterhouseCoopers in 2017, points to esti-

mates that greater Sydney will grow from 4.8 million people to about 8 million—the size of London—in the next forty years, creating a need for about 664,000 new homes across the next twenty years.

"So an increase in density isn't optional—it's unavoidable," the report says. "But densification does not necessarily mean more high-rise apartments. If we get densification right, we have the opportunity to address both housing affordability and what's referred to as the 'missing middle', a diverse array of housing options to meet the needs of a diverse community."

On July 6, 2018, "The Low Rise Medium Density Housing Code," created by the planning department of the State of New South Wales in Southeast Australia, went into effect and is operating within eighty-two councils across the state. "The Low Rise Medium Density Housing Code" allows well-designed two-story versions of the following Missing Middle types: dual occupancies (duplex), manor houses (fourplexes and small multiplexes), and terraces (town houses) to be carried out under a fast track complying development approval. This approval can be as quick as twenty days if the submittal meets the State's environmental planning policies.

REGIONAL PLAN FOR SOUTHEAST QUEENSLAND
Shaping SEQ

This regional plan for Southeast Queensland includes Brisbane and surrounding local governments, the Gold Coast, the Sunshine Coast to the north, and Toowoomba to the west. This plan does a very effective job of introducing the con-

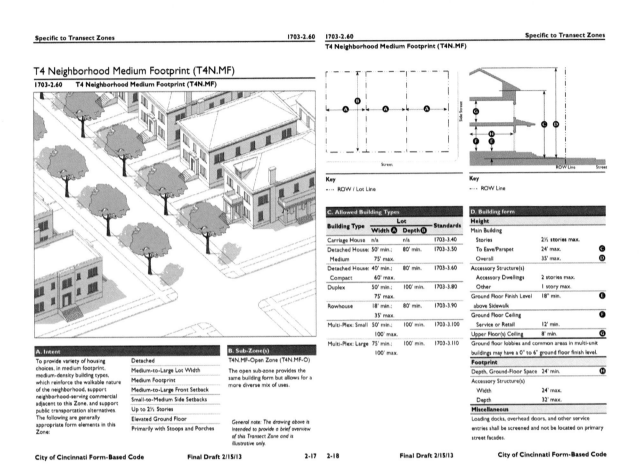

The Cincinnati Form-Based Code was calibrated to enable
more of the broad range of Missing Middle types inherent in
Cincinnati's historic neighborhoods. There were multiple now
form-based zones. This zone allows a broad range of Missing
Middle types, but requires larger front setbacks. This pattern
was identified in the micro-scale analysis.

cept early in the document and then reinforcing the concept through policies, actions, and implementation steps throughout.

BRISBANE GROWTH STRATEGY
Plan Your Brisbane

The City of Brisbane, Australia, has a population of approximately 1.2 million and is growing at around 1,300 people a month. The city council wanted to undertake a significant community-engagement exercise to address this growth and particularly wanted to engage with sectors of the community that do not traditionally participate. The process consisted of a series of both traditional engagement exercises and then an online interactive game, called *Plan Your Brisbane,* which aimed to illustrate the impacts of different growth options for the player related to the key themes identified by the community. Players were given a "game board" with approximately six city blocks within which they had to accommodate one thousand new housing units. The three scales of housing (on the lower left of the following image) that the player could choose from were large (mid-rise), medium (Missing Middle), and small (single family detached). The outcomes of lifestyle, travel time, green space, and affordability adjusted live based on the mix of housing types chosen by the player. For example, if more single-family housing was selected, travel times and green space increased and affordability decreased. In a scenario without single-family homes and a mix of Missing Middle and mid-rise housing, the outcomes for affordability are high, travel times are lower, and the lifestyle is medium, meaning that people may prefer to live in a different type but are willing to make the trade-off for the other outcomes.

The results were significant. City officials ended up with input from every suburb and every age group in the city, with one in five residents participating. All of that input was then aggregated and considered, and the council adopted a new corporate strategy known as Brisbane's Future Blueprint. As a next step, Brisbane is implementing the associated action plan, and one action is a housing strategy for the entire city, within which Missing Middle Housing plays a role in delivering more diverse housing choices and affordability.

ADELAIDE
The 30-Year Plan for Greater Adelaide

The 30-Year Plan for Greater Adelaide, which was first adopted in 2010 and updated in 2017, is a planning document intended to guide the development of the city. The recent update puts an emphasis on increasing residential densities through thoughtful infill, particularly with a focus on Missing Middle Housing types. The plan outlines a list of typologies that should be considered, including row houses, courtyard houses, granny flats, and laneway housing.

The interactive growth-scenario game used to engage community members in the discussion about trade-offs related to growth enables players to use single-family homes, Missing Middle, and high-rise buildings to test different growth scenarios. The outcomes adjust to show the impacts and benefits of the type of growth selected.

Box 7-3
Revitalization Strategies: Using Missing Middle Housing to Encourage Investment in Economically Challenged Neighborhoods

Missing Middle Housing was used as a strategy by the City of South Bend, Indiana, to help promote reinvestment in the Near Northwest Neighborhood, which had been in a steady state of decline for decades and had property values so low that it did not make economic sense to buy an existing single-family home and renovate it, because the cost of the renovation would ultimately be more than the value of the home. The local nonprofit the Near Northwest Neighborhood Association was the only group that was investing in the neighborhood, buying and repairing single-family homes and using federal subsidies to cover their cost gap and to sell them at affordable price points.

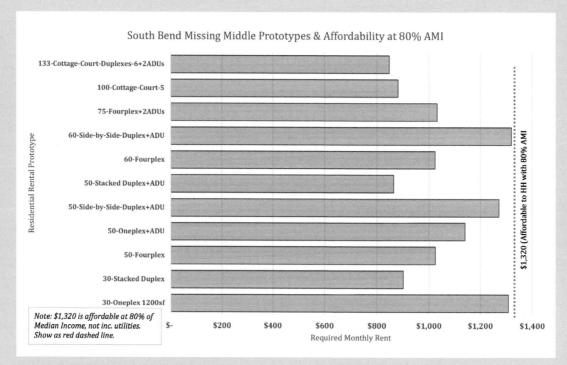

This proforma analysis by IDA illustrates that all of the housing types will generate housing affordable to households with 80 percent of AMI or higher with some types providing a higher level of affordability.

The question this planning effort was intended to answer was: If the zoning was tweaked to enable Missing Middle Housing, would construction of these housing types make economic sense and promote reinvestment and infill in the neighborhood and still deliver affordable housing choices for existing and new residents? Or, would the City still need to provide economic incentives to cover the gap between cost and potential revenue through rents or sales of the units? Within the larger neighborhood, a twenty-eight-acre target site was selected by the City to complete a detailed Missing Middle build-out and to assess economic performance.

Existing conditions:

- A target-market analysis had defined a strong demand for the full range of Missing Middle Housing types in this neighborhood.
- 48 percent of the existing lots were vacant or the homes on them were abandoned.
- 82 percent of buildings were single-family homes. The remaining 18 percent were duplexes.
- Typical lot depth was 126 ft. with alleys.
- 32 percent of lots were less than 40 ft. wide, informing the need for small Missing Middle types that could fit on these narrow lots without lot aggregation.
- An additional 35 percent of lots were under 50 ft. wide.

The City of South Bend worked with Opticos Design to develop a palette of Missing Middle building types to study. The types ultimately included in the economic analysis were duplex: stacked, duplex: side-by-side, fourplex, cottage court, and townhomes. The ultimate build-out for the target area included 44 percent duplexes, 24 percent fourplexes, 18 percent cottage courts, and the rest a mix of Missing Middle types. A pro forma analysis was performed on each of these types by the Incremental Development Alliance, including options with accessory dwelling units (ADUs) in addition to the types on each lot. The pro forma analysis assumed no land cost, because the City of South Bend owned many of the lots, and a 7.5 percent return. With a ten-year build-out, there would be an estimated $1.3 million annual tax revenue for the city. In addition, the pro forma analysis shows that newly constructed examples of the full range of Missing Middle types will deliver affordable rents for households that are at 80 percent of the city's medium income and above, and the stacked duplexes and cottage courts performed the best in terms of being able to bring them online at the lowest rents.

(Images, pages 290–291)
*These drawings illustrate
the incremental, locally driven
stabilization and build-out strategy
for the neighborhood that has been
in a state of decline for over thirty
years. Enabling Missing Middle
Housing is the key to allowing
private investment in
the neighborhood.*

Existing Condition

Phase I Build Out: 0–5 years

Phase II Build Out: 5–10 years

Phase III Build Out: 10–20 years

NOTES

INTRODUCTION

1   "U.S. Census Bureau Releases 2018 Families and Living Arrangements Tables," accessed February 19, 2020, https://www.census.gov/newsroom/press-releases/2018/families.html.

2   US Census Bureau, Population Division, "Projected Age Groups and Sex Composition of the Population: Main Projections Series for the United States, 2017–2060."

3   Joint Center for Housing Studies, "2016 Household Projections: Summary Household Growth Projected for 2015–2025."

CHAPTER 1: WHAT IS MISSING MIDDLE HOUSING AND WHY IS IT IMPORTANT?

1   Katherine Cole Stevenson and H. Ward Jandl, *Houses by Mail: A Guide to Houses from Sears, Roebuck and Company* (New York: John Wiley and Sons, 1986).

2   Chicago Architecture Center, "Two- and Three-Flats," Buildings of Chicago Resources page, http://www.architecture.org/learn/resources/buildings-of-chicago/building/two-and-three-flats/.

3   Anthony Cilluffo, A. W. Geiger, and Richard Fry, "More U.S. Households Are Renting than at Any Point in 50 Years," Pew Research Center, July 19, 2017, https://www.pewresearch.org/fact-tank/2017/07/19/more-u-s-households-are-renting-than-at-any-point-in-50-years/.

CHAPTER 2: DEMOGRAPHIC CHANGES AND GROWING PREFERENCE FOR MISSING MIDDLE HOUSING *(by Arthur C. Nelson)*

1. I use the term *growth* even though it can be both positive and negative. The term also needs context. Households last a long time. They start without children. Then they may have children. Then the children leave. So, when a householder ages from fifty-five to sixty-five years, the household becomes counted as sixty-five years or over even though it is the same household.

2. The year 2017 is our baseline because it is the most recent year for which we have walking and Missing Middle Housing demand and supply data.

3. Generation Alpha, born between 2016 and about 2031, will not have a substantial effect on housing markets until after 2040.

4. Andres Duany, Elizabeth Plater-Zyberk, and Jeff Speck, *Suburban Nation: The Rise of Sprawl and the Decline of the American Dream* (New York: North Point Press, 2000).

5. Although the Great Recession of 2008–2009 led to millions of foreclosures, the aftermath of the Great Recession was not realized fully until the early 2010s.

6. Housing-change figures for 1990 and 2000 are based on the Census of Housing, while the share of housing built on detached lots is based on the American Housing Survey for 1991 and 2011.

7. Jonathan Spader, Tenure Projections of Homeowner and Renter Households for 2018–2038 (Cambridge, MA: Harvard Joint Center for Housing Studies, 2019), accessed September 16, 2019, https://www.jchs.harvard.edu/research-areas/working-papers/tenure-projections -homeowner-and-renter-households-2018-2038-0.

8. According to the AHS, the average plex unit is fifty-two years old compared to forty years for all other units.

9. This is a stated-preference survey, meaning that respondents are forced to choose between roughly equally attractive options. Other housing-related studies are simply preferences: would you prefer marble or Formica countertops? The difference between preference and stated-preference surveys is this: a preference survey would ask if you prefer to live to

be eighty or one hundred, while a stated-preference survey would have you choose now between being healthy and active until eighty, when you keel over and die suddenly without pain, or live to one hundred after twenty years of dementia and incontinence.

10   Though surveys often ask respondents to choose between small and large or conventional lots, respondents are not given parameters, leaving them to define the terms in their local context. A "small lot" in Atlanta on one-quarter acre can be viewed as a large lot in Los Angeles. Nonetheless, in most contexts outside New York City, Los Angeles, and the Bay Area, small lot can be characterized as being one-eighth of an acre or less, which is the smallest lot category published by the AHS.

11   This is about the weighted average of Missing Middle Housing units making up 75 percent of attached units, with 32 percent of them being accessible by walking or biking to selected destinations, and 25 percent of large attached units where 40 percent are accessible to those destinations via walking or biking.

12   Mark J. Perry, "New US Homes Today Are 1,000 Square Feet Larger Than in 1973 and Living Space Per Person Has Nearly Doubled," American Enterprise Institute, accessed November 5, 2019, https://www.aei.org/carpe-diem/new-us-homes-today-are-1000-square-feet-larger -than-in-1973-and-living-space-per-person-has-nearly-doubled/.

13   See Price-to-Income Ratios Approaching Historic Highs, Harvard Joint Center for Housing Studies, accessed November 5, 2019, https://www.jchs.harvard.edu/blog/price-to-income -ratios-are-nearing-historic-highs/.

14   Barbara J. Lipman, "A Heavy Load: The Combined Housing and Transportation Burdens of Working Families" (Washington, DC: Center for Housing Policy, 2006).

CHAPTER 3: THE MISSING MIDDLE HOUSING AFFORDABILITY SOLUTION *(with case studies)*

1   National Low Income Housing Coalition, "Out of Reach 2019," https://reports.nlihc.org/oor.

2   Angie Schmitt, "How Much of Your Rent Covers the Hidden Cost of Parking?" Streetsblog USA, June 2, 2015, https://usa.streetsblog.org/2015/06/02/how-much-of-your-rent-covers -the-hidden-cost-of-parking/.

3   News Release from the Bureau of Labor Statistics, "Consumer Expenditures 2018," September 10, 2019, https://www.bls.gov/news.release/pdf/cesan.pdf.

4   City of Decatur, Georgia, "Decatur Affordable Housing Policy Feasibility Analysis," http://www.decaturhousing.org/City%20of%20Decatur-Affordable%20Housing%20Policy%20Analysis%205-26-16.pdf.

5   Emmeus Davis, John and Rick Jacobus, The City-CLT Partnership: Municipal Support for Community Land Trusts (Lincoln Institute of Land Policy, 2008).

6   Dan Whisenhunt, "Decatur Considering Lottery for Affordable Housing Project," Decaturish.com, Oct 19, 2016, https://decaturish.com/2016/10/decatur-considering-lottery-for-affordable-housing-project/.

CHAPTER 4: UNDERSTANDING BARRIERS TO MISSING MIDDLE HOUSING

1   Emily Badger and Quoctrung Bui, "Cities Start to Question an American Ideal: A House with a Yard on Every Lot," New York Times, June 18, 2019, https://www.nytimes.com/interactive/2019/06/18/upshot/cities-across-america-question-single-family-zoning.html?searchResultPosition=1.

2   Beth Mattson-Teig, "Why Aren't More Small Apartment Projects Built?" UrbanLand, April 14, 2017, https://urbanland.uli.org/planning-design/isnt-america-building-small-apartments/.

3   Margaret Morales, "Why Seattle Builds Apartment, But Vancouver, BC, Builds Condos," Sightline Institute, August 14, 2017, https://www.sightline.org/2017/08/14/why-seattle-builds-apartments-but-vancouver-bc-builds-condos/.

4   Ontario Construction Loans (website), "Cash Flow Management Is Key Aspect of Condo Construction Financing," https://www.ontarioconstructionloans.ca/construction-financing/condo-construction-financing.

5   Jann Swanson, "New FHA Rule Will Ease Condo Approval Process," Mortgage News Daily, August 15, 2019, http://www.mortgagenewsdaily.com/08152019_fha_lending.asp.

6   Ibid.

CHAPTER 5: MISSING MIDDLE HOUSING TYPES

1   United States Census 2010.

CHAPTER 6: CASE STUDIES

1   Dan Bertolet and Nisma Gabobe, "LA ADU Story: How a State Law Sent Granny Flats Off the Charts," Sightline Institute, April 5, 2019, https://www.sightline.org/2019/04/05/la-adu-story -how-a-state-law-sent-granny-flats-off-the-charts/.

2   Accessory Dwellings (website), "What Are the Rules Where I Live?" https://accessorydwellings.org/adu-regulations-by-city/.

3   Residential and commercial properties carried a high-risk cap rate of 14 percent at this time.

4   Living Cully (website), "Cully Neighborhood," http://www.livingcully.org/about-living-cully/ cully-neighborhood/.

CHAPTER 7: IMPLEMENTING MISSING MIDDLE HOUSING: OVERCOMING PLANNING AND REGULATORY BARRIERS *(with case studies)*

1   Harvard University, Joint Center for Housing Studies, "America's Rental Housing: Meeting Challenges, Building on Opportunities," April 26, 2011, https://www.jchs.harvard.edu/sites/ default/files/ahr2011-3-demographics.pdf.

2   City of Portland, Oregon, Department of Planning and Sustainability, "Better Housing by Design Project Overview," https://www.portlandoregon.gov/bps/article/618889.

3   Press Release from assembly member Todd Gloria, "Gloria Bill to Spur Production of Middle-Income Housing in San Diego Signed by Governor Brown," October 16, 2017, https://a78.asmdc.org/press-releases/gloria-bill-spur-production-middle-income-housing -san-diego-signed-governor-brown.

ABOUT
THE AUTHOR

DANIEL PAROLEK is an architect, urban designer, and the founding principal of Opticos Design, a B Corporation with a strong commitment to social, fiscal, and environmental responsibility. Opticos, founded in 2000, has grown into a sought-after company of thought leaders in urban place making, innovative housing design and policy, and zoning reform for walkable urbanism. They are leading the master plan and design of what will be the country's largest car-free, mobility-rich neighborhood.

Daniel has been featured in many high-profile publications, including the *New York Times*, *San Francisco Chronicle*, *Next City*, *Fast Company*, the *Wall Street Journal*, and *Curbed*. He created the concept of Missing Middle Housing, launched MissingMiddleHousing.com, and is a champion of the international Missing Middle Housing movement.

As a thought leader in zoning-reform efforts, Daniel coauthored the book *Form-Based Codes: A Guide for Planners, Urban Designers, Municipalities, and Developers* with Karen Parolek and Paul C. Crawford (named one of Planetizen's best books in 2009) and cofounded the nonprofit think tank the Form-Based Code Institute.

He has a bachelor's of architecture from the University of Notre Dame and a master's of urban design from the University of California at Berkeley. Daniel loves to travel internationally, especially in Italy. The seeds of his passion for walkable urban places sprouted while he was growing up in the small town of Columbus, Nebraska.